SUBTROPICAL AND DRY CLIMATE PLANTS

SUBTROPICAL AND DRY CLIMATE PLANTS

Martyn Rix

PLANTS PEOPLE
POSSIBILITIES

TIMBER PRESS

To those who have made gardens in Mediterranean climates around the world

SUBTROPICAL AND DRY CLIMATE PLANTS

Published in North America in 2006 by
Timber Press, Inc.
The Haseltine Building
133 S.W. Second Avenue, Suite 450
Portland, Oregon 97204-3527, U.S.A.
www.timberpress.com

ISBN-13: 978-0-88192-808-2
ISBN-10: 0-88192-808-9

A catalog record for this book is available
from the Library of Congress.

Page 1 illustration: *Nymphaea*
Page 2 illustration: Tresco Abbey, Isles of Scilly
Page 4 illustration: Castello di Volpaia, Tuscany

Commissioning Editor: **Michèle Byam**
Senior Editor: **Peter Taylor**
Executive Art Editor: **Penny Stock**
Design: **Jill Bryan**
Editorial Research: **Alison Rix**
Production: **Jane Rogers**
Project Editor: **Joanna Chisholm**
Indexer: **Sue Farr**

Set in Berkeley LT Book & Pie Charts for Maps

Repro by Chromographics, Singapore
Produced by Toppan Printing Co., (HK) Ltd
Printed and bound in China

Contents

Foreword

Temperate gardens and gardeners have always aspired to be a little more exotic than northern latitudes should permit – pushing the envelope of what will survive and thereby taking the risks that enhance horticultural experience. After all, if you don't try, how will you ever discover whether a given plant can perform? So, here's the book to give the ideas and encouragement to drive that grand experiment and set off on a voyage of gardening discovery and temptation. Its coverage is very extensive and every keen gardener will find something to their liking.

In Europe, at least, since the great winter of 1963, many who garden within the warming influence of the Atlantic or in more Mediterranean environments have started to experiment with subtropical plants and species from the world's drylands. In particular, those who garden in or near big cities – indeed the majority of us nowadays – have discovered that the protection from cold and wind afforded by tall buildings will enable a remarkable variety of exciting and beautiful plant forms to flourish. All this makes climate change seem more of a reality and while not wishing to minimize the threats it poses to all of us, it is true that in the shorter term we can indulge in a style of gardening that formerly was only to be seen inside great Victorian conservatories, like the Temperate House at Kew.

Climate change, of course, is not just about temperature, but most importantly also has a lot to do with water availability, both under- and over-abundance. The former is increasingly going to restrict some gardener's options, so growing exotic dryland plants may become a necessity and will definitely be in the interests of more sustainable living. The latter (over-abundance) will also bring challenges, especially in urban environments where so much of the ground surface is already impermeable, increasing the risk of flooding during downpours. Keeping the soil open and planted with large, thirsty exotic vegetation is a much better option than concrete and asphalt. And while we all need green space to enjoy, our native (and exotic) wildlife is increasingly taking to our gardens, as natural habitats are degraded and disappearing. The birds and insects will doubtless prefer the protection and cover offered by secluded islands of luxuriant subtropical vegetation within our urban jungle and give us pleasure too.

Growing subtropical plants is a world of discovery and can bring us into contact with new countries, habitats and cultures. Most importantly it can increase our awareness of the incredible diversity of plants on the planet and hopefully remind us that we need to do our bit towards its preservation. Gardening, almost by definition, is an environmentally "green" activity, especially if we can avoid some practices, such as the excessive use of peat or of fossil fuel energy to cut the traditional but increasingly unsustainable manicured lawn. If we are watchful and keep invasive and weedy species out of our gardens, the subtropical feel that our changing climate now allows us to create may even be a reason to stay relaxing at home and feel good about not burning all that globally-warming aviation kerosene on holiday travel to warmer climes. Why not enjoy the global world of plants in your back yard every day!

Nigel Taylor
Curator, Kew Gardens

Opposite: *Brunfelsia pauciflora* at Kew Gardens, London

How to use this book

The Plant Directory gives examples of suitable plants for a range of climates and uses in the garden. In most cases only one or two plants of each genus have been included, giving as wide a range of different-looking plants as possible. The text gives some of the main characters of the plant, its leaf and flower size, height, and width. Also included is the United States Department of Agriculture zones in which the plant might be expected to survive, and as a guidence for non-US readers, the coldest temperatures covered by these zones. Plant hardiness is little understood, and most of the figures shown are based on experience. Even in a small garden, a plant may survive cold in one place or be killed in another.

INDIVIDUAL SPECIES (SYNONYM)
The Latin name of the species, which is used throughout the world. If more than one Latin name is in common use, the second name, generally called a synonym, is given.

COMMON NAME
The English-language or local name where this is in common usage.

NATIVE GEOGRAPHICAL REGION
Shows the countries in the world where the species may be found growing wild and native, and not introduced by man.

PLANT USE
Indicates whether the plant has special uses in the garden.

INTRODUCTION TO GENUS
Gives the number of species in the genus, information on its origin, and its uses where this is of interest.

GROUP DESCRIPTION
This heading gives some idea of the main families, genera, or groupings of plants shown on the spread.

CULTIVATION INFORMATION
Gives a short guide to any unusual requirements the plant may have in order to thrive in a garden.

The Myrtle Family

Acca (Myrtaceae)

Acca is a genus of six species of evergreen shrubs and small trees, with guava-like fruit. They are native of South America.

Acca sellowiana (syn. *Feijoa sellowiana*)
PINEAPPLE GUAVA
This evergreen shrub is a native of South America. It has dark green leaves, with white felt on the underside, and solitary flowers, 4cm (1½in) across, with bosses of conspicuous red stamens, in summer. The red-tinged, green, egg-shaped fruit, 5cm (2in) long, is edible, and has a pleasant aroma. There are several cultivars available commercially, including 'Variegata', with its leaves edged creamy white, and 'Mammoth', which has larger fruits.

Cultivation Does best in moderately fertile, well-drained soil, with protection from cold drying winds. Good for coastal areas, as it will tolerate salt-laden winds. Makes a dense hedge if clipped.
Height to 3m (10ft); spread to 2m (6½ft). USZ 8–11, surviving -12°C (10°F) of frost when dormant. Tolerant of summer drought. ☻

Chamaelaucium (Myrtaceae)

Chamaelaucium comprises 21 species of evergreen shrubs, all from southwest Australia. The flowers of most species have waxy petals, hence the common name: wax flower. When each flower is fully open, the shining top of the ovary is exposed. *Chamaelaucium* is grown for the cut-flower trade in semi-desert areas, such as Israel.

Below *Acca sellowiana* (pineapple guava)

Chamaelaucium uncinatum
GERALDTON WAX
This tough upright shrub, native [to] Western Australia, has narrow le[aves] clusters of cup-shaped flowers i[n] of colours ranging from white th[rough] to mauve, purple, or red from la[te] through to early spring. *C. uncin[atum]* been planted to combat soil ero[sion] also grown as a cut flower plant [in] areas. It has a number of cultiva[rs] 'University', which bears vivid r[ed] and is a popular garden plant in [Australia] and elsewhere.
Cultivation Does well in full o[f] sun in sandy gravelly soil. Can [be pruned] immediately after flowering.
Height and spread to 5m (16ft). U[SZ] surviving -1°C (30°F) or more for [short] periods. Tolerant of summer drou[ght].

Leptospermum (Myrtac[eae])

The genus *Leptospermum* contai[ns] species of evergreen shrubs and [trees, the] majority of which originate in A[ustralia.] The leaves have been used as a [tea] substitute, hence the common n[ame.]

Leptospermum lanigerum
WOOLLY TEA TREE
This evergreen shrub, from Tas[mania and] southeast Australia, produces d[ense] greyish green leaves, and small [white] flowers, in spring. 'Silver Sheen' [is early] flowering, with more silvery lea[ves.]

Left *Leptospermum scoparium* 'Kiwi'
Far Left *Leptospermum lanigerum*

Above *Chamaelaucium uncinatum* 'University' (geraldton wax)

92

PLANT INFORMATION
Gives details of the plant, its flower and leaf, and where in the world it originates.

PLANT PORTRAIT/VIEW
Most of the pictures of plants were taken by the author or Roger Phillips in gardens around the world or in their natural habitat.

CAPTIONS
Show the name of the plant in the picture. We have tried to say if the plant photograph was taken in the wild.

PAGE HEADING
The plant directory is divided into sections, by plant habit and life form; this is the section heading.

HUMIDITY REQUIREMENT
This symbol indicates the type of climate to which the plant is best adapted. The meaning of the spot is explained below under KEY TO SYMBOLS.

SHRUBS

Below *Myrtus communis*

HARDINESS ZONES
Zones and minimum temperature ranges for North America and Europe

ZONE 1	*below −50°F (-46°C)*
ZONE 2	*50°C to 40°F (46°C to 40°C)*
ZONE 3	*50°C to 40°F (46°C to 40°C)*
ZONE 4	*50°C to 40°F (46°C to 40°C)*
ZONE 5	*50°C to 40°F (46°C to 40°C)*
ZONE 6	*50°C to 40°F (46°C to 40°C)*
ZONE 7	*10°F to 0°F (-12°C to -17°C)*
ZONE 8	*20°F to 10°F (-6.5°C to -12°C)*
ZONE 9	*20°F to 30°F (-1°C to 6.5°C)*
ZONE 10	*30°F to 40°F (4.5°C to -1°C)*
ZONE 11	*Above 40°F (above 4.5°C)*

KEY TO SYMBOLS
Climate in which the plants thrives best

◑ **Desert climate** (very hot, usually dry, low humidity, intermittent rain, and not much of it, in summer and even less in winter). Californian desert, central Mexico, central Australia, dry parts of sub-Saharan Africa, Karroo, etc.

◐ **Mediterranean climate**, (winter rainfall, hot and dry, with low humidity in summer) Mediterranean, Cape of South Africa, coastal California, coastal Chile, Western Australia and coast of South Australia.

◕ **Subtropical**; (summer rainfall, with some rain in winter. High humidity in summer only) Florida, New Zealand, coastal Mexico, the wetter parts of East Africa and the eastern Cape, southern China, and Japan.

● **Wet with rain and high humidity all year round.** Pacific northwest, Queensland, Tasmania. west coast of New Zealand, Cornwall, wet mountains in the tropics.

Cultivation Best in moist, well-drained soil in sun or light shade. Light pruning after flowering will help keep the bush neat. *Height and spread to 2m (6½ft). USZ 8–11, surviving -12°C (10°F) of frost. Tolerant of summer drought.* ◑

Leptospermum scoparium
NEW ZEALAND TEA TREE, MANUKA
This fast-growing, evergreen shrub or small tree is a native of Australia (including Tasmania) and New Zealand. It has very narrow, dark green leaves and masses of white, pink, or red flowers, from late spring to summer. 'Kiwi' is a popular dwarf form; it bears red flowers and purple leaves.
Cultivation Grow in well-drained, acid, sandy soil. Prune after flowering to maintain a good shape.
Height and spread to 2m (6½ft). USZ 9–11, surviving -6.5°C (20°F) of overnight frost for short periods only. Tolerant of summer drought once established. ◑

Myrtus (Myrtaceae)
MYRTLE

This genus of two species of aromatic evergreen shrubs or trees is from the Mediterranean region and northern Africa. The South American species previously found under *Myrtus* have been transferred to *Luma* and other genera.

Myrtus communis
This evergreen shrub, native of the Mediterranean region and western Asia, has dark green leaves, which are aromatic when crushed. The white flowers with masses of stamens, in summer, are followed by purple berries. Subsp. *tarentina* is more compact, with narrower leaves and white berries.
Cultivation Grow in well-drained soil in full sun. Water sparingly in the growing season. Can be clipped to form a hedge.
Height and spread to 4m (13ft). USZ 8–11, surviving -12°C (10°F) of overnight frost. Tolerant of summer drought. ◐

Rhodomyrtus (Myrtaceae)

This genus comprises 11 species of evergreen shrubs and trees from China, southeast Asia, and Australia.

Rhodomyrtus tomentosa
This evergreen shrub or small tree is a native of China and southeast Asia. It has leathery, green, oval leaves, around 7.5cm (3in) long, downy on the underside. Pink, saucer-shaped flowers, around 5cm (2in) across, are borne in early summer.
Cultivation Best in deep, lime-free soil in a sheltered place.
Height to 4m (13ft), spread to 2m (6½ft). USZ 10–11, surviving -1°C (30°F) of occasional overnight frost. Tolerant of summer drought. ●

Above *Rhodomyrtus tomentosa* growing wild on The Peak in Hong Kong

93

GENUS HEADING (FAMILY NAME)
The name of the plant genus and family.

DROUGHT TOLERANCE
Gives an indication of whether the plant will survive dry summers or whether extra watering will be needed in dry areas.

HARDINESS RATING
The key for the zones is in the upper pink box. As a rough guide, the Atlantic coasts of the British Isles and Europe, fall into zones 8 and 9; the coast of the Mediterranean Sea into zones 9 and 10. Zones 10 and 11 are essentially frost-free. Olives thrive in zone 9; white daturas survive the winter in zone 10. Bermuda, southern Florida,and the West Indies are zone 11.

HEIGHT & SPREAD
Indicates the overall size of the plant, although this may depend on the availability of water. In the case of trees, some years may elapse before the final height is reached.

Gardening in Warm Climates

Summer-dry Climates

Warm and subtropical climates, that is, those with very little or no winter frost but with seasonal rain, present many opportunities to gardeners, as well as a few challenges. For some familiar plants, for example apple trees, winter may not be cold enough; for others the summers may be too hot. But many of the most beautiful garden plants, such as *Wisteria* or lavender, do better in such warm climates than in colder ones, where they survive yet are commonly grown. Knowledge of native habitats will therefore help the gardener grow plants successfully.

The favoured climate for many people is one in which most rain falls in winter, and the summers are hot and dry. This climate type is generally called Mediterranean and is found around the Mediterranean Sea, as well as along the Californian coast outside the fog belt. Other areas include the Cape area of South Africa, Western and South Australia, and central Chile. Wine and olive growing is becoming more and more popular in these areas, and this, as well as housing, is putting pressure on the remaining areas of wild country and on scarce water supplies.

Where these climates merge into the desert, the flora tends to be dominated by bulbs, annuals, and succulents, which exploit good winter rains, yet still survive if the rains fail. The wonderful floras of Namaqualand or northern Chile have evolved in this apparently inauspicious environment.

The challenge for the gardener is to keep the garden going through the dry summer season; lawns are irrigated to keep them green, and plants from areas with wet summers are watered to keep them flowering, or even alive. Scarce water supplies are needlessly used when, by growing plants from a suitable climate, the garden could survive unwatered until the autumn rain.

Above This wonderful view of white Compositae and Umbelliferae, combined with variously coloured Leguminosae, growing between olive trees, is at Aphrodisias in Turkey on the Mediterranean coast in April. It is also a good habitat for bulbs and orchids. Winter rainfall is exploited by the annuals, which make most of their growth and foliage in the wet months, and then flower in spring and early summer, when the weather is becoming hot and dry.

Left Around Nieuwoudtville in north Western Cape, in South Africa, the winter rainfall has produced an explosion in the evolution of small bulbs and annuals, often with spectacularly colourful flowers. In this small patch are salmon-pink *Sparaxis elegans*, blue *Moraea elegans*, purple *Senecio cakilefolius*, and the yellow buttons of a *Cotula*.

Winter-dry Climates

A warm wet summer and dry cool winter creates the reverse climate to the summer-dry one. This climate is found in southeastern North America, in northern Argentina, in Eastern Cape in South Africa, in much of eastern Africa and in eastern Australia. In Europe this climate type is rare, mainly being found in the warm valleys of the southern Alps by the Italian lakes, but in Asia it is the most common type, found in the subtropical parts of those areas affected by the summer monsoon.

This is an ideal climate for the gardener, as most plants will make good growth without extra watering in summer, and the plants can stay dormant and dry in winter. Even trees and shrubs from summer-dry climates, such as Californian *Ceanothus*, will probably grow well. It is only those smaller plants particularly adapted to dry summers, such as tulips and many other bulbs, that cannot survive summer rainfall and tend to rot. On the whole, Mediterranean climates seem to be recent, from a geological perspective, and only plants with short generations, such as annuals and some bulbs and tuberous perennials, have become so highly adapted that they cannot survive summer rain.

Deserts that have evolved from summer-rainfall climates usually have a rich and diverse natural, mainly succulent, flora. In America the Cactaceae (*see* pp. 224–44) have become dominant, accompanied in some areas by annuals. In the Arizona desert, annuals from the tropical south germinate after summer storms; those with northern Californian affinities germinate in winter. The areas of the world where dry and subtropical climates are found are described in more detail below, so that gardeners can choose plants adapted to their own type of climate.

In some parts of the world rain is evenly distributed throughout the year: for example, in the North Island of New Zealand, and the warmer parts of the Atlantic coast of Europe. In the next few pages I discuss some of these areas in more detail.

Left The annual *Lupinus pilosus* makes a fine display in the mountains of western Crete, where it is contrasted with the bold leaves of *Colchicum macrophyllum* and clumps of yellow-green spurge *Euphorbia characias*. The *Colchicum* disappears in summer, before flowering with the first autumn rain; the spurge remains green throughout summer.

Below Summer flowers in the summer-rainfall zone of Natal, South Africa, on Mount Ngeli, an outlier of the Drakensberg, include *Agapanthus campanulatus*, *Watsonia densiflora*, and a *Dierama* species. These grasslands are dry in winter, and rich with herbaceous and bulbous plants in summer.

Wild Origins of Garden Plants

Mediterranean

The typical Mediterranean climate, of warm wet winters with little frost and hot dry summers, has lent its name to similar climates around the world. Although these areas are small in extent, they are exceptionally rich in species, and evolution is still particularly active there.

In such a climate many plants start growing in autumn, and the first storms or even cool nights trigger autumn flowers in some familiar genera such as *Cyclamen*, *Crocus*, and *Colchicum*. In general trees and shrubs remain dormant until spring, and this probably reflects the relatively recent development of this climate in the area, probably within the last 100,000 years. There is also the uncertainty of the frost-free winter; even the warm coastal strip can sometimes freeze. In Europe the Mediterranean climate is considered to coincide with the extent of olive cultivation:

from southwest Portugal, inland through southern Spain, then north along the coast to France, western Italy, and Sicily. Cold arctic air and summer rainfall reach the northern Adriatic, so it is only the southern part that is truly Mediterranean. The climate then extends through Greece and down the Aegean coast of Turkey east to Syria and the Lebanon. From there the coastal strip in Palestine, Egypt, and along the North African coast to Morocco has the typical climate. There is an interesting outlier on the coast of Somalia, where there are species of *Cyclamen* and *Anemone*, suggesting that the Mediterranean flora may once have been more widespread. In the north, the Mediterranean blends into the wetter Alps, in Turkey into dry cold Anatolia, and in the Middle East and North Africa into desert. Soils are variable, but relatively soluble limestones are particularly common.

Many beautiful garden plants originate from this area, and basically the same type of vegetation is found all round the

Above *Phlomis fruticosa* (Jerusalem sage) is an evergreen shrub with large yellow flowers in spring and early summer. It is a common plant on limestone near the Mediterranean coast.

Right In the wild *Nerium oleander* (oleander) always grows in stream beds, as the seeds germinate only in running water. Here it thrives near Antalya, in Turkey.

Mediterranean Sea: low shrubby vegetation in the driest places or poorest soils – the garrigue – with *Cistus*, *Phlomis*, lavender, rosemary, *Euphorbia acanthothamnos*, *Quercus coccifera*, and many others. They are often kept low by frequent fires or heavy grazing. In deeper soils, or areas less subject to burning, a taller scrub may develop – the maquis – with strawberry tree and *Viburnum tinus* as two of the main components. In areas where woods form, pines and oaks are the major species. Along streams are found plane trees, alders, oleander, and, in one area in Turkey, the rare *Liquidambar orientalis*, a relic of ancient pre-Ice Age forests. Many garden flowers originated here too. Madonna lilies, irises, tulips, crown imperials, hyacinths, florists' anemones, and *Ranunculus* were grown by the Turks, and cornflowers, mignonette, marigolds, sweet peas, carnations, and *Acanthus* are annuals or perennials developed from Mediterranean ancestors.

By growing species from this area, the Mediterranean gardener can be sure of success with little artificial watering in summer (once the plants are established) and with less heartache caused by losses in winter from unexpected cold.

Below Wild *Tulipa saxatilis* carpets the Omalós plain in western Crete. Many tulips, including this one, spread by stolons and grow in cornfields, which may have been cultivated since Neolithic times.

Left *Echium candicans* is a native of Madeira, where it is very rare. It is widely grown elsewhere, as here in the Giardino Botanico Hanbury, La Mortola, in Ventimiglia, Italy, and has naturalized in South Africa.

Below Shrubby daisies, *Argyranthemum foeniculum*, grow in the mountains of Tenerife. There are about 24 species of *Argyranthemum* in the Canaries and Madeira, differing from one another mainly in leaf colour and shape and size of flower.

Canary Islands & Madeira

Though they are only a group of small islands off the coast of northwestern Africa, the Canaries have a rich and unique flora. Because of their position and geological history, these islands, together with Madeira, which lies 500km (300 miles) to the northwest, have acted as a refuge for a remnant of the subtropical forest that lived in Europe before the Ice Ages (from three to two million years ago). At the same time they have harboured desert and montane species from Africa, survivors from a time when the Sahara was less arid than it is today. Because of the mountainous topography of the islands – Mount Teide on Tenerife is 3,717m (12,198ft) high, and was once thought to be the highest mountain in the world – there is great diversity of habitat and climate in a very small area, from both hot and cold semi-desert and total desert, to humid forests and numerous gorges and cliffs. This encourages a large number of ancient species to survive, and new endemic species to develop.

Because there is a tendency for shrubby species of normally herbaceous plants to evolve on islands, many good examples of this are found in the Canaries and Madeira. Shrubby *Echium* species, *Cheiranthus*, *Convolvulus*, *Sonchus*, *Argyranthemum*, and *Isoplexis* (a shrubby foxglove) are among those commonly cultivated. The genus *Aeonium*, related to *Sempervivum*, has also developed tall species with almost woody trunks.

The climate of both the Canaries and Madeira is basically Mediterranean, but the eastern islands, which are closest to Africa, are very dry. The western side of the western islands has a well-developed fog belt at 400–1,300m (1,300–4,300ft), where the trade winds hit the mountains; the forests condense the fog, feeding numerous small streams. This is the area where ancient tree species have survived, in the so-called laurisilva or laurel forest, because many of the trees belong to the Lauraceae, the family of the bay and laurel tree. They include *Persea indica* (a relative of *P. americana*, avocado), *Laurus azorica*, *Apollonias barbusana*, *Ocotea foetens*, and *Picconia excelsa* (a relative of olive).

On Madeira the same trees occur, with *Clethra arborea*, whose nearest relatives are in Mexico and China. Surviving subtropical ferns include large *Woodwardia radicans* and creeping epiphytic *Davallia canariensis*. Fossil remains of leaves of these trees have been found in central and southern Europe, mostly from the Pliocene, when this evergreen subtropical forest would have surrounded the Tethys Sea. The uplift of the Himalayas caused the Ice Ages in Europe, killing off this forest and causing the drying of the Sahara. Because of the area's mountainous nature and the warming effect of the sea, this little remnant has survived.

Other plants seem to be survivors of what is now a mainly African flora; these include orange *Canarina canariensis*, whose close relatives are found on mountain forests in Ethiopia, Kenya, and Tanzania, and *Draceana draco* (dragon tree), which still survives in one place – on the African mainland.

When brought into cultivation in a Mediterranean climate, most of these Canary plants do very well, tolerating rain and drought. Many other examples will be found in this book.

Top *Euphorbia canariensis* is one of the succulent spurges common on the eastern Canary islands, and has African affinities. *Opuntia* was introduced for the production of cochineal, and is now common.

Above Around 35 species of *Aeonium* occur in the Canaries and Madeira, ranging from shrubs to dwarf succulents. *A. glandulosum* is one of several genera that have evolved rapidly in these islands.

15

South Africa

South Africa is the richest country in the world for the beauty, wealth, and diversity of its flowers. Within the country, too, there is a contrast between the winter-rainfall and summer-rainfall areas. Best of all is the winter-rainfall, summer-dry area of the Cape, which stretches in an arc along the coast from the Orange River to Port Elizabeth, and roughly between the mountains and the sea. The countryside consists of wide valleys and steep rocky hills, usually with poor sandy soil, sometimes peaty where there is more rainfall, at other times drier and desert-like, as in the Karroo. Rainfall is heaviest near the coast and on the south-facing mountain slopes; inland many areas soon merge into desert. Fire has been of great significance in the evolution of this unparalleled explosion of species, and pollinating insects and birds have pushed floral diversity even further.

There have been no periods of recent ice or major climate changes, as have been experienced in Europe, and the flora is therefore much richer. The numbers are striking: the Cape region has 9,000 species of flowering plants, while Sicily (the most florally rich Mediterranean island) has 2,700, and California (in an area three times the size) 4,200. Only southwestern Australia approaches the Cape, with perhaps 8,000 species. The major

Above *Protea cynaroides* has the largest flowerhead of any of the species of this purely African genus. It grows wild throughout the winter-rainfall area of the Cape, between southern Namibia and Port Elizabeth, in South Africa. Its family, Proteaceae, is found all round the southern hemisphere.

Below *Protea roupelliae* here flourishes near Cathedral Peak, in the Natal Drakensberg. This species is confined to subalpine parts of the summer-rainfall region, which stretches from Natal northwards to tropical eastern Africa.

Left The speed with which *Cyrtanthus angustifolius* (firelily) can appear after a bush fire in the Langkloof, in the Cape, and the flowers open, is astonishing. The half-burnt reeds are probably *Arundo donax*, a weed introduced from the Mediterranean.

Below *Pelargonium longicaule* is a lovely member of this popular genus, which reaches its peak of diversity in the Cape area of South Africa, with around 150 species out of a total of 250 from around the world.

Bottom The flora of the area around Nieuwoudtville, in the north Western Cape, is exceptionally rich, both in number of species and in their sheer quantity. Here, seen growing in the protected area of Glenlyon Farm, is *Gazania rigida*.

vegetation is the fynbos, which is roughly equivalent to the Mediterranean garrigue, though usually taller, much more diverse in species, and modified and enhanced by periodic fire.

With such floral richness, it is difficult to select a few genera, but *Pelargonium* must have made the biggest impact in gardens. Annuals such as *Osteospermum*, *Gazania*, *Nemesia*, and *Lobelia* are commonly cultivated, as are bulbs including *Nerine*, *Lachenalia*, and *Amaryllis belladonna*. Shrubby *Proteas* are popular as cut flowers, while the Karroo is the home of specialized succulents such as the pebble-mimicking *Lithops* and *Fenestraria*.

The reverse climate to the summer-dry one is that with a dry, often cold, winter and a warm wet summer. This type of climate is found from east of Port Elizabeth, northwards and eastwards through eastern Africa to Kenya. In some areas the seasons are less pronounced, and there may be a short rainy season as well as a longer one. Summer-wet climates usually produce more herbaceous plants and fewer bulbs, annuals, and shrubs, though in Africa summer-growing bulbs are common. There are forest areas protected from fire – the habitat of *Clivia* – and open grassland, where *Agapanthus*, *Watsonia*, *Galtonia*, *Gladiolus*, and *Eucomis* are found. Cliff ledges and stream beds are the habitat of *Schizostylis* and *Crocosmia*, among other plants.

California

The western Californian landscape consists of dry rolling hills rising slowly from the sea to the foothills and peaks of the Sierra Nevada. In some areas the hills are covered with park-like woodland, with heavy clay soil and grasses under spreading oaks. In other places pines and small-leaved shrubs such as *Ceanothus* survive on the dry rocky hills. Patches of woodland, with alders and *Platanus* (planes; in America sycamore) can survive along streams, with redwoods in deep valleys near the coast, where they trap the summer fog. The main period of rainfall is in winter and spring – the annuals, bulbs, and shrubs relying on water stored in the soil to survive into early summer.

A Mediterranean climate is found mostly along the coast, though some areas, notably north of San Francisco, are affected by summer fogs. Exceptional frosts can also be a limiting factor, and these occasionally reach as far south as Santa Barbara. Inland in the north the land soon climbs into the foothills and finally the high ridge of the Sierra Nevada, which is cooler but still has a little summer rain. East of the mountains are the dry pinyon pine zones, and the hollows of Death Valley and the deserts. A considerable number of popular garden plants originate in coastal California: for example, annuals such as *Clarkia*, *Nemophila*, and *Eschscholtzia* (Californian poppy); bulbs such as *Calochortus* (Mariposa tulip), *Erythronium*, and *Triteleia*; shrubs such as *Ceanothus*, *Carpenteria*, and *Ribes speciosum* (fuchsia currant); and drought-tolerant perennials such as *Romneya* (tree poppy) and *Zauschneria* (Californian fuchsia). Spectacular species of *Yucca* are found in the drier warmer habitats.

Summer rainfall increases further north into Oregon and Washington, and decreases south into the deserts, where rainfall is low and unreliable, often falling in summer storms. Wild plants have adapted to withstand long periods of low humidity and drought, and to make the best of the rain when it comes. The Sonoran desert in Arizona and northern Mexico is an interesting transition zone between winter rainfall (from the Pacific in California) and summer rainfall (in storms from the Gulf of Mexico). Winter annuals such as *Phacelia* (desert bluebell) germinate in cool weather and have northern affinities, while summer annuals germinate after summer storms, and have migrated from the south. Cactuses, which are so dominant, can make use of rain in either season; *Opuntia*, *Echinocereus*, and *Ferocactus* are common in the Mojave desert and other dry locations (*see also* pp.238–41).

Above *Zauschneria californica* is a variable and common plant in the Californian foothills. Its red flowers, with a long tube and exserted stamens, show that it is designed for pollination by hummingbirds. This plant is now sometimes considered not to be distinct from *Epilobium* (willowherb).

Right *Yucca whipplei* (Our Lord's candle) was photographed in May near Bakersfield. The inflorescence develops in early spring, and after flowering the rosette dies. Of its two subspecies, one forms suckers, the other relies on seed for propagation.

Left This typical Californian desert scene includes tree *Y. whipplei*, *Opuntia echinocarpa* (silver cholla), and the grey bushes of *Artemisia* (sagebrush).

Below One of the most characteristic flowers of California is *Escholzia californica* (California poppy), here flowering in the native plant garden in Santa Barbara Botanic Garden. It usually grows as an annual inland, but coastal forms in cooler areas may be short-lived perennials.

domesticated: *Dahlia, Zinnia*, African marigolds, *Cosmos, Epiphyllum,* French and runner beans, tomatoes, and maize were all cultivated in Mexico. Later introductions, mainly from the wild, include *Cobaea, Laelia, Passiflora mollissima, Bomarea*, and ornamental shrubby *Salvia*. The climate in these temperate parts of Mexico, and equivalent parts of South America, is the key to growing the plants successfully: winter is cool and dry; spring is also dry; and the majority of rain comes in summer, from June until August, when temperatures are high. Therefore plants from these areas can be kept dry and dormant until late spring, and only watered as growth begins in warm weather. After September the weather becomes drier, and many Mexican plants have their maximum flowering periods from September and October into November and even December.

The majority of the rainforest areas of Brazil and tropical South America are too tropical to furnish many plants suitable for cooler areas. However, in the hills around Rio de Janeiro conditions become more suitable, and many genera from here,

Mexico to Chile & Argentina

It is not surprising that the vast area of Central and South America, from Mexico to Chile and Argentina, should be home to many good garden plants. At sea level the majority of the area is tropical, yet the abundance of mountains, mostly part of the great Andes range, means that there are wet and dry, and cold and hot areas in close proximity, and the diversity of plants matches this topography. The actual lines of the tropics run through central Mexico and just south of Rio de Janeiro, thus included within the tropics are the northern ends of Argentina and Chile.

Although the junction of North and South America occurred only recently in geological terms, there are many ornamental genera in common between Mexico and South America. Some genera of southern affinities appear to have migrated northwards, while other genera, such as *Alnus* (alder), have moved the other way, with one species, *A. acuminata*, common along the eastern flank of the Andes as far south as Argentina.

The influence of hummingbird pollination has been very strong in the development of red-and-green flowers, as it has in North American plants. This colour combination, unusual to European eyes, is common throughout Central and South America.

The northern part of Mexico is one of the most important sources of garden plants. The pre-Columbian inhabitants of Mexico were keen gardeners, growing both vegetables and ornamentals, and the early introductions to Spain and later to northern Europe consisted predominantly of plants already

Top Left *Salvia* x *jamensis*, here flowering near Saltillo, in northeastern Mexico, is found in the wild in a range of colours from red to pink, apricot, and pale yellow. Many colour forms of this hybrid have been named, and are excellent plants for hot dry gardens.

Above Shrubby, scrambling *Mutisia acuminata*, from the mountains of Bolivia and northern Argentina, has dark-green, vetch-like leaves and spectacular red flowers. It is one of the potentially excellent plants from South America still to be introduced to gardens.

Right *Verbena microphylla* is widespread in the Altiplano of Argentina, Bolivia, Chile, Ecuador, and Peru. Here it covers an area of high-altitude, sandy plain in the province of Jujuy, Argentina.

such as *Bougainvillea, Passiflora, Clysostoma, Fuchsia,* and *Cleome,* provide useful garden plants.

The eastern Andean foothills, which extend from Peru into Bolivia and northern Argentina, are more temperate still and therefore an excellent source of even more garden plants, many of which have become popular in Europe and North America. Perhaps the commonest subtropical tree from this area is the beautiful blue *Jacaranda.* Epiphytic, bird-pollinated *Begonia boliviensis,* yellow *B. pearcei,* and other species were the forerunners of the cultivated, tuberous, large-flowered, and pendula begonias. Large-flowered *Fuchsia boliviana* grows in the same forests, and in drier areas are the wild species from which garden petunias, verbenas, and spectacular *Puya* were obtained.

Central Chile has a Mediterranean climate and is a rich source of garden plants: bulbs such as *Hippeastrum*; tuberous perennials including *Alstroemeria* and *Tropaeolum*; and the annuals *Salpiglossis* and *Schizanthus.* Wet-loving plants such as *Embothrium, Eucryphia,* and *Lapageria* come from wet coastal areas further south.

Below *Fuchsia fulgens* 'Rubra Grandiflora', from southern Mexico (on the right), and bulbous *Phaedranassa dubia*, from Peru (on the left), are typical green-and-red, hummingbird-pollinated flowers.

China & India

The climate of eastern Asia, from southern Japan to Taiwan and westwards across China to the Himalayas and India, is dominated by the summer monsoon. Warm moist air from the southeast trade winds hits the coast and is precipitated in heavy rain, mist, and cloud. This is a typical summer-rainfall area, with distinct wet and dry seasons. Spring is generally warm and dry, with little return to winter once it has begun. The climate of Yunnan, in southern China, is typical of the area, being dry until the end of May or beginning of June, when the monsoon arrives with heavy showers at the same time every afternoon, and often again in the night. From September onwards the weather is drier, though sometimes rain, which falls as snow in the mountains, may come from the north. Winter is cool and dry, being frost-free below around 1,500m (5,000ft). This climate type is found in India too. In all areas there are wetter places on mountains that catch the rain and drier places to the leeward of mountains; indeed the base of some of the deep river valleys in the Himalayas, such as the upper Yangtze, Salween, and Irrawaddy, are nearly desert.

The flora of these subtropical monsoon areas is huge, yet collectors from Europe and North America have tended to concentrate on hardier plants from higher altitudes. Above

Below *Luculia intermedia* is a lovely, scented, winter-flowering shrub or small tree from the foothills of the Himalayas, in India and China.

Bottom *Quercus, Ilex, Lithocarpus, Carpinus,* and *Acer,* and a rich ground flora with *Begonia, Epimedium, Arisaema, Iris,* and *Impatiens,* occur in this subtropical mixed forest in western Sichuan, China.

Left These diverse ferns grow in subtropical rainforest at the foot of Omei Shan, in western Sichuan. Because this mountain is sacred, its vegetation, which ranges from subtropical to temperate and is affected by the summer monsoon, has been wonderfully preserved.

Below Little rain reaches the desert near Jodhpur, Rajasthan, where this shrubby *Capparis aphylla* grows. It is at the other end of the Himalayas from Omei Shan.

1,800–3,000m (6,000–10,000ft) the majority of trees, shrubs, and herbaceous plants can survive the frosts of western Europe, or US Zone 7. For example, the most magnificent flowering trees must be *Magnolia campbellii* from northern India and its Chinese counterpart, subsp. *mollicomata*. These survive in southern England and western Scotland, but their whole display and growth rate is much better in warmer areas such as New Zealand, Natal, or the sheltered subalpine valleys of northern Italy; here also the flowers are not constantly threatened by unseasonal frost. In the same forests are found the largest of all roses, *Rosa gigantea*, parent of the large-flowered varieties that do so well in Australia and the Mediterranean. Camellias are also finer where summers are warmer, and winters less unpredictable. The large-flowered cultivars of *C. japonica*, *C. reticulata*, and the exciting, yellow-flowered *C. nitidissima* are all best in warm climates, and do well in the Californian coastal belt in places cooled by fog. Of the herbaceous plants that come from this area, the ginger family is particularly diverse, and of these *Hedychium* with its large heads of scented flowers make excellent garden plants.

Drier woods in these climates provide trees and shrubs that can do better in Mediterranean gardens, surviving on ground water throughout the summer months. Trees such as *Bauhinia variegata* (orchid tree) and *Koelreuteria paniculata* (golden rain) grow in drier parts of these monsoon climates, and are commonly cultivated in California and the south of France. Once established, they need little watering. Other good growers appear to be the larger species of *Mahonia*, such as *M. siamensis*, and *Buddleja* such as white, freesia-scented *B. asiatica*.

Warmer and wetter monsoon climates are found in the islands of southeast Asia, in the Philippines, Indonesia, Borneo, and New Guinea. Some good garden plants come from these places, but being more tropical they are generally less easy to cultivate outside the tropics. *Rhododendron* from the highlands of New Guinea and Borneo, however, do seem relatively easy to grow, and can be found in warm parts of coastal California, Australia, and New Zealand, as well as in the cool moist greenhouses at the British Royal Botanic Gardens, in Kew and in Edinburgh.

These summer-rainfall plants require ample water in the hottest months. Where the ambient air, which in nature is cooled by the monsoon rain, is hot and dry, they need placing on the shaded side of a wall or a bank of trees. They are beautiful and worth growing, but should they be attempted in summer-dry areas? The purpose of this book is to show which plants can be grown without extensive use of scarce water.

Australia & New Zealand

Australia is the largest remnant of the great continent of Gondwanaland, and its vegetation has evolved in isolation for millions of years, developing many special genera. Some families such as Myrtaceae (for example, *Eucalyptus* and *Callistemon*), Proteaceae (*Banksia, Hakea, Grevillea*), and Leguminosae (*Acacia,* and many pea flowers) have exploded, producing hundreds of species; others, such as the recently discovered Wollemi pine, have just managed to survive.

All the main climate types are found in Australia: desert, tropical rainforest, subtropical summer rainfall, Mediterranean-type winter rainfall, and temperate rainforest. Most of the east coast has a summer-rainfall climate, varying from the rather dry scrubland and open *Eucalyptus* forest around Sydney to wetter forests in the Blue Mountains. In Tasmania the rain falls all year round, producing temperate rainforest full of tree ferns (*Dicksonia antarctica*), now exported in large numbers.

In Western Australia, however, evolution has been remarkably active, producing around 8,000 species. The flowers of this area are still underrepresented in gardens in other parts of the world, even though red-flowered *Eucalyptus ficifolia* and the even more striking *E. rhodantha* are frequently grown elsewhere. *Banksia, Lechenaultia,* and, among perennials, *Anigozanthus* (kangaroo paws) are also popular abroad.

Above *Prostanthera saxicola* var. *montana* is a free-flowering species of mint-bush from New South Wales, in Australia.

Left *Phormium tenax* (New Zealand flax) grows wild on the cliffs above Cape Reinga, New Zealand. Its tubular flowers contain thick nectar and are pollinated by birds.

Bottom Left *Banksia media* flourishes in the Moore River National Park, near Perth, in Western Australia.

Below Damp forests on both North and South islands of New Zealand are home to the broad-leaved cabbage tree *Cordyline indivisa*.

New Zealand appears close to Australia on maps, yet at its closest is around 1,500km (900 miles) away – that is, about the distance between London and Rome. Its climate is less diverse than Australia, with subtropical moist forest in the North Island, while the South Island has temperate rainforest on the west coast and the drier Canterbury plains on the east of the Southern Alps.

Many of the subtropical garden plants come from the North Island, where *Clianthus puniceus* (parrot beak) is one of the most spectacular types. *Phormium* (New Zealand flax) and *Cordyline* (cabbage tree) are both popular garden genera, and come from both islands, where they are common features of the landscape. It is interesting to note that both *Clianthus* and *Phormium* are bird pollinated, though the birds involved are very different from the American hummingbirds. In the wetter areas of New Zealand are wonderful forests with stands of tree ferns, and in drier parts are gnarled stands of *Leptospermum scoparium* (tea tree); many varieties of this are grown in other areas of the world.

Gardeners living in New Zealand are very fortunate, as they seem to be able to grow, without difficulty, plants from all over the temperate, subtropical, and Mediterranean parts of the world.

Water Regimes & Water Saving

The title of this book, *Subtropical and Dry Climate Plants*, indicates the basis of the selection in the plant directory, which comprises a good range of plants for different subtropical climates, with particular emphasis on those that can survive unwatered. In summer-rainfall climates, water is rarely a problem, and enough rainwater can be stored to survive any dry spells. But summer-dry climates have much greater difficulties. Even in reputedly wet England, drought is often a problem in summer, and public water resources are inadequate for the use of a fast-growing, urban, and suburban population in southern England, so the watering of gardens is sometimes banned before the growing season has even started. In parts of the world with totally dry summers water may be even scarcer and more expensive, and expanding populations, for instance in southern California, put pressure on supplies that have to be brought from a long way off. As the Roman aqueducts and Persian qanats demonstrate, this is not a new phenomenon, but the arrival of accelerating climate change has stimulated gardeners all over the world into rethinking the type of plants that they can grow.

The purpose of the book is to help gardeners choose those plants that will survive in their own climate, firstly by cultivating those that are wild locally, often called native plant gardening. The logical extension of this idea is to plant species from climates similar to one's own: plants from Mediterranean areas in summer-dry climates; and plants from summer-rainfall areas in areas with adequate summer rain. This may seem so obvious, as to be hardly worth saying, but it is common to see sprinklers trying to keep lawns green in Palm Springs. The ideal of a garden seems to be that which might have been found at a Victorian English country house on a fine day in a wet summer: green lawns like velvet; scented roses; and borders of stately delphiniums, lupins, and other flowers – an ideal seldom achievable even in England.

Those who live in a summer-dry climate and want to make a Mediterranean garden are fortunate to have a vast supply of suitable plants from which to choose. Low shrubs are ideal for covering large areas of poor soil, with varied colours, scents, and textures. Avoid clumping the plants of each sort. It is most important to plant in a natural way, so that one or two species are dominant, and others meander through this matrix as if growing wild.

Within this base of low shrubs might be planted the smaller flowers (irises, cyclamen, anemones, bulbs, and annuals), which give colour in autumn, spring, and early summer. Trees such as olives, pines, cedars, oaks, or eucalyptus can grow through the scrub, providing an extra dimension and some summer shade.

In very hot, dry areas, cactus gardens can be exciting. They can be filled not only with cactuses but also with succulents of all

Above *Euphorbia coerulescens* from Namaqualand and Namibia is one of the cactus-like spurges found throughout Africa and in the Canary Islands.

Left The Cactus Garden at the Huntington Botanic Garden in California is a wonderful example of a dry garden, which needs little watering. A wide range of American cactuses and other succulents from around the world give interest and colour throughout the year.

sorts and drought-tolerant bromeliads including *Puya*. Short-lived annuals such as South African daisies, American *Mimulus*, or Australian *Rhodanthe* will give colour after a few weeks of rain. In *Gardens of the Sun*, the Australian Trevor Nottle suggests keeping only a very small area well watered, near the house, and leaving the rest to nature. Plants that need summer water can be grown in large pots, and provided with drip irrigation; waste is eliminated, and water is concentrated at the roots where and when it is needed. Protection from hot, dry, summer winds is vital for newly planted trees or shrubs; they should be provided with shelters, and watered until they can cope on their own. Sinking a pipe to the roots will help direct water to where it is required.

Water can also be preserved by a deep mulch. This is often made up of wood chippings or some ugly material, but flat stones and coarse gravel, of varied size and 15cm (6in) or more deep, and as locally sourced as possible, are much more natural and attractive. Any rain that does fall is protected from evaporation, and in the driest areas the stones can be laid around a depression, so they direct rain to the roots of the plants.

Top This natural garrigue in western Crete boasts scented, flowering shrubs such as *Lavandula stoechas* and *Cistus salvifolius* beneath olive trees. Openings or path edges in a planting of this sort would be an ideal habitat for bulbs and low-growing annuals.

Above A colourful display of South African annuals, bulbs, and low shrubs can be seen in the Cape Rock Garden at Berkeley Botanic Garden, California, in spring.

Planting & Design

The Formal Garden

In this very brief discussion, the formal garden is contrasted with the natural garden (*see also* pp.30–1). Of course a garden can combine both styles, and I believe that the best gardens do this: the pavements and avenues, steps and terraces of the formal areas are placed near the house, and around the perimeter is the natural garden – the Jardin Anglais, nature artfully tamed.

In the Mediterranean climate the most important part of the garden is the outdoor room, for taking meals and drinks on warm evenings. This requires a roof for shade, either open and planted with vines or creepers, or an area roofed over but with open sides to catch breezes and scents from the garden. In areas prone to strong winds, such as the mistral, the outdoor room such as a verandah, condi, or loggia should be sheltered. So should an orangerie or squiffa, set apart from the house. In both of them, scented plants can be grown, either in pots or as climbers: *Pelargonium*, lilies, *Gardenia*, *Datura*, or *Hedychium* are suitable for large pots; and roses, jasmines, *Quisqualis*, or *Ipomoea* are good for climbing up walls or over a roof.

Other formal areas near the house are useful for short, easy walks. Therefore there should be a terrace, level with the house or joined to it by a flight of wide and shallow steps, and ideally partly shaded. Many of the plants shown within this book at the

Above Longwood Gardens in Pennsylvania were created by the industrial tycoon Pierre S. Dupont. They combine a wide range of subtropical planting with numerous formal features and a huge conservatory, in an area with hot humid summers and cold winters. *Victoria* 'Longwood Hybrid', waterlilies, and a large clump of *Nelumbo nucifera* (sacred lotus) dominate the planting in the lake.

Left Succulents, mostly *Aloe* and *Agave*, have been planted along a path, with steps leading up to a gazebo on a shaded terrace at La Mortola, in Italy. In this large garden, built on the side of a cliff overlooking the Mediterranean, there are numerous avenues, steps, pools, terraces, and covered walks.

Giardino Botanico La Mortola, on the coast of northwestern Italy, are suitable for the shaded backdrop of such a terrace, which has been cut into the hillside, or for a sunny wall and may be used to build up its front. The terrace is also a suitable place for statues, pillars, or a large urn or other container with a formal plant such as *Agave*.

The presence of flowing water has always been an important feature of gardens in dry climates. The medieval Moorish gardens of the Generalife in Spain are famous for their use of water. There are fast-flowing rills along flights of steps, and bubbling pools, as well as rows of small fountains, which give the impression of wetness without needing great quantities of water. Numerous small fountains of equal size give a better effect than one large one; in a shaded courtyard, a single jet can be set to fall back into a shallow basin. Even in the desert of Rajasthan, in the Indian palace fort at Chokhelao, near Jodhpur, there were water gardens with rills and moving sheets of water which ran inside the buildings, all fed by run-off carefully stored in tanks. Flowers were planted in small, rectangular beds, which could be watered easily. In these dry areas, great ingenuity was used to make the best of a limited flow.

In climates with wet summers, there can be larger areas of water – either in square, rectangular, or circular tanks, or larger sheets of water. These can be planted with waterlilies, or with the Amazonian *Victoria*, as at the Longwood Gardens, in eastern USA, as well as with reed-like marginal plants such as *Thalia*. The tall leaves and flowers of sacred lotus contrast with the floating waterlilies. In the Shalamar Gardens in Kashmir, terraces with pavilions and gravity-fed tanks and small plumes of water descend in steps to the lotus-filled Dal lake.

Above This simple terrace in Ronda, in southern Spain, is enhanced by a pot planted with variegated *Agave americana*. Light and shade, simplicity and proportions are important elements in the formal garden.

Left Fountains play in a courtyard in the gardens of the Generalife, originally built in the mid-13th century, in Granada, southern Spain. These fountains, though in keeping with the spirit of a Moorish garden, are a relatively recent addition, as are the modern roses framed by hedges of myrtle.

29

Left Subtropical Tasmania and China have been transported to Heligan, in Cornwall, England, where the tree fern *Dicksonia antarctica* has naturalized, in a gully leading down to the sea.

Below *Cyclamen graecum* subsp. *graecum*, seen here in western Crete, is happy in the driest rockiest places. It flowers with the first rains of autumn.

Bottom *Allium neopolitanum* and *Bellavalia paradoxa* bloom in spring under the olives at La Mortola, in Italy.

Right A Judas tree provides a focal point by the river at the wonderful Ninfa gardens, south of Rome, in Italy.

The Natural Garden

Away from the house and beyond the terraces and flights of steps a garden can become more natural. The plants used can be those found in the vicinity, ones chosen from another part of the world with a similar climate, or a mixture. In general, plants that come from similar climates look natural and appropriate when planted together. The purist, however, may like to have small areas of species from one location, and there are several examples that show how successful this can be. The Botanic Garden in Santa Barbara in California grows mainly plants from the chaparral, and the Living Desert Garden near Palm Springs boasts a fine collection of Californian cactuses and desert shrubs. In South Africa the National Botanic Garden at Kirstenbosch near Cape Town specializes in plants from the fynbos, while a smaller garden near Worcester, in Western Cape, concentrates on succulents from the Karroo. The former is one of the most attractive gardens in the world, and the restriction of planting only South African native species has, if anything, enhanced its beauty.

The design of natural planting relies on avoiding straight lines, creating changes of level and meandering paths from which the garden can be enjoyed. For the purpose of growing different plants it is desirable to create as many microhabitats as possible: shady cliffs, sunny cliffs, steep slopes, and moist places with damp rich soil as well as water. If a spring can be found or brought into the garden, a whole different range of plants, particularly ferns, can be grown.

A natural garden can be made in an old olive grove, with a slightly meandering and sunken path, like an ancient track between the trees. The native underplanting can be enhanced by spring-flowering bulbs, such as tulips, hyacinths, *Cyclamen persicum*, and *Muscari*, and with annuals including *Nigella* (love-in-a-mist) and scented *Reseda* (mignonette). Shrubs such as lavender and *Cistus* can be planted in the background, with drought-tolerant perennials including *Euphorbia characias*, *Iris unguicularis*, and *Acanthus*. In the heat of summer this garden is dormant, but the autumn rains bring out the first *Cyclamen neapolitanum* and yellow *Sternbergia*, whose flowers appear before the leaves.

PLANT DIRECTORY

Opposite Tresco Abbey, Isles of Scilly

Trees

A TREE IS A NECESSITY even for the smallest garden, to give shade and that feeling of coolness which is so welcome in a hot climate. Many conifers are tolerant of drought; cedars and pines are particularly suitable, as they cast a gentle shade and take little water.

Above *Schotia brachypetala* (see p. 57)

Pines

Pinus (Pinaceae)
PINE

Pinus is the most important conifer genus for planting in dry, hot climates, though, of course, many types tolerate cold and wet. Their narrow, wax-covered leaves make them exceptionally tough. Of around 100 species found in the northern hemisphere, half are native of Mexico and dry parts of western North America.

Above *Pinus ayacahuite* (Mexican white pine)

Above An ancient *Pinus bungeana* (lacebark pine) in a courtyard in the Forbidden City in Beijing, China

Pinus ayacahuite
MEXICAN WHITE PINE

This graceful, soft-needled pine from Mexico and Guatemala eventually forms a large tree. Its grey-green needles, 15–20cm (6–8in) long, are in groups of five; the narrow, soft, brown cones hang down and can reach 40cm (16in). These long cones are characteristic of white pines, which are also found in the Himalayas, the habitat of similar-looking but hardier *P. wallichiana*, which has shorter needles and cones.

Cultivation Best in good deep soil.
Height to 45m (150ft); spread to 15m (50ft). USZ 9–11, surviving -3°C (27°F) of overnight frost. Best with summer rainfall. ◗

Pinus bungeana
LACEBARK PINE

This elegant pine is ideal for a small space, and it is widely used in its native China for planting in temple courtyards and palace gardens. It is easily recognized by its silvery and pinkish flaking bark and short, grey-green needles, 6–8cm (2½–3in) long, in groups of three. The brown cones are around 5cm (2in) long, and shed their nut-like seeds in late autumn.

Cultivation Easy to grow in light soil, but slow to establish; very hardy and resistant to atmospheric pollution.
Height to 20m (65ft); spread to 6m (20ft), but usually less and often multistemmed. USZ 6–11, surviving -20°C (-4°F) of overnight frost. Tolerant of drought in summer or winter. ◗

Pinus coulteri
BIG-CONE PINE

This coarse, fast-growing pine is handsome when young, probably reaching its optimum after 30 years, before becoming a bit gaunt. It grows wild in southern California, for

Above *Pinus coulteri* (big-cone pine) in the hills above Pasadena, California

example, in the dry foothills above Los Angeles and is easily recognized by its huge, pale brown, spiky cones, to 30cm (1ft) long, and stiff, grey-green needles, more than 20cm (8in) long, held in threes, mainly towards the ends of the branches.

Cultivation Needs a hot, sunny site and dry, well-drained soil.

Height to 20m (65ft); spread to 6m (20ft). USZ 7–11, surviving -10°C (14°F) of overnight frost. Tolerant of summer drought. ◑

Pinus halepensis
ALEPPO PINE

This graceful, very hardy pine has yellowish green needles, 6–11cm (2½–4¼in) long, in pairs. The brown cones are 10cm (4in) long. It is native of the western and southern Mediterranean coastline, and its relative *P. brutia* is commoner in the east.

Cultivation Grow in dry soil.

Height to 20m (65ft); spread to 6m (20ft). USZ 8–11, survives -5°C (23°F) of overnight frost. Tolerant of summer drought. ◑

Pinus montezumae
MONTEZUMA PINE

This is one of the most magnificent of all trees for a mild and moist subtropical garden. The branches form a rounded head, with dense whorls of grey-green needles towards their ends; these are up to 25cm (10in) long, drooping or spreading and mostly in groups of five. The cones, green turning brown, are smooth and woody, up to 15cm (6in) long, and take two years to ripen. As its name suggests, *P. montezumae* is native of Mexico, and grows in moist mountain areas mainly in the south and centre, as far north as Saltillo. The specimen

shown here, in the subtropical garden at Mount Usher, was planted in 1909.

Cultivation Needs deep rich soil, ample water, and shelter from wind to grow into a perfect specimen.

Height to 30m (100ft); spread to 18m (60ft). USZ 9–11, surviving -5°C (23°F) of overnight frost. Needs water in summer. ●

Pinus patula
MEXICAN WEEPING PINE

This is an elegant but delicate pine, easily recognized by its long, slender needles, which hang like sheaves of grass, sticking together when wet; they can reach 30cm (1ft) long and are grass-green, in groups of three. The green, smooth, woody cones, 6–10cm (2½–4in) long, mature to brown. This lovely pine is native of southern Mexico; in tropical areas it is very fast

Above *Pinus halepensis* (Aleppo pine) on the Italian coast at La Mortola

growing and can reach 50m (165ft) in less than 40 years. Even in cooler zones it can make 6m (20ft) in 10 years.

Cultivation Needs well-drained but fertile soil for the best growth and longest needles.
Height to 50m (165ft); spread to 6m (20ft). USZ 9–11, surviving -6°C (21°F) of overnight frost. Needs summer water. ●

Pinus pinea

STONE PINE, UMBRELLA PINE

P. pinea is one of the most characteristic trees of the Mediterranean and Black Sea coasts, and is widely planted in areas with similar climates around the world. The characteristic shape is like an umbrella, with a single trunk and rounded head, yet old trees often have several stems and form a huge dome. The grey-green needles are sharp, around 12cm (5in) long, and in

Above *Pinus pinea* (stone pine) in the garden at Serre de La Madone near Menton, France

pairs. The round, knobbly, green cones turn brown and take two years to ripen. They have large, hard-shelled, edible seeds, which are the pine nuts of Mediterranean cooking. A good specimen of *P. pinea* makes a fine shade tree or focal point in a warm-climate garden.

Cultivation Needs well-drained soil, and thrives on sand.
Height to 25m (80ft); spread to 20m (65ft). USZ 7–11, surviving -10°C (14°F) of overnight frost. Tolerant of summer drought. ◑

Above The famous specimen of *Pinus montezumae* (Montezuma pine), Mount Usher, Ireland

Above *Pinus patula* (Mexican weeping pine), ten years after planting

Cedars & Cypresses

Cedrus (Pinaceae)
CEDAR

The four species of *Cedrus* are some of the best of all garden trees for subtropical and Mediterranean climates, growing reasonably fast to a great size, and often with a beautiful shape. They cast light shade, and many plants grow well beneath them, particularly bulbs that flower in autumn or spring, or drought-tolerant shrubs such as *Cistus* or rosemary. The species have an interesting disjunct distribution, with three species from the Mediterranean region and one, *C. deodara*, in the western Himalayas.

Cedrus atlantica f. *glauca*
BLUE ATLANTIC CEDAR
C. atlantica is found wild in the Atlas Mountains in Morocco and Algeria. Most wild trees have green leaves, 2–3cm (¾–1¼in) long, in clusters of 10–50 on spur shoots, while the blue forms are popular in cultivation. They make huge trees, pyramidal when young, but later becoming rounded, with layered, blue-green branches set with rounded, pale brown cones.

Above *Cedrus atlantica* f. *glauca* (blue Atlantic cedar)

Cultivation Needs well-drained soil.
Height to 40m (130ft); spread to 15m (50ft).
USZ 7–11, surviving -10°C (14°F) of overnight
frost. Survives summer drought. ◑

Cedrus libani
CEDAR OF LEBANON
This cedar is found wild in the mountains of southern Turkey, in Syria, and in the Lebanon, where the oldest trees are thought to be more than 2,000 years old. It tolerates most soils; indeed our picture shows it growing in Turkey on bare serpentine soil, which is poisonous to most other trees. All cedars develop their characteristic flat tops with increasing age, but *C. libani* in Turkey tends to grow taller and narrower than it does in the Lebanon. The green shoots are rather stiff, with clusters of 30–45 needles, 2–3cm (¾–1¼in) long, on short shoots. The pale brown cones are rounded, with densely overlapping scales, and they break up on the tree.
Cultivation Once young trees have become established, they are very tough and easy to grow in well-drained soil.
Height to 36m (120ft); spread to 18m (60ft).
USZ 7–11, surviving -10°C (14°F) of overnight
frost. Tolerant of summer drought. ◑

Above A wild *Cedrus libani* (cedar of Lebanon)

Cupressus (Cupressaceae)
CYPRESS

The genus *Cupressus* has 16 species, found around most of the northern hemisphere, south to Honduras. It is recognized by its very small, overlapping leaves and quite large, round cones. Some species are very drought resistant; others need moisture and shelter to thrive.

Cupressus cashmeriana
KASHMIR CYPRESS
This lovely graceful tree is said to be wild in Bhutan, not in Kashmir, as was originally thought. It is often planted elsewhere in warm, moist climates, and was popular as a foliage plant in Victorian conservatories. In the usual cultivated form the branches hang in long, narrow, fan-like sprays of soft bluish-green needles, 1–2mm (½–⅙in) long, a lovely foil for flowering shrubs. The cones are 1cm (⅜in) across and green.
Cultivation Given shelter, warmth, and fertile leafy soil, it is fast growing.
Height to 20m (65ft); spread to 6m (20ft).
USZ 9–11, surviving -6.5°C (20°F) of
overnight frost. Needs water in summer. ●

Above **Cupressus sempervirens** (Italian cypress) in Hurst castle, California

Below *Cupressus cashmeriana* (Kashmir cypress)

Cupressus sempervirens

ITALIAN CYPRESS

Large areas of Mediterranean scenery are dominated by the dark upright spires of cypresses and the silvery rounded clouds of olives. *C. sempervirens* grows as a wild tree from the eastern Mediterranean and north Africa eastwards to Iran, where it often makes a wide spreading tree. The rounded, dark green leaves are 0.5mm (¹⁄₃₂in) long, and knobbly brown cones are 2–2.5cm (¾–1in) long.

Cultivation Easily grown in any well-drained soil, and good for rocky places. *Height to 30m (100ft); spread to 6m (20ft). USZ 8–11, surviving -12°C (10°F) of overnight frost. Tolerant of summer drought.* ◗

Cupressus macrocarpa

MONTEREY CYPRESS, MACROCARPA

This species is as common in cultivation as *C. cashmeriana* is rare. It is one of the best trees to form a fast-growing windbreak in coastal areas, and is often planted as a vigorous hedge in mild climates. It is native only in a few places on the California coast around Monterey, where it grows on cliffs and sandy bluffs, dwarfed by salt winds and drought. The dark green shoots are round, not flattened, and the brown cones are up to 3.5cm (1½in) across. Leaves are 1.5mm (¹⁄₁₆in) long. Young trees are narrowly pyramidal when growing fast, but with age and in exposed sites develop a flat spreading top, like that of a dark *Cedrus libani*.

Cultivation Easily grown in any soil. *Height to 36m (120ft); spread to 15m (50ft). USZ 8–11, surviving -12°C (10°F) of overnight frost. Tolerant of summer drought.* ◗

Above A wild stand of *Cupressus macrocarpa* (Monterey cypress), south of Monterey in California

Small Palms

Chamaerops (Arecaceae)

The genus *Chamaerops* consists of a single species of fan palm, often suckering to form thickets of small trees. The fibres from the leaf bases were used as a coarse substitute for horsehair, in upholstery.

Chamaerops humilis
This palm is native only in western Europe, particularly in Spain, and in north Africa, though it is often planted elsewhere, as a dwarf, slow-growing palm with a curving trunk. In dry places, or when frequently burnt, it may fail to make much of a trunk. Its dark bluish green, fan-shaped leaves, 70cm (28in) long, are borne in rosettes. The pale creamy yellow flowers are followed by inedible fruit, 1–3cm (⅜–1¼in) long, which is orange-brown when ripe.
Cultivation Easily grown in any soil. *Height to 6m (20ft); spread to 1.2m (4ft). USZ 9–11, surviving -6.5°C (20°F) of overnight frost. Tolerant of summer drought.* ◑

Dypsis (Arecaceae)
FEATHER PALM

Dypsis is a genus of about 140 species of palm, found wild in Madagascar, and on

Above A fine clump of *Chamaerops humilis* at the Jardin Thuret on Cap d'Antibes, France

other islands in the Indian Ocean. It now includes the genera *Neodypsis*, *Neophloga*, and *Chrysalidocarpus* and is very variable in size, from 30cm (1ft) to 10m (33ft).

Dypsis lutescens
(syn. *Chrysalidocarpus lutescens*)
BUTTERFLY PALM, ARECA PALM
This very graceful palm is often cultivated in frost-free climates and as a potted plant.

The stems are slender, around 15cm (6in) across, and sucker freely, often forming thickets, while the arching, pinnate, bright green leaves can reach 2.5m (8ft) long.
Cultivation Easily grown in moist soil in shade and shelter, or in a pot that is kept well watered. *Height to 6m (20ft); spread to 4m (13ft). USZ 10–11, surviving -1°C (30°F) of overnight frost. Needs summer water.* ●

Above *Dypsis lutescens* (butterfly palm)

Above *Trachycarpus fortunei* (Chusan palm) in the subtropical garden at Trebah on the Cornish coast

Phoenix (Arecaceae)

Phoenix is an important genus of 17 species of pinnate-leaved palms from Arabia and north Africa, central Africa to Malaysia and southeast Asia, and coastal Crete and Turkey. Most grow in apparently dry areas, but may have their roots reaching to the water table; some species even grow along rivers or in swamps.

Phoenix canariensis
CANARY ISLAND DATE PALM
This short, thick-trunked palm bears very long, luxuriant, green leaves and large bunches of small orange fruit, 3cm (1¼in) long, which ripen in spring. It is very commonly planted along the coasts of the Mediterranean, as well as in the warmer parts of California, as a garden specimen or a street tree. The narrowly pinnate, mid- to dark green leaves can reach 6m (20ft) long.
Cultivation Easily cultivated in any soil.
Height to 20m (65ft); spread to 10m (33ft). USZ 9–11, surviving -6.5°C (20°F) of overnight frost. Tolerant of summer drought. ◗

Trachycarpus (Arecaceae)

This genus comprises around four species of fan palm from the Himalayas and China. They are among the hardiest of their family, and are often cultivated in warm-temperate climates. The very fibrous leaf bases have

Below *Phoenix canariensis* (Canary Island date palm) growing wild in Tenerife

been used for cordage, and as long waterproof capes in western Yunnan.

Trachycarpus fortunei
CHUSAN PALM, HEMP PALM
This palm is native of China, Burma, and Japan. It grows in the mountains up to 2,400m (8,000ft) in western China and is commonly cultivated in the villages there. It develops rather slowly when young, but eventually forms a rough trunk covered in old leaf bases; these can be peeled off, as they are in China, to improve the look of the tree. The dark green, fan-shaped leaves form rather soft fans, 80cm (32in) across. The spherical to kidney-shaped fruits, 1.2cm (½in) long, are bluish when mature.

Left *Trachycarpus martianus* in Yunnan, China

Cultivation Easily grown in woodland or a sheltered site, in partial shade in hot areas.
Height to 9m (30ft); spread to 3m (10ft). USZ 8–11, surviving -12°C (10°F) of overnight frost. Needs water in summer. ◗

Trachycarpus martianus
This native of the Himalayas, from Nepal to Burma, is closely related to *T. fortunei* but has a taller, narrower, naked trunk, bluish stiffer leaves, and oblong–ovoid, glossy blue fruit, 1.2cm (½in) long.
Cultivation Requires fertile moist soil and a sheltered position.
Height 15m (50ft) or more; spread to 3m (10ft). USZ 9–11, surviving -6.5°C (20°F) of overnight frost. Needs water in summer. ◗

Medium-sized Palms

Butia (Arecaceae)

This genus consists of around eight species from eastern South America. The leaves are pinnate with leaflets in two rows, the very coarse leaf bases remaining attached to the trunk. Sweetly scented flowers, in long arching bunches, are followed by round, grape-like, edible fruit, orange when ripe.

Butia capitata
BUTIA PALM, JELLY PALM
This low, spreading palm with its blue-green leaves, 3m (10ft) long, is native in southern Brazil, Uruguay, and northern Argentina. The small, three-petalled flowers are yellow or tinged reddish.
Cultivation In fertile deep soil, this palm is very tough and heat tolerant.
Height to 9m (30ft); spread to 6m (20ft). USZ 9–11, surviving -6.5°C (20°F) of overnight frost. Tolerant of summer drought. ◗

Copernicia (Arecaceae)
COPPER PALM

The genus *Copernicia* comprises around 25 species of large fan palms with thick trunks

Above *Livistona chinensis* (Chinese fan palm), Bermuda

often covered by dead leaves and thorny leaf stalks, from the West Indies, especially Cuba, southwards to Argentina and Paraguay. One species, *C. cerifera* from Brazil, is an important source of wax.

Copernicia baileyana
YAREY
This palm is a native of Cuba and makes a tall, impressive tree in Florida. The fan-shaped, narrow, hard and leathery, green leaves, around 1m (3ft) in diameter, are produced on thorny stalks and have tiny yellowish teeth on the margins. The small flowers are yellow and are carried in a branching inflorescence.
Cultivation Grows in sandy soil that is deep and moisture retentive.
Height to 12m (40ft); spread to 3m (10ft). USZ 10–11, surviving -1°C (30°F) of overnight frost. Needs water in summer. ●

Dypsis (Arecaceae)

Around 14 of the 140 species of *Dypsis* (see p.40) from Madagascar were formerly separated into the genus *Neodypsis*.

Dypsis decaryi (syn. Neodypsis decaryi)
This strange-looking palm has the leaves twisted so that they appear to be arranged in three rows, although, from the angle at

Above *Butia capitata* (Butia palm)

Left *Copernicia baileyana* (yarey) in the Fairchild Botanic Garden, Florida

which our picture was taken, the leaves and leaf bases appear to be in two rows. The bluish green, pinnate leaves are around 2.5m (8ft) long, covered with dark brown hairs when young, and arch over as they age. The plant eventually forms a short stout trunk, marked with horizontal rings.
Cultivation This tough palm is tolerant of heat and drought and grows well in full sun.
Height to 4m (13ft); spread to 3m (10ft). USZ 10–11, surviving -1°C (30°F) overnight. Needs some water in summer. ◗

Livistona (Arecaceae)

Livistona is a genus of around 30 species of palm, from Malaysia, China, Japan, and the Philippines south to Australia. They have fan-like leaves and conspicuous flowers.

Livistona chinensis
CHINESE FAN PALM
This is a large fan palm with characteristic floppy tips to the leaf segments and long arching leaf stalks. The slightly greyish green leaves, 1.2m (4ft) across, have their spreading and curling leaflets joined in the basal third. This native of southern China, Taiwan, and Japan as far north as Shikoku is slow growing, and impressive when

Above The spectacular Madagascan palm
Dypsis decaryi in Florida

young; later it develops a strong trunk. The numerous, pale yellowish, flowers, 1cm (⅜in) long, are followed by bluish green or grey fruit, 2.5cm (1in) across.
Cultivation Grow in fertile moist soil.
Height to 5m (16ft); spread to 3m (10ft). USZ 9–11, surviving -6.5°C (20°F) of overnight frost. Needs water in summer. ◗

Phoenix (Arecaceae)
DATE PALM

The genus *Phoenix* of pinnate-leaved, tender palms is described on p.41.

Phoenix sylvestris
WILD DATE PALM
This is a tall elegant palm with slender, narrow, greyish leaves, to 5m (16ft) long, with leaflets arranged in several rows. It is found growing wild in India, Nepal, and Burma. Juice from the trunk, 30cm (12in) across, is used to make palm wine and sugar. The inflorescence is to 90cm (3ft) long, and the yellow-orange to red-brown, cylindric fruit are about 3cm (1¼in) long.
Cultivation Easily cultivated in any soil.
Height to 18m (60ft); spread to 3m (10ft). USZ 9–11, surviving -6.5°C (20°F) of overnight frost. Tolerant of summer drought. ◑

Below *Phoenix sylvestris* (wild date palm) on Mount Abu in Rajastan, northwest India

43

Large Palms

Bismarckia (Arecaceae)

The genus *Bismarckia* contains only one species. Male and female flowers are formed on separate trees.

Bismarckia nobilis
This dramatic palm produces huge, stiff, fan-like leaves, about 2m (6ft) long and whitish or blue-green all over. It is native of Madagascar, where it grows in open savannah. The fruits are freely formed in cultivation and are like large purple dates.
Cultivation Easily grown in dry sandy soil in full sun in warm areas.
Height to 18m (60ft); spread to 6m (20ft). USZ 10–11, surviving -1°C (30°F) of overnight frost. Tolerant of summer drought. ◗

Hyophorbe (Arecaceae)

Hyophorbe is a genus of around five species, often called *Mascarena*, from the Mascarene

Above *Bismarckia nobilis* in California

Islands in the Indian Ocean, where many of these species are native. All have smooth thickened trunks and flowers emerging from the base of the spineless leaf sheaths.

Hyophorbe verschaffeltii
SPINDLE PALM
This palm is native of Mauritius, but is now commonly planted in the Caribbean, where the picture here was taken. The upper part of the trunk is covered by smooth sheathing leaf bases, and the inflorescence emerges from below these sheaths. The greyish green, pinnate leaves are around 2.5m (8ft) long.
Cultivation Easily grown in any soil and tolerant of coastal conditions.
Height to 9m (30ft); spread to 6m (20ft). USZ 10–11, surviving -1°C (30°F) of overnight frost. Tolerant of summer drought. ◗

Roystonia (Arecaceae)
ROYAL PALM

The genus *Roystonia* comprises 11 species found in Florida, the Caribbean, and Central America south to northeastern South America. *R. oleracea* grows from Trinidad southwards and is the source of edible growing points, which are sold as palm hearts or *palmitos*.

Left *Hyophorbe verschaffeltii* (spindle palm) planted in the Virgin Islands

1m (3ft) or more in diameter, and the dark green, fan-shaped leaves, 2m (6½ft) or more across, have hanging fibrous tips to the segments and long threads, which give it its name, *filifera*. The inflorescence appears among the leaves and bears plum-like, brownish black fruit.
Cultivation Easily grown in dry soil, where there is sufficient water beneath. *Height to 25m (80ft); spread to 5m (16ft). USZ 9–11, surviving -3°C (27°F) of overnight frost. Needs ample water at the roots.* ◑

Washingtonia robusta
MEXICAN FAN PALM
This is similar in leaf to *W. filifera*, but has a taller, narrower trunk, being less than 80cm (32in) in diameter, and fewer threads among the leaves, which are 1.25m (4ft) long. It is wild in northwest Mexico, in Sonora, and in Baja California.
Cultivation Easily grown in dry soil, where there is sufficient water beneath. *Height to 33m (110ft); spread to 3m (10ft). USZ 9–11, surviving -3°C (27°F) of overnight frost. Needs ample water at the roots.* ◑

Above Washingtonia filifera (California fan palm) growing by a stream in Indian Canyon, Palm Springs, California

Roystonia regia
CUBAN ROYAL PALM, FLORIDA ROYAL PALM
This tall palm, commonly planted in warm areas, is native of Cuba, southeast Mexico, the West Indies, and Florida, where it grows in swamps. The smooth grey trunk tends to be slightly thicker towards the middle. Its dark green, pinnate leaves have very long sheaths and reach 6m (20ft) long, later arching over and hanging down. The inflorescence, to 1m (3ft) long, emerges below the lowest leaf sheath; the round fruits are 2cm (¾in) across and purplish when ripe. Closely related *R. oleracea* has a narrow, parallel-sided trunk.
Cultivation Easily grown in fertile soil. *Height to 30m (100ft); spread to 12m (40ft). USZ 9–11, surviving -6.5°C (20°F) of overnight frost. Needs water in summer.* ●

Washingtonia (Arecaceae)
FAN PALM

The genus *Washingtonia*, named after George Washington (1732–99), contains only two species. These are native in western North America and northwest Mexico, and are widely cultivated.

Washingtonia filifera
CALIFORNIA FAN PALM, DESERT FAN PALM, PETTICOAT PALM
This sturdy fan palm, with its untidy leaves and hanging, straw-like "skirt", is native of the extreme south of Arizona, Nevada, California, and Baja California. It grows in the desert and foothills, usually by springs and along permanent streams. The trunk is

Above Washingtonia robusta (Mexican fan palm) above; *Roystonia regia* (Cuban royal palm) below

Cycads

Though many of them look distinctly palm-like, the cycads are a very ancient group of gymnosperms, and therefore more closely related to conifers and *Ginkgo*. They often have very large male and female cones, the latter with nut-like seeds. Their most remarkable feature, however, is their huge swimming sperm, the largest known, with a spiral band of flagella (thin, whip-like shoots). Fossil cycads have been found from the Triassic Period, and reached their peak in the Jurassic one. Many cycads are now rare and endangered, though individuals are very long-lived.

Cycas (Cycadaceae)

There are 17 species of *Cycas* found wild from East Africa and India to Japan and Australia. The orange seeds are formed on short, brown, leaf-like stems. Many species are tall and palm-like.

Cycas revoluta
This short, palm-like plant bears whorls of stiff, dark green, pinnate leaves on a short

Above *Cycas revoluta:* female cones

trunk. It is found wild in Japan, growing on rocky slopes and cliffs. The leaves all uncurl together, like fern fronds, and are around 1m (3ft) long. Male and female organs are formed on different plants, and in females the centre of the leaf whorl can be filled with seed leaves.

Cultivation Easily grown in good soil, and tolerant of coastal conditions in Mediterranean climates.
Height to 4m (13ft); spread to 2m (6½ft). USZ 9–11, surviving -6.5°C (20°F) of frost. Tolerant of summer drought. ◐◑

Above *Dioon purpusii*

Dioon (Zamiaceae)

The genus *Dioon* contains 10 species, from Mexico and Central America. The leaf pinnae are all the same width, and do not narrow towards their base, so they have a very ancient, undeveloped appearance.

Dioon purpusii
This very slow-growing, palm-like cycad has pinnate, blue-green leaves, around 1.2m (4ft) long. The stiff pinnae are

Above *Cycas revoluta* in the garden of Elbow Beach Hotel, Bermuda

5–10cm (2–4in) long, with a spiny tip, and a few spines on the edge. The cones are large; the cylindric brown females mature to 45cm (18in) long.

Cultivation Grow in well-drained soil.
Height to 2m (6½ft); spread to 1.5m (5ft). USZ 9–11, surviving -3°C (27°F) of overnight frost. Tolerant of summer drought. ◗

Encephalartos (Zamiaceae)

Encephalartos comprises 46 species, which are native in tropical and southern Africa. They have thick knobbly trunks, which often form small side plants.

Encephalartos horridus
This distinct showy cycad has blue-green, very stiff and prickly, upright leaves, around 1m (3ft) long, and is generally stemless; old specimens can have a short thick trunk. It is native of the Eastern Cape in South Africa, where it grows in dry rocky grassland and scrub. The cylindric brown female cones are 40cm (16in) long.

Cultivation Easily grown in well-drained soil and full sun.
Height to 2m (6½ft); spread to 1.2m (4ft). USZ 9–11, surviving -6.5°C (20°F) of overnight frost. Needs some summer water. ◗

Below *Encephalartos horridus* in the Karoo Botanic Garden, Worcester, South Africa

Lepidozamia (Zamiaceae)

The genus comprises two species of palm-like cycads from northeastern Australia. The male cones are particularly large, to 25cm (10in) in diameter.

Lepidozamia peroffskyana
This is one of the larger cycads, found in the rainforests near the coast from northeast New South Wales to southeast Queensland. The trunks are rough and corky, with the remains of old leaf bases. The green leaves, up to 1m (3ft) long, have pinnae around 1.2cm (½in) wide. Male and female cones are produced on different plants: the male to 75cm (30in) long; the female to 90cm (3ft), with red seeds.

Cultivation Needs dry sandy soil in a sheltered, humid, partially shaded site.
Height to 6m (20ft); spread to 4.5m (15ft). USZ 10–11, surviving -1°C (30°F) of overnight frost. Needs watering throughout the year. ◑

Zamia (Zamiaceae)

Zamia is a genus of 40 species, native in tropical America and Florida. Several species are pollinated by beetles. They usually have short thick trunks.

Left *Lepidozamia peroffskyana* in the West Indies

Zamia furfuracea
This dwarf cycad from eastern Mexico to Colombia has a tuberous stem and stiff hairy, green leaves with spiny stalks and blunt-tipped pinnae. The male cones are green and cylindric, 10cm (4in) long; the female ones, cylindric, brown, and pointed.

Cultivation Easily grown in any soil.
Height to 1m (3ft); spread to 2m (6½ft). USZ 9–11, surviving -6.5°C (20°F) of overnight frost. Needs some water in summer. ◑

Above *Zamia furfuracea* in the Virgin Islands

Magnolias

Magnolia (Magnoliaceae)

Magnolias are some of the most beautiful of the flowering trees and shrubs. The genus includes more than 120 evergreen and deciduous species, and originates in areas as diverse as southeast Asia and northeast USA. In addition to species, many hybrids and cultivars are available to gardeners. Many produce enormous, sometimes scented flowers. Magnolias do exceptionally well in sheltered, warm, moist areas, where their rate of growth is often phenomenal – more than 1m (3ft) per growing season.

Magnolia 'Caerhays Belle'

This deciduous hybrid was raised at Caerhays Castle, Cornwall. It is fast growing and flowers freely, producing light pink, nodding flowers, to 30cm (1ft) wide. in early spring. The obovate leaves, 20–25cm (8–10in) long, are green.
Cultivation Does well in a reasonable depth of fertile, moist but well-drained soil in sun or semi-shade. A mulch of compost or leaves will help to conserve moisture. *Height to 10m (33ft); spread to 6m (20ft). USZ 7–11, surviving -17°C (2°F) of overnight frost. Needs summer water.* ❧

Magnolia campbellii 'Betty Jessel'

Magnolia campbellii is native to the Himalaya, where it makes a huge deciduous tree, with enormous, waterlily-like flowers, varying in colour from white through pink to rose-purple. There are many forms and hybrids of this magnificent species. The clone shown

Above *Magnolia campbellii* 'Betty Jessel'

Above *Magnolia* 'Caerhays Belle'

Below *Magnolia* 'Caerhays Belle'

Below *Magnolia delavayi* outside the Yufeng temple near Lijiang, in China

Above *Magnolia grandiflora*

Above *Magnolia yunnanensis*

here was raised by Sir George Jessel, of Kent, UK, from a seedling of a very dark form of *M. campbellii*, which grew in the Botanical Garden of Darjeeling. 'Betty Jessel' flowers are borne in late spring and can measure as much as 25cm (10in) across. Its green obovate leaves are to 30cm (12in) long.
Cultivation Does well in a reasonable depth of fertile, moist but well-drained soil. Add a mulch of compost or leafmould to help conserve moisture.
Height to 9m (30ft); spread to 6m (20ft). USZ 7–11, surviving -17°C (2°F) of overnight frost. Requires summer water.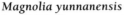

Magnolia delavayi

This evergreen Chinese species makes a spreading tree, usually with a flat top, but is otherwise quite similar in appearance to *M. grandiflora*. In the wild it grows in rocky sandstone or limestone areas, which accounts for the fact that it is tolerant of chalky soils. Depending on the conditions in which it is growing, it will eventually make a good-sized tree, with beautiful, cup-shaped, creamy white, slightly scented flowers, to 20cm (8in) across, during late spring and summer. The mainly elliptic to ovate, leathery leaves, 13–20cm (5–8in) long, are dull green on the upper side, and greyish coloured and downy underneath.
Cultivation Grow in sun or partial shade. Does best when sheltered from strong wind, because of its large leaves. Prefers fertile soil, but tolerates chalk.
Height to 9m (30ft); spread to 6m (20ft). USZ 8–11, surviving -12°C (10°F) of overnight frost occasionally. Needs water in summer. ●

Magnolia grandiflora

This is one of the best-known, evergreen magnolias, with its scented, cream, cup-shaped flowers, to 25cm (10in) wide, produced during summer. It originates from southeastern North America, where it grows in humid forests near the coast. In warm gardens, freestanding trees attain a magnificent pyramidal shape. The variable, usually narrowly elliptic to ovate, leathery leaves, to 20cm (8in) long, are a glossy dark green on the upper side, with a reddish brown felt on the underside. 'Exmouth' has a slender pyramidal habit and rather narrow leaves; 'Goliath' has short blunt leaves, and flowers in late summer.
Cultivation Grow in fertile, deep, moist but well-drained soil in sun or partial shade. Will not tolerate chalk. The shallow roots resent disturbance, and an annual mulch is beneficial.
Height to 30m (100ft); spread to 25m (80ft). USZ 7–11, surviving -17°C (2°F) of frost. Needs summer watering when young. ●●

Magnolia yunnanensis
(syn. *Michelia yunnanensis*)
This evergreen shrub is a native of southwestern China, where it grows on rocky hills. It has thick, shining, leathery leaves. Star-shaped, cream flowers, to 9cm (3½in) across, are borne in spring; they emerge from velvety, red-brown bud scales.
Cultivation Does well in fertile soil in sun or partial shade.
Height to 4m (13ft); spread to 2.1m (7ft). USZ 8–11, surviving -12°C (10°F) of overnight frost. Requires water in summer. ●

Palm-like Trees

Cordyline (Agavaceae)

This small genus of evergreen trees and shrubs has around 15 species in Australasia and one in tropical America. The two species shown here are both from New Zealand, and are widely available.

Cordyline australis

NEW ZEALAND CABBAGE TREE, TORBAY PALM
If left unpruned, this evergreen tree eventually makes a single trunk up to 3m (10ft), from the top of which arise many stout ascending branches. These are crowned with dense tufts of arching, sword-shaped, light green leaves, to 60cm (2ft) long. If kept cut back, *C. australis* can be forced to produce several trunks. The star-shaped, creamy white, fragrant flowers are borne in terminal panicles, 1.5m (5ft) long, in early summer and are followed by small white berries.
Cultivation Grow in any soil in a humid maritime climate. Dislikes sudden changes in temperature and moisture levels. *Height to 9m (30ft); spread to 4m (13ft). USZ 9–11, surviving -6.5°C (20°F) of frost. Drought tolerant, but will probably need water when first planted.* ◗●

Cordyline indivisa

BLUE DRACAENA
This species is less hardy, and slightly less well known, than *C. australis*, yet is often

Above *Cordyline australis* (New Zealand cabbage tree)

more spectacular. It generally has a single unbranched stem and a dense head of sword-shaped, green to bluish green leaves, to 1.5m (5ft) long, glaucous below, and wider than those of *C. australis*. The small translucent flowers are flushed purple, and are carried in summer in stiff pendulous panicles, 1m (3ft) long (*see* p.25).
Cultivation Does well in any soil in a maritime climate, but because of its large leaves it needs shelter from gales.

Above *Cordyline indivisa* (blue dracaena) in Devon

Height to 8m (25ft); spread to around 4m (13ft). USZ 10–11, surviving -1°C (30°F) of overnight frost. Tolerant of summer drought, but needs moisture when newly planted. ●

Dasylirion (Dracaenaceae)

This genus of 18 species of evergreen shrubs and bushy trees is related to *Agave* and is native of the southern USA and Mexico. In

Below *Dasylirion acrotrichum* in the Abbey Gardens, Tresco, Isles of Scilly

Below *Dracaena draco* in a garden on Beverley Hills, California

most species the rosettes of leaves emerge from a woody underground stem. Some dasylirions are now known as *Nolina*.

Dasylirion acrotrichum
This unbranched shrub has a thick trunk, to 4m (13ft) wide, and a round head of numerous, very narrow, dull green leaves, to 90cm (3ft) long, with hooked spines on the toothed margins. As the name indicates, there is also a tuft of fibres on the point of each leaf. The tiny, white, bell-shaped flowers are carried in an inflorescence, 3–4m (10–13ft) long, in summer.
Cultivation Does well in dry rocky places or sandy soil in full sun.
Height to 1.8m (6ft); spread to 1m (3ft). USZ 10–11, surviving -1°C (30°F) of frost for short periods. Tolerant of summer drought. ◑

Dracaena (Dracaenaceae)
DRAGON TREE

There are around 40 species of *Dracaena*, several of which are grown for their foliage. They are evergreen shrubs or trees, native of Africa and the Canaries.

Dracaena draco
This stout, branching, slow-growing tree is native of the Canary Islands, but is now very rare in the wild. It has a silvery trunk and clusters of mid-green, sword-shaped leaves, up to 60cm (2ft) long, while the greenish flowers are borne in an erect terminal panicle, 0.8–1m (2½–3ft) long, in summer. The dark red resin, which seeps from the trunk, looks similar to blood.
Cultivation Grow in any dry rocky soil in sun. Tolerates partial shade. Can also be cultivated as a houseplant.
Height to 9m (30ft); spread to 6m (20ft). USZ 9–11, surviving -3°C (27°F) of overnight frost. Fairly tolerant of summer drought. ◑

Pandanus (Pandanaceae)
GRAPE TREE

There are around 700 species of palm-like trees and shrubs in the genus *Pandanus*, which is native of northern Australia, Africa, India, Malaysia, and the Pacific Islands. Many species grow in mangrove swamps or near the coast, and the fruits are dispersed by the tides.

Pandanus utilis
SCREW PINE
This native of Madagascar has stilt-like, aerial roots, a twisted stem, and pineapple-like fruits, which are edible when ripe.
Cultivation Needs well-drained soil in sun.
Height to 20m (65ft); spread to 4.5m (15ft). USZ 10–11, surviving -1°C (30°F) of frost for short periods only. Needs water in summer. ●

Above *Pandanus utilis* (screw pine) in Bermuda

Bananas

Ensete (Musaceae)

There are seven species of these giant monocarpic evergreens from tropical Africa and India. They are closely related to bananas, but differ in that they do not sucker, most have a swollen stem base, and larger seeds. All species have large leaves and can make huge plants in favourable conditions; they can also do well as pot plants in conservatories in cooler climates.

Ensete ventricosum
ABYSSINIAN BANANA

This evergreen perennial produces a cluster of huge, exotic-looking, arching, broadly linear, dark green leaves, to 6m (20ft) long, atop a massive single upright "trunk" (strictly speaking a pseudostem), which can be 2–6m (6½–20ft) high. The whitish flowers are inconspicuous on horizontal then drooping inflorescences with dark red bracts. The banana-like, inedible fruits contain large, glossy, black seeds. Although fast growing, *E. ventricosum* is not very long-lived as it usually flowers after a few years and then dies back to its roots.

Cultivation Easily raised from seed. Grow in fertile soil in full sun, with shelter from strong winds.

Height to 6m (20ft); spread to 3m (10ft).
USZ 11, with a minimum of 4.5°C (40°F).
Needs generous summer watering. ●

Above A young plant of *Ensete ventricosum* (Abyssinian banana) at Rosemoor in Devon

Musa (Musaceae)

The genus *Musa* comprises around 40 evergreen species originating from Asia and Australia. Though most people consider bananas to be trees, botanically speaking they are all large suckering perennials producing clumps of pseudostems, which are formed by the stiff overlapping leaf stalks. Their distinctive large leaves make an attractive focal point in warm gardens, but need shelter as they very soon become shredded in windy conditions. In tropical areas many species are grown for their fruit, generally called bananas if small and sweet, plantains if long and starchy. In Africa they are a reliable source of food. The male flower is at the apex of the inflorescence, and the female in whorls above it. Cultivated bananas are mostly hybrids of *M. acuminata*, found wild in forests in southeast Asia, from Thailand to northern Australia.

Musa acuminata 'Dwarf Cavendish'
This relatively small variety, probably a form or hybrid of *M. acuminata,* is grown commercially for its small fruit, the so-called "Canary" banana, but is also good for ornamental use. The yellow flowers, with dark reddish purple bracts, are carried in a hanging inflorescence, 1–2m (3–6½ft) long, and in warm enough situations will bear

Left *Musa acuminata* 'Dwarf Cavendish'

delicious, edible fruit. The elliptic to lance-shaped, green leaves are to 2m (6½ft) long.
Cultivation Best in fertile soil in full sun, with shelter from strong winds.
Height and spread to 2m (6½ft). USZ 11, with minimum of 4.5°C (40°F) overnight. Needs summer watering. ●

Musa x sapientum

This is one of the most commonly grown edible bananas, an ancient hybrid probably between M. *acuminata* and M. *balbisiana*. The arching, oblong–elliptic, slightly bluish green leaves can reach 2m (6½ft) long. White or pinkish flowers, with dull purple bracts, are borne in a hanging inflorescence, 1–2m (3–6½ft) long. The fruit is short and fat.
Cultivation Best in fertile soil in full sun and a sheltered situation.
Height to 3m (10ft); spread to 2m (6½ft). USZ 11, with minimum of 4.5°C (40°F) overnight. Needs summer watering. ●

Above *Musa x sapientum* growing in the subtropical valley of the Dado river, Sichuan, China

Musa velutina

This small species from northeast India has a pseudostem, which grows to 1.5m (5ft) or more. Its narrowly elliptic, slightly bluish green leaves, 1m (3ft) long, are around two and a half times as long as broad, and have a particularly striking, pink midrib on their underside. The pale yellow flowers are borne in an erect inflorescence, 60cm (2ft) long. The male bud is rather slender, with purplish bracts. The female flowers are in a single row per bract and form pinkish red, upright fruits with a velvety skin.
Cultivation Best in fertile soil in full sun and a sheltered situation.
Height to 1.5m (5ft) or more; spread to 1m (3ft) . USZ 11, with minimum of 4.5°C (40°F) overnight. Needs summer watering. ●

Above *Musa velutina*, fruiting at Kew
Right A young plant of *Musa velutina* at Kew

Flowering Bean Trees

Bauhinia (Leguminosae)

This genus of around 300 species has a wide distribution around the world, Europe being the only continent in which it does not occur in the wild. It is a very variable group and encompasses climbers, shrubs, and trees, some of which are evergreen; all bear distinctive, twin-lobed leaves. The genus was named after the botanical brothers Johannes and Caspar Bauhin, who lived in the late 16th century.

Bauhinia tomentosa

This evergreen shrub, or small tree, from southeast Asia and east Africa carries pale yellow, bell-shaped flowers, with a reddish spot inside, almost throughout the year. The leaves are pale green, hairy on the underside, and 3–4cm (1¼–1½in) long.

Cultivation Does best in fertile, moist but well-drained soil. Can be kept clipped. *Height to 5m (16ft), but often less; spread to 3m (10ft). USZ 10–11, surviving -1°C (30°F) of overnight frost for short periods. Needs water during the growing season.* ◗

Above *Bauhinia tomentosa*

Bauhinia variegata

ORCHID TREE, MOUNTAIN EBONY
This spreading, usually deciduous, flowering tree originates from Pakistan and India to south China, where it is considered to be sacred by Buddhists; it is often found growing near temples. It is a popular garden plant, and fast growing, to the extent that in some areas it is considered an invasive nuisance. The dull green, veined leaves grow to 20cm (8in) long, setting off exotic, rose-purple, fragrant flowers, which are superficially similar to some orchids (hence the common name) and are borne in late winter and spring. The long, reddish brown pods persist for many months.

Cultivation Does well on fertile, well-drained soil in full sun. Occasional pruning of the many stems improves the general

Above *Senna alata*
Left *Bauhinia variagata* (orchid tree) on Mount Abu in Rajasthan, India

Below *Cercis siliquastrum* (Judas tree)

Above *Senna spectabilis* in Malawi

shape and overall size of this lovely tree.
*Height to 10m (33ft); spread to 8m (25ft).
USZ 9–11, occasionally surviving -6.5°C
(20°F) of frost. Tolerant of summer drought.* ◑

Cercis (Leguminosae)

The small genus of *Cercis* comprises only
six species of deciduous trees and shrubs,
which originate from east Asia, south
Europe, and North America. They have
distinctive, round or heart-shaped leaves.

Cercis siliquastrum
JUDAS TREE
The generally accepted explanation for the
common name of this spectacular tree,
native of the Mediterranean region, is that
the red buds emerging from the trunk
commemorate the tree from which Judas
hanged himself. It is a wide-spreading tree
or shrub with pea-like, purplish pink
flowers bursting out from almost bare stems
in spring, followed by delicate, light green,
heart-shaped leaves. The flat green seed
pods ripen to purplish brown.
Cultivation Best in fertile, moist but not
waterlogged soil, in full sun or partial
shade. Plant out into its final position when
young because it dislikes transplanting.
*Height to 10m (33ft); spread to 4.5m (15ft).
USZ 7–11, surviving -17°C (2°F) of overnight
frost. Needs summer watering when young.* ◐

Senna (Leguminosae)
SENNA

The genus *Senna* contains around 350
species of evergreen and deciduous trees,
shrubs, and climbers, distributed across the
tropics. Some, such as those shown here,
were previously known as *Cassia*, a genus
differentiated only by its stamens. Many
Senna species have medicinal uses.

Senna alata (syn. *Cassia alata*)
This deciduous shrub or tree originates
in tropical Africa, Central America, and
southeast Asia, and has naturalized in many
tropical areas. The dark green, pinnate
leaves, to 1m (3ft) long, have been used to
treat ringworm. The striking, bright yellow
flowers are carried in erect spikes during
late summer and early autumn.

Cultivation Grows readily in any type of
soil. Is good by the coast.
*Height to 10m (33ft); spread to 6m (20ft), but
often less. USZ 10–11, surviving -1°C (30°F)
of overnight frost occasionally. Tolerant of
summer drought.* ◑

Senna spectabilis (syn. *Cassia spectabilis*)
This spreading, fast-growing, deciduous
shrub or tree, which is native of Central
and South America, has a stout trunk
topped by a roundish crown of lush, green,
pinnate leaves, 45cm (18in) long. The
abundant, pale yellow flowers, in loose
erect spikes in summer and autumn, are
followed by long, narrow, black fruit pods.
Cultivation Tolerates most soils in full sun.
*Height to 20m (65ft); spread to 6m (20ft).
USZ 10–11, surviving -1°C (30°F) of overnight
frost. Tolerant of drought.* ●

Delonix (Leguminosae)

This small genus of 10 species of tropical trees is closely related to *Cassia*. Some species are evergreen, others deciduous.

Delonix regia
FLAMBOYANT TREE

This large, wide-spreading, deciduous tree originates in Madagascar but has become common in India and southeast Asia, and is naturalized in parts of south Florida. Most of the pale green, feathery leaves are shed before the flowers appear. These are bright orange-red, and are carried in large clusters at the ends of the branches in summer. They are followed by large, flat, reddish brown seed pods, which take two years to ripen. *D. regia* is a beautiful shade tree and is frequently planted in private gardens and as a street tree in the tropics. Var. *flavida* bears golden-yellow flowers.

Cultivation Does well on fertile, well-drained soil, and is good in coastal areas. Has greedy roots, which spread out a long way, so needs plenty of space.

Height and spread to 9m (30ft). USZ 11, needing minimum of 4.5°C (40°F). Tolerant of summer drought once established. ●

Erythrina (Leguminosae)
CORAL TREE

This genus consists of around 110 tree and shrub species, mostly deciduous but some semi-evergreen, originating in the warm-temperate and tropical regions of the world.

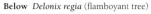
Below *Delonix regia* (flamboyant tree)

Erythrina caffra

This spreading, semi-evergreen tree or shrub, which is native of eastern South Africa, has angular spiny branches. Dense racemes, 10cm (4in) long, of red, pea-like flowers appear at the tips of the branches, just before the leaves, in spring (autumn in Africa). The red seeds are used as beads, and the ovate green leaflets, 7.5cm (3in) long, for medicinal purposes, by local people. This species is used as a street tree in California.

Cultivation Easily grown in any soil. Prune after flowering.

Height to 20m (65ft); spread to 10m (33ft). USZ 9–11, surviving -3°C (27°F) of overnight frost. Tolerant of summer drought. ●

Erythrina crista-galli
COCKSPUR CORAL

This deciduous shrub or multistemmed small tree has spiny branches. It is a native of eastern South America. The loose

Above *Erythrina caffra* in South Africa

racemes, to 30cm (1ft) long, of large, pea-like, red flowers are produced from summer to autumn in the wild, and from spring to summer in the northern hemisphere. They are a good source of nectar, and are bird pollinated. The ovate to circular, green leaflets are 10cm (4in) long.
Cultivation Grow in any soil in sun. Benefits from hard annual pruning after flowering. If grown in cooler areas, it will die back to the ground, and reappear in spring.
Height to 9m (30ft); spread to 6m (20ft). USZ 9–11, surviving -3°C (27°F) of frost. Requires summer watering when young. ◗

Schotia (Leguminosae)

This small genus originates from southeast Africa and consists of four or five (no one seems able to decide how many!) species of deciduous or semi-evergreen shrubs or trees. They are admired for their striking flowers arising from almost bare stems.

Schotia brachypetala
AFRICAN WALNUT, TREE FUCHSIA
This wide-spreading, slow-growing, semi-evergreen tree or large shrub has pinnate leaves, which are flushed pink when they first appear in spring, becoming pale green later. As the leaves begin to fall, the small, bright red, fragrant flowers emerge; these are full of nectar and attract birds as pollinators. The fruits are flat brown pods. *S. afra* is smaller than *S. brachypetala*, eventually making a shrub or small tree up to about 6m (20ft); it also has showy bright red flowers.
Cultivation Needs fertile, well-drained soil in full sun.
Height to 12m (40ft); spread to 6m (20ft). USZ 9–11, surviving -3°C (27°F) of frost occasionally. Tolerant of summer drought. ◗

Above *Erythrina crista-galli* (cockspur coral)

Above *Schotia brachypetala* (African walnut) flowering in Adelaide, Australia

Acacia

Acacia (Leguminosae)
MIMOSA, WATTLE

Acacia is a large and variable genus with around 1,200 species of deciduous and evergreen trees and shrubs, chiefly originating from Australia, but with species also native of South Africa and Central and South America, where they are important trees in savannah areas. Most mimosas are very beautiful, but they can also be extremely invasive, and some species form suckers a surprising distance from the parent plant. There are many species and hybrids freely available from commercial sources, with white, cream, or yellow flowers and widely varying foliage. Occasional heavy watering when mimosas are becoming established is better than frequent spraying, because it encourages the roots to penetrate deeply and become better anchored in the ground.

Above *Acacia dealbata* (silver wattle) in Lawrence Johnston's garden at Serre de La Madone in Menton, France

Acacia dealbata
SILVER WATTLE, MIMOSA
This is one of the hardiest of all mimosas, and is a fast-growing, evergreen, upright tree or large shrub, originating from Australia and Tasmania, where it flowers in winter. The branches are silvery grey, and hairy when young. The greyish feathery leaves are doubly pinnate, and small, fluffy, globose, yellow, scented flowerheads are arranged in spikes. *A. dealbata* is one of the best known of all mimosas, and is frequently grown both in warm gardens and for cut flowers, particularly along the French Riviera. Cultivars include 'Mirandole' (said to be hardier than the species), 'Pendula' (a weeping form), and 'Kambah Karpet' (a prostrate, ground-covering form, grown chiefly in Australia). *A. dealbata* subsp. *subalpina* is a small form, which is hardy, pretty, and desirable for gardens; it was formerly very rare but is now becoming more freely available.
Cultivation Does best in slightly moist but well-drained soil in full sun.
Height 10m (33ft) or more; spread to 8m (25ft). USZ 8–11, surviving -12°C (10°F) of frost for short periods. Tolerant of summer drought. ◗

Acacia fimbriata
BRISBANE WATTLE, FRINGED WATTLE
This small evergreen tree or bushy shrub, native to eastern Australia, often has low drooping branches. The dark green leaves

Above *Acacia dealbata* (silver wattle)

Above *Acacia dealbata* subsp. *subalpina*

Above *Acacia fimbriata* (Brisbane wattle) in Menton, France

Below *Acacia melanoxylon* (blackwood)

Acacia saligna (syn. *A. cyanophylla*)

BLUELEAVED WATTLE, GOLDEN WREATH
WATTLE

This fast-growing, evergreen shrub or
small spreading tree, native to southwest
Australia, has drooping reddish branches
and narrow, blue-green leaves. It is free
flowering with spikes of globose, bright
orange-yellow flowerheads from late winter
to late spring. This shelter plant tolerates
some exposure to coastal conditions, and
has been use to combat sand-dune erosion.
It can become very invasive, as has
happened in parts of South Africa.
Cultivation Tolerates most reasonably
well-drained soils in sun or partial shade.
Height to 10m (33ft); spread to 6m (20ft), but
often less. USZ 9–11, surviving -3°C (27°F) of
overnight frost. Tolerant of summer drought. ◐

are narrowly oblong. The fluffy, globose,
golden-yellow, slightly scented flowerheads
appear in late winter and spring.
Cultivation Tolerates most soils, as long
as they are well drained, and is happy in
sun or partial shade. Can be clipped to
make a good hedge.
Height to 6m (20ft); spread to 5m (16ft) if left
to develop as a tree. USZ 9–11, surviving -3°C
(27°F) of frost. Tolerant of summer drought. ◐

Acacia melanoxylon

BLACKWOOD

This evergreen, upright or spreading tree
or large shrub originates from eastern
Australian and Tasmania, and is naturalized
in Madeira. The flat, elliptic-shaped leaves
(phyllodes) are downy when young. Large,

globose, pale creamy yellow flowerheads
are carried in short spikes in the leaf axils
in spring. The greyish, rough, furrowed
bark is good for tanning, and the hard
timber is used in furniture-making. In some
areas *A. melanoxylon* is rather short-lived.
Cultivation Best in slightly moist but
well-drained soil in full sun, preferably in
a sheltered position, as the branches are
susceptible to wind damage. Tolerates
partial shade. Produces suckering roots,
which has made it popular for erosion
control. The dense, rather upright growth
can be pruned back to give the desired
shape, and it makes a handsome specimen.
Height to 30m (100ft); spread to 6m (20ft).
USZ 9–11, surviving -3°C (27°F) of frost.
Needs a little water in summer when young. ◐

Above *Acacia saligna* (blueleaved wattle)

Tree Hibiscus

Dombeya (Sterculiaceae)

Dombeya is a genus of around 225 species of evergreen and deciduous trees and shrubs from Africa, Madagascar, and the Mascarene Islands. Many species and hybrids are grown for their flowers.

Dombeya cacuminum
This very beautiful small tree or large shrub is a native of Madagascar, where it grows in scrub or woodland margins. It thrives in southern California. The smooth, shiny, maple-like leaves are usually five-lobed and around 10cm (4in) across. In early spring, the cupped flowers, in shades of red or pink, are held in clusters of about 10, usually hanging down.
Cultivation Easily grown in any fertile soil in sun or partial shade.
Height to 5m (16ft); spread to 6m (20ft). USZ 10–11, surviving -1°C (30°F) of overnight frost. Best with summer rainfall. ●

Hibiscus (Malvaceae)

Hibiscus is one of the most popular genera of garden plants, especially in the tropics.

Below *Hibiscus tiliaceus* (mahoe)

There are around 300 species, from large evergreen and deciduous trees and shrubs to herbaceous perennials and annuals. Some species are minor crops, for food, oil, timber, or for fibre in the stems.

Hibiscus tiliaceus
MAHOE, MANGROVE HIBISCUS
This evergreen tree or large shrub is now common on the coast in subtropical areas and is planted as a street tree. Originally it came from the eastern Pacific from Japan to Australia. The unlobed green leaves are 7.5–15cm (3–6in) long. Yellow flowers, around 10cm (4in) across, and often with red centres, are produced all year; they turn orange and red as they fade. The seed pods are egg shaped, with spreading sepals.
Cultivation Easily grown in an open sunny site. Tolerates wind and damp soil in coastal conditions.
Height to 12m (40ft); spread to 8m (25ft). USZ 9–11, surviving -6.5°C (20°F) of overnight frost. Needs water in summer. ●

Below *Dombeya cacuminum* in the Huntington Botanical Gardens, in Los Angeles

Above *Lagerstroemia indica* (crepe myrtle)

Lagerstroemia (Lythraceae)

Lagerstroemia contains around 53 species of evergreen and deciduous trees, which are natives from Asia to Australia. A few species and their hybrids are commonly planted elsewhere in areas with hot summers.

Lagerstroemia indica
CREPE MYRTLE
L. indica, a large deciduous shrub or multistemmed tree has particularly beautiful, smooth, peeling bark in grey and chestnut-brown. Its smooth, oval, dark green leaves turn yellow or red in autumn. The large showy flowers, with their frilly petals, are produced in summer in shades of white, pink, magenta, or crimson.
L. indica is native of China, while the hardier *L. faurii* comes from Japan. Hybrids between them are popular in southeastern USA.
Cultivation Easily grown in any soil type in areas with warm summers.
Height to 14m (45ft); spread to 6m (20ft). USZ 7–10, surviving -17°C (2°F) of overnight frost. Needs summer water. ◗

Melia (Meliaceae)

Melia contains three species from India, China, and southeast Asia to Australia. These deciduous and evergreen trees bear star-shaped flowers.

Melia azedarach
CHINABERRY, PERSIAN LILAC, PRIDE OF INDIA
This upright deciduous tree, from India to Australia, has scented, pale purplish blue flowers. They are followed by bead-like, pale orange fruits, 1cm (⅜in) across, which hang on the bare tree through winter. The much-divided leaves have toothed leaflets; lower leaves are often lobed.
Cultivation Easily grown in any soil.
Height to 12m (40ft); spread to 6m (20ft). USZ 8–11, surviving -12°C (10°F) of overnight frost. Tolerant of summer drought. ◑

Thespesia (Malvaceae)

Thespesia comprises 17 species of evergreen trees and shrubs from around the tropics. It is closely related to *Hibiscus*.

Thespesia populnea
PORTIA TREE
This fast-growing, evergreen, pantropical coastal tree has leathery leaves, pale yellow flowers turning purple, and rounded fruit.
Cultivation Easily grown in wet but well-drained soil. Tolerates salt water.
Height to 9m (30ft); spread to 6m (20ft). USZ 10–11, surviving -1°C (30°F) of overnight frost. Needs summer water. ◗

Above *Thespesia populnea* (portia tree)

Above *Melia azedarach* (chinaberry)

Small Mediterranean Trees

Arbutus (Ericaceae)

Arbutus contains around 14 species of evergreen trees and shrubs from the Mediterranean, western Europe, and western North America south to Mexico. All species have fleshy, strawberry-like but insipid fruit.

Arbutus andrachne
This small tree or large shrub has smooth, mahogany-brown bark and bell-shaped, greenish white flowers, 3–5mm (⅛–¼in) long, in early spring. It is a native of the coasts of the eastern Mediterranean. The ovate leathery leaves are almost untoothed and around 7.5cm (3in) long.
Cultivation Easily grown in dry rocky soil, especially on limestone, but slow to establish itself and therefore seldom seen.
Height to 6m (20ft); spread to 5m (16ft). USZ 9–11, surviving -6.5°C (20°F) of overnight frost. Tolerant of summer drought. ◑

Arbutus unedo
STRAWBERRY TREE
This gnarled twisted tree, from Killarney in Ireland to the eastern Mediterranean, has rough, dark greyish brown bark. The white, pink, or greenish, bell-shaped flowers, 6mm (¼in) long, appear in winter, in hanging bunches. The fruit ripens in

Above *Arbutus andrachne* at Phaselis, southwest Turkey

autumn, and looks good but is virtually tasteless, hence the specific name, *unedo* ("I eat one"). The ovate to narrowly elliptic leaves, 7.5cm (3in) long, have blunt shallow teeth. The flowers on f. *rubra* are dark pink.
Cultivation Easily grown in a sheltered sunny position in well-drained soil. Tolerates alkaline soils.
Height to 9m (30ft); spread to 6m (20ft). USZ 9–11, surviving -3°C (27°F) of overnight frost. Tolerant of summer drought. ◐

Above *Arbutus unedo* f. *rubra* (strawberry tree)

Ficus (Moraceae)
FIG

The genus *Ficus* is one of the largest in the world, containing around 750 species. Most of these are tropical evergreen trees. Many are familiar houseplants such as *F. elastica* (rubber plant), *F. benjamina*, and the sacred *F. religiosa* (peepul tree), beneath which the Buddha found enlightenment.

Above *Ficus carica* 'Brown Turkey'

Below Old *Olea europaea* (olive) trees with *Euphorbia characias* subsp. *wulfenii* in the Peloponnese, Greece

Ficus carica 'Brown Turkey'

This fig is an ancient cultivated deciduous tree, whose leaves have rounded lobes. It was grown by the Egyptians in 4000BC or earlier, and is native by springs on cliffs and rocks in southwest Asia. Most edible cultivars are parthenocarpic: they do not require pollination to form their seedless fruit. The minute flowers develop inside the young figs, which become elongated, pear-shaped, and edible as they mature. 'Brown Turkey', with dark brown fruits, is one of the hardiest cultivars.
Cultivation Easily grown in well-drained, poor soil, in warmth and shelter. Needs water in summer only when newly planted. *Height and spread to 6m (20ft). USZ 8–11, surviving -12°C (10°F) of overnight frost. Tolerant of summer drought.* ◑

Olea (Oleaceae)
OLIVE

A genus of about 30 species of evergreen trees and shrubs with small greenish flowers and fruit with a single large seed. They are found wild from the Canary Islands, across Asia to the Himalayas and south to the Cape. As well as the cultivated olive, some wild species are valued for their hard, heavy wood.

Olea europaea
OLIVE

The cultivated olive is a native of the Mediterranean region and remains one of the most familiar trees in that landscape, with its gnarled trunk and silvery, narrowly elliptic leaves. Pale green flowers in spring are followed by edible, egg-shaped fruits, which are black-purple when ripe.
Cultivation Though long-lived, olives are not slow growing if given fertile soil and water in summer. Old trees may need their branches thinned to produce a good crop. *Height to 9m (30ft); spread to 6m (20ft). USZ 9–11, surviving -6.5°C (20°F) of overnight frost. Tolerant of summer drought.* ◑

Punica (Lythraceae)
POMEGRANATE

This genus of deciduous trees comprises only two species: one is described here; the other is from the island of Socotra.

Punica granatum

This shrub or short tree has elliptic-ovate leaves, 10cm (4in) long, and red flowers, 3–4cm (1¼–1½in) wide, in summer, then round, orange, red, or pink-streaked, edible fruit with a tube at the apex. It is wild in northeast Turkey and northern Iran, where it grows in gorges and on cliffs. The smooth, reddish brown bark peels in thin flakes.
Cultivation Easily grown in any soil and drought tolerant once established. In recent years old trees from redundant orchards have been sold as ornamentals, a desirable but expensive way to cultivate old trees. *Height to 9m (30ft); spread to 6m (20ft). USZ 8–11, surviving -12°C (10°F) of overnight frost. Tolerant of summer drought.* ◑

Above *Punica granatum* (pomegranate)

Aesculus, Laurus, Liquidambar, & Platanus

Aesculus (Hippocastanaceae)
HORSE CHESTNUT

The genus *Aesculus*, called buckeye in North America, contains 13 species of deciduous trees and shrubs with palmate leaves. One species is native only in a few places in northern Greece, while the other ones are native of the Himalayas and China or are found in woods in North America.

Aesculus californica
CALIFORNIAN BUCKEYE

This shrub or neatly rounded tree is native of the foothills in coastal California from the Oregon border to north Los Angeles. In late spring it bears dense spikes of white flowers. It is free flowering even when young. The narrow, inversely lance-shaped leaflets are 20–25cm (8–10in) long.
Cultivation Easily grown in fertile soil.
Height to 6m (20ft); spread to 6m (20ft). USZ 9–11, surviving -6.5°C (20°F) of overnight frost. Tolerant of summer drought. ◗

Above *Aesculus californica* (Californian buckeye) near San Francisco

Aesculus pavia
RED BUCKEYE

This large shrub or small tree from southeastern USA looks striking in late spring with its spikes of bright crimson flowers – an adaptation, like so many red flowers in North America, to pollination by hummingbirds. The narrowly lance-shaped leaflets are 15–20cm (6–8in) long.
Cultivation Grow in any soil.
Height to 9m (30ft); spread to 6m (20ft).

USZ 8–11, surviving -12°C (10°F) of overnight frost. Needs water and heat in summer. ●

Laurus (Lauraceae)
BAY

The genus *Laurus* contains two species of evergreen trees: one is from mainland Europe, and the other from the Canaries and Azores. The related genus *Persea* (which contains the avocado tree, *P. americana*) is also found in the Canaries, a relic of Tertiary forests (*see* p.14).

Laurus nobilis

This robust, fast-growing tree sprouts freely from the base after a fire or frost. It is wild in the Mediterranean region. The ovate to narrowly elliptic leaves are aromatic. Small, creamy yellow flowers are clustered along the branches, and are followed by black fleshy fruit.
Cultivation Easily grown in any soil in sun or partial shade. Can be clipped or trained to make formal shapes.
Height to 9m (30ft); spread to 6m (20ft). USZ 9–11, surviving -6.5°C (20°F) of overnight frost. Tolerant of summer drought. ◗

Above *Aesculus pavia* (red buckeye)

Above *Liquidambar formosana* in southern California

Liquidambar (Hamamelidaceae)
CHINESE SWEET GUM

The genus *Liquidambar* contains five species of deciduous trees from southwest Turkey, North and Central America, and eastern Asia. All species are valued for their red and purple autumn colour. Some species are a source of aromatic gum.

Liquidambar formosana
This fast-growing tree, which is a native of eastern China, grows better than the more common *L. styraciflua* in warm climates. The leaves are generally three-pointed and around 10cm (4in) across. The young reddish foliage matures to green, then turns reddish in autumn. The small green flowers are in spherical heads in late spring, and are followed by spiky brown fruits, 2cm (¾in) across.
Cultivation Easily grown in any fertile soil in sun for best autumn colour. Is often planted as a street tree in hot areas, such as southern California.
Height to 9m (30ft); spread to 6m (20ft). USZ 9–11, surviving -6.5°C (20°F) of overnight frost. Tolerant of summer drought. ◗

Platanus (Platanaceae)
PLANE TREE

The genus *Platanus* contains around eight species of deciduous trees in Asia and North America, usually growing by springs or along streams. DNA studies have shown the plane trees to be a very isolated family, most closely related not to any other trees but to the aquatic *Nelumbo* (*see* p.154).

Platanus orientalis
ORIENTAL PLANE
This native of western Asia, forming a huge spreading tree, is often planted in village squares. It has rough bark and deeply divided leaves, around 15cm (6in) across. The insignificant flowers, hanging in spherical heads, are followed by small brown seeds surrounded by a plume of hairs. The London plane, a hybrid or cultivar of *P. orientalis*, is the commonest street tree, famous for its tolerance of air pollution in 19th-century London.
Cultivation Easily grown in any fertile soil.
Height to 30m (100ft); spread to 20m (65ft). USZ 7–11, surviving -17°C (2°F) of overnight frost. Tolerant of summer drought. ◗

Below *Platanus orientalis* (oriental plane) growing wild

Below *Laurus nobilis* (bay) at Portmeirion, Wales

65

Small, Late-flowering Trees

Cornus (Cornaceae)
DOGWOOD, CORNEL

The genus *Cornus* contains around 65 species of mainly deciduous trees and shrubs in three main groups: flowering dogwoods, such as *C. capitata*, with white, petal-like bracts around a tight head of very small flowers; red-fruited cornelian cherries, such as *C. mas*, with small, bright yellow flowers and red, cherry-like fruit; and the swamp dogwoods often grown for their coloured winter shoots, which have a flat head of white flowers, followed by blackish or white fruit.

Cornus capitata

This evergreen tree is native of the Himalayas and China, growing in woods and by streams. The leaves, around 6cm (2½in) long, have 3–5 veins. In late spring and summer the flowers, to 5–7cm (2–3in) across, are borne with 4–6 creamy yellow, obovate, pointed bracts. The fruit is round and strawberry-like. The rather similar *C. nuttallii*, from northern California and Oregon, has flowers to 15cm (6in) across, and 4–8 flatter, broader bracts, and single-seeded fruits held at the base.
Cultivation Easily grown in any soil in a moist position, sheltered from drying wind. *Height to 15m (50ft); spread to 9m (30ft). USZ 9–11, surviving -6.5°C (20°F) of overnight frost. Needs water in summer.* ◖

Above *Cornus capitata*

Eucryphia (Eucryphiaceae)

Eucryphia is a small genus of six species of mainly evergreen trees from South America and Australia including Tasmania. All species produce white or pale pink, simple, rose-like flowers in late summer.

Eucryphia cordifolia
ULMO

This evergreen tree has simple, stiff, oblong leaves, which are dark green above and silvery beneath, and white flowers around 5cm (2in) across. It grows wild in woods in south Chile.

Cultivation Needs damp peaty soil. Tolerates limestone if the rainfall is high. *Height to 20m (65ft); spread to 6m (20ft). USZ 9–11, surviving -6.5°C (20°F) of frost. Needs ample summer water.* ●

Eucryphia moorei
STINKWOOD, PLUMWOOD

Found in the rainforests near the coast in New South Wales and eastern Victoria, Australia. It forms a rugged evergreen tree and produces dark green, pinnate leaves, greyish beneath, with 11–13 leaflets. The white flowers are around 2.5cm (1in) across.
Cultivation Needs acid sandy soil and a damp sheltered position, preferably by a stream, with shelter from drying wind. *Height to 15m (50ft); spread to 10m (33ft). USZ 9–11, surviving -6.5°C (20°F) of overnight frost. Needs ample summer water.* ●

Hymenosporum (Pittosporaceae)

Hymenosporum has only one species of evergreen tree, which is native of rainforests in northern Australia and New Guinea.

Hymenosporum flavum
NATIVE FRANGIPANI

This upright tree produces narrow shining leaves, to 15cm (6in) long, and, in early summer, hanging bunches of scented, yellowish, long-tubed flowers, which are 4cm (1½in) across the lobes.
Cultivation Easily grown in a subtropical climate, in full sun in any soil. *Height to 20m (65ft); spread to 6m (20ft). USZ 10–11, surviving -1°C (30°F) of overnight frost. Needs water in summer.* ◖

Left *Eucryphia cordifolia* (ulmo) in Cornwall

Above *Eucryphia moorei* (stinkwood)

Koelreuteria (Sapindaceae)

Koelreuteria has three species of deciduous trees, which are native in China and Taiwan.

Koelreuteria bipinnata

This deciduous tree has bipinnate leaves, to 60cm (2ft) long, with numerous leathery leaflets. Yellow, narrow-petalled flowers, 1cm, (⅜in) wide, borne from summer to autumn, are followed by huge bunches of inflated, reddish, papery fruit, 10–15cm (4–6in) long.
Cultivation Easily grown in any soil in a sunny sheltered position.
Height to 10m (33ft); spread to 6m (20ft).
USZ 9–11, surviving -6.5°C (20°F) of
overnight frost. Tolerant of summer drought. ◗

Pittosporum (Pittosporaceae)

Pittosporum contains around 150 tree and shrub species from South Africa to Japan, and south to New Zealand. Many are evergreens, with simple, leathery or soft leaves, often with a wavy edge. The flowers sometimes smell of orange blossom.

Pittosporum undulatum

This spreading tree has evergreen, wavy-edged, lance-shaped leaves, 7.5–10cm (3–4in) long, and small, whitish, scented, five-petalled flowers in spring. It is wild in Australia, from Queensland to New South Wales and Tasmania, growing in forests. It has been much planted in southern California, particularly around Los Angeles, where it seeds itself on bare hills.
Cultivation Easily grown in any soil. Soon creates a pleasant light shade.
Height to 10m (33ft); spread to 6m (20ft).
USZ 9–11, surviving -6.5°C (20°F) of
overnight frost. Tolerant of summer drought. ◗

Above *Koelreuteria bipinnata*

Above *Hymenosporum flavum* (native frangipani)

Above *Pittosporum undulatum*

Australian Gum Trees & Myrtles

Eucalyptus (Myrtaceae)
GUM

Eucalyptus is a large and important genus of evergreen trees and shrubs, with around 600 species in Australia. Some 113 of the species, including *E. ficifolia*, sometimes now separated into the genus *Corymbia*, have a compound inflorescence.

Eucalyptus ficifolia
RED-FLOWERING GUM

This is one of the most beautiful eucalyptus, with its large, rounded heads of bright red, crimson, pink, or white flowers, about 5cm (2in) across, in summer. It is wild in southwestern Australia, in sandy soil. It makes a very good, small tree or large shrub in the Mediterranean or near the coast in California. The broadly lance-shaped leaves are 10–20cm (4–8in) long.
Cultivation Grow in acid sandy soil.
Height to 15m (50ft); spread to 6m (20ft). USZ 9–11, surviving -6.5°C (20°F) of overnight frost. Tolerant of summer drought. ◑

Eucalyptus leucoxylon
YELLOW GUM, WHITE IRON BARK

This graceful upright tree, native of southeast Australia, has hanging branches and narrow, greyish or green leaves, around 15cm (6in) long. It is popular for its habit and nectar-rich flowers for honey. The red, pink, or white flowers, 3cm (1¼in) across, hang in threes, from autumn to spring.
Cultivation Easily grown in any soil.
Height to 30m (100ft); spread to 6m (20ft). USZ 9–11, surviving -6.5°C (20°F) of overnight frost. Tolerant of summer drought. ◑

Above *Eucalyptus ficifolia* (red flowering gum)

Above *Eucalyptus leucoxylon* (yellow gum)

Grevillea (Proteaceae)

The genus *Grevillea* contains around 260 species of evergreen trees and shrubs, nearly all from Australia, but with a few species in the Pacific islands and New Guinea. It is named after Robert Kaye Greville (1794–1866), who specialized in algae and ferns, and was a friend of W.J. Hooker, first director of Kew. Many *Grevillea* species are shrubs (*see* pp.78–9).

Grevillea robusta
SILKY OAK

This fast-growing, upright tree produces stiffly horizontal, one-sided, comb-like spikes, 15cm (6in) long, of yellow flowers, the colour of a good egg yolk. The bark is rather smooth and dark brown. The ferny leaves, to 20cm (8in) long, are dark green above, pale and silky beneath, and deeply divided with flat segments. It is native of Queensland and New South Wales, where it grows in dry forest, flowering in spring. *G. robusta* is widely planted in warm areas, sometimes as a street tree, and was formerly used as fast-growing cover in tea gardens or coffee plantations.
Cultivation Grow in any soil. Is tough in warm climates.
Height to 40m (130ft); spread to 10m (30ft). USZ 9–11, surviving -6.5°C (20°F) of overnight frost. Tolerant of summer drought. ◑

Metrosideros (Myrtaceae)
CHRISTMAS TREE (NZ)

The genus *Metrosideros* contains around 50 species from east Malaysia and the Pacific Islands (including Hawaii) to New Zealand, with one isolated species in South Africa. It appears to be absent from Australia, but is very close to the largely Australian genus *Callistemon* (*see* p.94). Some species are dwarf, ivy-like creepers and climbers when young; others form large evergreen trees. The Hawaian species have evolved the unusual capability of closing their stomata in the presence of sulphur dioxide, so that they can survive on volcanoes in places where most plants would be killed.

Metrosideros excelsa

In midsummer, this large evergreen tree bears heads of crimson flowers at the tips of the branches, so that the whole tree may appear red. The flowers have short petals and red stamens, 1–1.5cm (⅜–½in) long. This native of New Zealand grows along the coast of North Island, sometimes on cliffs, sometimes in the edge of the sand. The bark is very spongy, and the trees can form conspicuous hanging aerial roots. The tough, leathery, oval leaves, 5–10cm

Below *Metrosideros excelsa*

(2–4in) long, are dark green above and silvery beneath.

Cultivation Easily grown in moist sandy soil in full sun. This is an excellent tree for coastal planting in cool, frost-free areas, as it is very tolerant of salt-laden wind. It grows well on the Isles of Scilly, where it is occasionally defoliated by frost, sprouting again in spring.

Height to 30m (100ft); spread to 20m (65ft). USZ 10–11, surviving -1°C (30°F) of overnight frost. Needs water in summer. ●

Below *Metrosideros kermadecensis* 'Variegatus'

Metrosideros kermadecensis

This is a rather similar tree to *M. excelsa*, but is less hardy and has broader leaves, 3–5cm (1¼–2in) long, brighter crimson flowers in midsummer, and flower stalks and sepals covered in white indumentum. It is found wild on the Kermadec islands. 'Variegatus' has creamy margins.

Cultivation Grow in moist sandy soil.

Height to 9m (30ft); spread to 6m (20ft). USZ 10–11, surviving -1°C (30°F) of overnight frost. Needs water in summer. ●

Above *Grevillea robusta* (silky oak) in Yunnan, China

Above Aerial roots of *Metrosideros excelsa* in the garden at Tresco, Isles of Scilly

Ornamental Fruits

Citrus (Rutaceae)
CITRUS FRUITS

The genus *Citrus* contains such popular fruits as oranges, lemons, limes, and grapefruit, and numerous hybrids. These evergreen trees and shrubs are excellent in gardens, either potted, in areas where they need extra protection in winter, or planted in the open ground. The waxy whitish flowers are produced in early spring soon after the fruits ripen, and their sweet scent is the delight of the Mediterranean. *Citrus* contains around 16 species in southern China and the Malay peninsula.

Citrus auriantium
SEVILLE ORANGE, BITTER ORANGE
This spreading evergreen tree produces dark green, ovate leaves and round orange fruits, which are used mainly for making marmalade. It is native of southeast Asia.
Cultivation Grow in slightly acid, very well-drained soil. Use rainwater where

Above *Citrus medica* 'Etrog' (citron)

Above *Citrus aurantium* (Seville orange) in the garden of the Villa Gamberaia, Florence, Italy

possible, and feed with a citrus fertilizer.
Height to 12m (40ft); spread to 6m (20ft). USZ 9–11, surviving -5°C (23°F) of overnight frost. Needs regular water. ◗

Citrus medica
CITRON, ETROG
This is a very leafy, aromatic tree, producing thick-peeled, hanging, egg-shaped, pale yellow fruit, 20–25cm (8–10in) long, and green ovate leaves. It was the earliest citrus to be brought to the west from China, possibly by Alexander's troops; soon it came to be used in the Jewish Feast of Tabernacles. 'Etrog' is the extra large-fruited variety, which is used for candied peel. There is a smaller-fruited variety, 'Corsican', and a weird Chinese variety with lobes like crooked fingers, called 'Buddha's hand'.
Cultivation Needs acid, well-drained soil, and shelter from very hot, dry wind.
Height and spread to 5m (16ft). USZ 9–11, surviving -5°C (23°F) for short periods. Needs water through the summer. ◗

Crataegus (Rosaceae)
HAWTHORN

The genus *Crataegus* contains around 200 species. Most are hardy, temperate, deciduous trees or shrubs bearing small,

Left *Fortunella margarita* 'Nagami' (kumquat)

inedible fruit, with stone-like seeds. A few species in Mexico and central America, the Mediterranean, and in China have large, fleshy fruit like small apples, which can be eaten when ripe or made into jam.

Crataegus pubescens
This semi-evergreen tree is found in eastern Mexico, in the Sierra Madre Orientale. The ovate leaves are dark green and leathery, on horizontally spreading branches. White large flowers are borne in spring. The apple-like fruit is red, orange, or yellow.
Cultivation Easily grown in any well-drained soil and full sun.
Height and spread to 6m (20ft). USZ 8–11, surviving -12°C (10°F) of overnight frost. Tolerant of summer drought. ◗

Eriobotrya (Rosaceae)
LOQUAT

The genus *Eriobotrya* contains 26 species of evergreen trees and shrubs, from the Himalayas and eastern Asia.

Eriobotrya japonica
This tree or shrub is native of China. The dark green, ribbed, ovate to lance-shaped leaves, 15–20cm (6–8in) long, are often red when young. Whitish flowers are borne in

bunches in autumn, then orange fruit, with edible flesh and 1–3 large shining pips.
Cultivation Easily grown in fertile soil, partial shade, and shelter.
Height and spread to 5m (16ft). USZ 9–11, surviving -6.5°C (20°F) of overnight frost. Tolerant of summer drought. ◗

Fortunella (Rutaceae)
KUMQUAT

The genus *Fortunella* contains four or five species of evergreen tree and shrubs from eastern Asia and is closely related to *Citrus*.

Fortunella margarita
KUMQUAT
This very bushy, evergreen tree, from southeast Asia, is sometimes used to make a dense hedge. It has smaller, narrower leaves than most oranges, and smaller round or oval fruit; the first taste is very sour, but the sweetness comes out as the peel is chewed. 'Nagami' grows to only 2m (6½ft).
Cultivation Needs slightly acid, well-drained, fertile soil.
Height to 4m (13ft); spread to 3m (10ft). USZ 9–11, surviving -6.5°C (20°F) of overnight frost. Needs summer water. ◗

Above *Eriobotrya japonica* (loquats) in fruit with wisteria in Madeira in spring

Above *Crataegus* (hawthorn) with *Tillandsia* (Spanish moss) in Mexico

71

Colourful Flowering Trees

Chorisia (Malvaceae)

The genus *Chorisia* has two species of semi-evergreen and deciduous, succulent trees from Brazil and Argentina. This genus is sometimes united with *Ceiba*.

Chorisia speciosa
SILK FLOSS TREE

This fast-growing, stiff, semi-evergreen tree has a green trunk covered in thick spines and divided leaves, to 12cm (5in) long. It is a native of southern Brazil to Argentina. The flowers usually appear in autumn, after the leaves have fallen. They are usually pink with a white centre, but some cultivars have been raised with bright red flowers. The seeds are surrounded by silky fibres.
Cultivation Easily grown in any rich soil. Needs summer water when young.
Height to 20m (65ft); spread to 6m (20ft). USZ 9–11, surviving -6.5°C (20°F) of overnight frost. Tolerant of summer drought. ◑

Above *Chorisia speciosa* (silk floss tree) planted in Buenos Aires, Argentina

Jacaranda (Bignoniaceae)

The genus *Jacaranda* contains around 34 species of deciduous and evergreen trees in tropical South America.

Jacaranda mimosifolia
JACARANDA

This is one of the loveliest and most commonly planted of all subtropical trees, both for its soft ferny foliage and for its beautiful, pale-throated, bluish lavender, tubular flowers, which often cover the whole tree from spring to summer, when it is leafless; no photograph can do justice to the subtle colour. The branching panicles are 25cm (10in) long, and the seed pods are flat and oval, with winged seeds. The deciduous leaves are about 30cm (1ft) long, with narrow pinnate leaflets. *J. mimosifolia* is native of dry, open, savannah-type woodland in southern Brazil and northern Argentina.
Cultivation Easily grown in any soil, but needs a warm summer and a dry cool winter to flower freely. In northern Natal and other parts of Africa, flowering is exceptionally good.
Height to 15m (50ft); spread to 6m (20ft). USZ 9–11, surviving -6.5°C (20°F) of overnight frost. Tolerant of summer drought. ●

Above *Paulownia fargesii* in Sichuan, China

Above *Jacaranda mimosifolia* (jacaranda)

Paulownia (Scrophulariaceae)

This genus contains six species of deciduous trees, all Chinese. They are known for fast growth, huge leaves, and autumn flower buds.

Paulownia fargesii

This tree from western China grows in rocky valleys, flowers in late spring. The tubular, pale lavender flowers have darker spots and white throats. The fruit is like a greenish pecan nut, with small, dry seeds. The adult leaves, 15–20cm (6–8in) long, are ovate, unlobed, and hairy beneath.

Cultivation Easily grown in fertile soil. *Height to 20m (65ft); spread to 6m (20ft). USZ 8–11, surviving -12°C (10°F) of overnight frost. Needs summer water.* ◗

Above *Tabebuia impetiginosa* (ipe)

Tabebuia (Bignoniaceae)

This genus contains some 100 evergreen and deciduous species from tropical America. They are often small trees of semi-desert areas. Many of them are used in town planting and flower in spring before the leaves develop. Other species have very long-lasting timber, and are particularly useful for furniture-making.

Tabebuia impetiginosa

IPE, TOLEDO

This native deciduous tree of South America bears tubular, pale-throated, purple, red, or pink flowers during the spring months. The palmate leathery leaves have between five and seven leaflets.

Cultivation It is easily grown in fertile moist soil, but slow when young. *Height to 9m (30ft); spread to 6m (20ft). USZ 9–11, surviving -6.5°C (20°F) of overnight frost. Needs water in summer.* ◑

Above *Jacaranda mimosifolia* (jacaranda) in Cradock, East Cape Province, South Africa, flowering in late October

73

Shrubs

SHRUBS ARE VALUABLE to the gardener for providing structure
throughout the season. Many are particularly drought-tolerant, and
the summer-dry vegetation of the Mediterranean (the garrigue),
South Africa (the fynbos), and Western Australia is mainly
composed of shrubs. Many of these also have beautiful flowers,
and most of them have the advantage of coming to flowering size
more quickly than trees, as well as being very long-lived.

Above *Iochroma australe* (see p. 119)

Plumbago

Plumbago (Plumbaginaceae)

The genus *Plumbago* contains 10 species of shrubs. Most are evergreen but *P. europaea* is deciduous; it was formerly used to treat eye disease, but made the skin lead-coloured, hence the name *Plumbago* from *plumbum* (Latin for "lead").

Plumbago auriculata

LEADWORT, PLUMBAGO

This is one of the most commonly planted shrubs in dry, frost-free climates. It has a sprawling habit and produces its blue tubular flowers, 3cm (1¼in) long, almost continuously in warm weather. *P. auriculata* is found wild on dusty hills and rocky slopes in the eastern Cape province, Natal, and Transvaal of South Africa, and is especially common in the dry areas between the summer- and winter-rainfall Cape climates.

Cultivation Easily grown in fertile soil. Responds to hard pruning in early spring. *Height to 3m (10ft); spread to 6m (20ft). USZ 9–11, surviving -6.5°C (20°F) of overnight frost. Tolerant of drought.* ◐

Plumbago indica

This is a more tropical species than *P. auriculata*, and has tubular flowers, about 5cm (2in) long, in deep pink, scarlet, or purple. It is a perennial or scrambling shrub, perhaps native of India but usually found cultivated there and elsewhere in dry tropical areas. Flowers in winter.

Cultivation Grow in any soil. Needs heat in the growing season to flower well. *Height to 1m (3ft); spread to 3m (10ft). USZ 10–11, surviving -1°C (30°F) of overnight frost. Needs water in summer.* ●

Above *Plumbago indica*

Above *Plumbago auriculata* (leadwort) trained on a wall in the south of France

Poppies & Related Families

Dendromecon (Papaveraceae)

Dendromecon is a small genus of two closely related species of evergreen shrubs confined to California and northwestern Mexico. It is one of the few shrubby members of the poppy family.

Dendromecon rigida
TREE POPPY

This upright shrub or small tree, wild in the coastal ranges of most of California south to Baja California, grows on dry rocky slopes and cliffs. The narrow, greyish green leaves are stiff and leathery. Yellow, poppy-like flowers, around 5cm (2in) across, are produced in spring and summer.
Cultivation Easily grown in dry rocky soil. Is short-lived except in very rocky soil. *Height and spread to 3m (10ft). USZ 9–11, surviving -6.5°C (20°F) of overnight frost. Tolerant of summer drought.* ◗

Loropetalum (Hamamelidaceae)

Loropetalum consists of one to three species of small shrubs, evergreen in warm winters. They grow wild in Assam, southern China (from Hong Kong to Yunnan), and southern Japan, on rocky hills and dry open woods.

Loropetalum chinense
LOROPETALUM

This low, spreading shrub from China has green,ovate leaves, 2.5–4cm (1–1½in) long,

Above *Dendromecon rigida* (tree poppy)

and scented flowers, 2cm (¾in) wide, with strap-like petals in spring. The wild plant has white flowers, but pink-, red-, and crimson-flowered forms are very popular in gardens, particularly in southern USA. Some, such as 'Burgundy' and 'Plum Delight', have purple leaves too. 'Bicolor' produces white flowers and purple leaves.
Cultivation These tough plants are easy to grow anywhere, but are best in fertile soil with summer water. *Height to 2m (6½ft); spread to 3m (10ft). USZ 7–10, surviving -17°C (2°F) of overnight frost. Tolerant of drought.* ◗

Above *Mahonia siamensis*

Mahonia (Berberidaceae)

Mahonia has 55 species of evergreen shrubs, with stiff ornamental leaves and scented yellow flowers in winter, followed by blue berries. They are from eastern Asia from the Himalayas and southern India, to Japan and western North America south to Mexico, and mostly found in open woods.

Mahonia siamensis
The more spectacular subtropical species of *Mahonia* come from Asia, from the Nilgiri

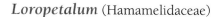

Above *Loropetalum chinense* (loropetalum)

Above *Melianthus major*

Above *Mahonia siamensis* in January in Lawrence Johnston's old garden at Serre de La Madone in Menton, France

Hills in India to China and Japan.
M. siamensis is one of the tallest and most striking, with its prickly pinnate leaves, 50–60cm (20–24in) long, and spikes, to 20cm (8in) long, of scented, deep yellow flowers in winter. Other species and cultivars such as M. *japonica* and M. x *media* 'Charity' are hardier and smaller but have less spiny and wavy leaves.
Cultivation Grows well in fertile leafy soil in partial shade and shelter from drying wind. It needs water in summer until it is well established.
Height to 3m (10ft); spread to 2m (6½ft). USZ 9–11, surviving -6.5°C (20°F) of overnight frost. Tolerant of summer drought. ◗

Melianthus (Melianthaceae)

Melianthus is a South African genus of around five species of evergreen shrubs. All are fine foliage plants, with pinnate, jaggedly toothed leaves, and have weird rather than beautiful flowers, adapted for pollination by sunbirds; in the Americas they attract hummingbirds into the garden.

Melianthus major
This soft, suckering shrub is grown mainly for its blue-grey leaves, 40cm (16in) long. The dark reddish maroon flowers, to 6cm (2½in) long, are borne in an upright arching spike, 1m (3ft) long, in spring.
Cultivation Easily grown and happiest by a water source in deep sandy soil. It responds well to cutting back in early spring or after flowering, and mulching with warm wood ash.
Height to 4m (13ft); spread to 3m (10ft). USZ 9–11, surviving -6.5°C (20°F) of overnight frost. Tolerant of summer drought. ◗

Paeonia (Paeoniaceae)
PEONY

The genus *Paeonia* has around 30 species of deciduous shrubs and herbaceous perennials, mostly from eastern Europe and western Asia but with two species from California. Hardy herbaceous peonies are familiar to gardeners. The tough shrubby species from China do best in warm climates with cool winters and no spring frost.

Paeonia rockii
TREE PEONY
This shrubby peony from northwestern China has dissected leaves and white, purple-centred, single flowers, in spring.
Cultivation Easily grown in deep fertile soil in a sheltered site.
Height and spread to 2m (6½ft). USZ 9–11, surviving -3°C (27°F) of frost. Tolerant of short periods of summer drought. ◗

Right *Paeonia rockii* (tree peony) at Kew

Southern Hemisphere Flowering Shrubs

Banksia (Proteaceae)

Banksia bears upright, cone-like heads crowded with small flowers. The genus has around 70 species of evergreen shrubs and trees, most of them found in dry sandy soils in Western Australia.

Banksia marginata
SILVER BANKSIA

This is one of the toughest banksias, as it will withstand some frost, and survive salt winds on the coast; it grows well on Tresco in the Scilly Isles. It is a shrub or small tree, native of New South Wales, Victoria, South Australia, and Tasmania, where it flowers in summer. Its cylindrical flowerheads are pale to bright yellow, to 10cm (4in) long. The green leaves are 2.5–10cm (1–4in) long, and silvery beneath.

Cultivation Is best in acid sandy soil, with no phosphatic fertilizer. Bonfire or wood ash, however, is beneficial.
Height to 10m (33ft); spread to 6m (20ft). USZ 9–11, surviving -6.5°C (20°F) of overnight frost. Tolerant of summer drought. ◗

Above *Banksia marginata* (silver banksia)

Embothrium (Proteaceae)

This genus comprises a single species of evergreen or deciduous shrubs and trees from temperate South America, in Chile and southern Argentina.

Embothrium coccineum
FIREBUSH

This beautiful shrub or tree has rather narrow climatic requirements, but is worth every effort. It grows on well-drained, often volcanic soils, in areas that are cool and wet in summer and not very cold and wet in winter, so it thrives in Ireland and the northwest coasts of England, Scotland, and France, as well as in Tasmania and New Zealand, and the Pacific coast of North America. *E. coccineum* flowers during late spring. The flowers, which can cover last year's new stems, are red, orange, or, very rarely, yellow, and around 3cm (1¼in) long.

Cultivation Best in sandy acid soils with ample water. Avoid fertilizer.
Height to 10m (33ft); spread to 3m (10ft). USZ 8–11, surviving -12°C (10°F) of frost overnight. Not tolerant of summer drought. ●

Grevillea (Proteaceae)
GREVILLEA

This is a large and important Australian genus of evergreen trees and shrubs. There are around 250 species, and many garden hybrids; all but a few are wild in Australia. Many species are cultivated for their attractive flowers, which are sometimes in long, hanging or upright, cone-like inflorescences. Red, yellow, and white are

Above *Embothrium coccineum* (firebush)

Above *Embothrium coccineum* (firebush)

the commonest colours. In addition to those shown here, other popular species of *Grevillea* are *G. banksii*, which forms a rounded shrub with upright heads of red flowers, and its many hybrids, and the commonly planted tree *G. robusta* (*see* p.68).

Grevillea juniperina f. sulphurea

This is a yellow form of a common red variety from New South Wales. It forms a stiff, rather upright shrub, with stiff, narrow leaves and pale sulphur-yellow flowers produced throughout the year. This is one of the toughest *Grevilleas*, tolerant of cold, wet, and drought. Some varieties are used as ground cover.

Cultivation Easily grown in poor soils, and better without fertilizer.

Height to 2m (6½ft); spread to 3m (10ft). USZ 8–11, surviving -12°C (10°F) of overnight frost. Tolerant of summer drought. ◗

Grevillea rosmarinifolia

ROSEMARY GREVILLEA

This is a very popular shrub, in Europe, in America, and in Australia, where it is native of New South Wales and Victoria, growing in rocky places and open forest on poor soil. It has soft, narrow, flat leaves, which are silvery beneath, and pink-red flowers almost throughout the year. Few garden shrubs are more free-flowering.

Cultivation Easily grown in any poor sandy soil. Avoid too much fertilizer.

Height to 3m (10ft); spread to 5m (16ft). USZ 8–11, surviving -12°C (10°F) of overnight frost. Tolerant of summer drought. ◗

Below *Grevillea rosmarinifolia* (rosemary grevillea)

Telopea (Proteaceae)

Telopea is a small but lovely and very popular genus of evergreen shrubs from Australia, in New South Wales, Victoria, and Tasmania. There are seven species, which include the spectacular *T. speciossisima*, with its huge heads surrounded by red bracts. All species grow in open *Eucalyptus* forest, but in the uplands the forest is cooler and more ferny. As with so many of the red-flowered Proteaceae, *Telopea* plants are visited by nectar-feeding birds.

Below *Grevillea juniperina* f. *sulphurea*

Telopea truncata

TASMANIAN WARATAH

An upright shrub from the mountains of Tasmania with narrow, dark green leaves, to 10cm (4in) long, with paler undersides. The flowerheads are about 8cm (3in) across and are produced on the tips of the shoots in late spring. They comprise red flowers with four equal-sized sepals.

Cultivation Easily grown in poor, well-drained but moist soils. Avoid heavy applications of fertilizer.

Height and spread to 3m (10ft). USZ 9–11, surviving -6.5°C (20°F) of overnight frost. Needs summer water. ●

Below *Telopea truncata* (Tasmanian waratah)

The Protea Family

Leucadendron (Proteaceae)

The genus *Leucodendron* contains 83 species, mostly evergreen shrubs, all of which are natives in South Africa. They have small heads of flowers surrounded by stiff, often brightly coloured bracts. The male and female flowers are produced on different trees.

Leucadendron argenteum
SILVER TREE

This beautiful large shrub or small tree has long branches densely covered with silvery, silky, narrow, lance-shaped leaves. It is wild in the southern Cape, from the Cape peninsula to the Hottentots-Holland mountains. The small, greenish flowerheads, 5cm (2in) across, are borne in spring.
Cultivation This has not proved easy to cultivate, needing sandy, peaty soil with no great heat in summer. It is an excellent coastal plant, thriving in sea winds, and grows well in the Isles of Scilly and extreme western coasts of Europe.
Height to 10m (33ft); spread to 4m (13ft).
USZ 9–11, surviving -6.5°C (20°F) of
overnight frost. Tolerant of summer drought. ◑

Leucospermum (Proteaceae)
PINCUSHSION

Leucospermum is a genus of 48 species of evergreen shrubs from South Africa north to Zimbabwe. Most species have rounded

Above *Leucadendron argenteum* (silver tree) in Kirstenbosch Botanic Garden, Cape Town, with Table Mountain behind

Above *Leucospermum conocarpodendron*

heads tightly packed with bright red, orange, or yellow flowers, with the long pollen presenter of each flower looking like a pin stuck into a pincushion.

Leucospermum conocarpodendron
This rounded shrub or small tree has wedge-shaped, sometimes felted leaves with 3–10 short, blunt teeth. The flowerheads, 5–9cm (2–3½in) across, are yellow when fresh in spring, fading to red.

This species grows wild on dry rocky slopes from the Cape peninsula north to Stamford.
Cultivation Grows best in sandy, acid soil. Avoid fertilizer, except for wood ash.
Height to 5m (16ft); spread to 6m (20ft).
USZ 9–11, surviving -6.5°C (20°F) of
overnight frost. Tolerant of summer drought. ◑

Leucospermum cordifolium
This shrub has short, stiff, overlapping leaves. Orange or scarlet flowerheads,

Above *Leucospermum cordifolium*

10–12cm (4–5in) across, are borne in spring and early summer. The styles and pollen presenters curve inwards, giving the flattened head a very neat effect. This species grows wild in the extreme southwest of Cape Province.
Cultivation Needs sandy soil and moisture in spring. Avoid fertilizer.
Height to 1.5m (5ft); spread to 2m (6½ft).
USZ 9–11, surviving -3°C (27°F) of overnight frost. Tolerant of summer drought. ◑

Protea (Proteaceae)
PROTEA

The genus *Protea* contains around 115 species, mostly in the winter rainfall area of Cape Province in South Africa, but spreading east and north into the summer rainfall area, as far north as Kenya. Most species are low evergreen shrubs; some, known as snow proteas, hug the ground; a few are small trees. *Protea* flowers are very long-lasting and often sold as cut flowers, sometimes imported from the wild in South Africa, where the locals make a business of selling them, thereby saving areas of fynbos from being cleared for grapevines. *P. roupelliae* (*see* p.16) is a stout small tree, growing at high altitudes in the Drakensberg in Natal, so it should be able to withstand frost, possibly into zone 8.

Protea cynaroides
KING PROTEA
This low shrub has the largest flowerhead of all the proteas, up to 30cm (1ft) across, surrounded by pale or deep pink, often silky bracts, produced from mid- to late summer. It is regularly burnt to the ground by fire, but resprouts quickly from a woody

underground tuber. Elliptic leathery leaves have a long slender stalk. *P. cynaroides* is wild throughout the winter rainfall area of the Cape, east to Port Elizabeth.
Cultivation Needs sandy acid soil, and moisture in spring. Avoid artificial fertilizer, especially phosphates; a dressing of wood ash is beneficial.
Height to 3m (10ft); spread to 2m (6½ft).
USZ 9–11, surviving -6.5°C (20°F) of overnight frost. Tolerant of summer drought. ◑

Protea eximia
Produces oblong leaves, heart-shaped at the base, and, in spring, pink-bracted flower-heads, 10cm (4in) across; the florets have black bearded tips. It is found wild, mainly on mountain slopes in the south Cape region.

Above *Protea eximia*

Cultivation As for *P. cynaroides*.
Height to 4m (13ft); spread to 3m (10ft).
USZ 9–11, surviving -6.5°C (20°F) of overnight frost. Tolerant of summer drought. ◑

Protea lacticolor
This shrub is found growing wild in fynbos in the southern Cape, in the Bainskloof and Hottentots-Holland mountains, and flowering during the summer months. Its flowerheads, 10cm (4in) across, are surrounded by pink bracts. The leathery, stalkless leaves are heart-shaped with rounded tips.
Cultivation As for *P. cynaroides*.
Height to 4m (13ft); spread to 5m (16ft).
USZ 9–11, surviving -6.5°C (20°F) of overnight frost. Tolerant of summer drought. ◑

Above *Protea cynaroides* (king protea) at Kew

Above *Protea lacticolor* in the Hottentots-Holland mountains, Western Cape, South Africa

Ceanothus & Related Plants

Above *Ceanothus* 'Cascade' in Eccleston Square, London, with white *Viburnum plicatum* 'Mariesii'

Above *Ceanothus* 'Concha' with the grass *Briza maxima*

Ceanothus (Rhamnaceae)
CALIFORNIAN LILAC

This genus of 55 species of evergreen and deciduous shrubs and small trees is found throughout North America. The loveliest species come from California, and most of these have blue flowers in spring, on stiff shrubs with shining evergreen leaves. They do well in sun or light shade, and are very tolerant of summer drought, but tend to be rather short-lived both in the wild and in gardens. A few species from eastern North America and hybrids such as 'Gloire de Versailles' are partly deciduous, and flower in late summer; they need summer water.

Ceanothus 'Cascade'
One of the older and still one of the best hybrids, this is probably derived from evergreen *C. thyrsiflorus*, which is found in redwood forests in northern California. In spring the arching branches bear pale blue flowers. The coastal form, *C. thyrsiflorus* f. *repens*, is good for planting in exposed windy sites and tolerant of salt wind.
Cultivation Easily grown in well-drained soil in sun or partial shade, but needs shelter from wind. Is short-lived (around 10 years) but can readily be increased from cuttings of the new growth.
Height to 3m (10ft); spread to 4m (13ft). USZ 8–11, surviving -12°C (10°F) of overnight frost. Tolerant of summer drought. ◑

Ceanothus 'Concha'
This is one of the best of the deep blue-flowered *Ceanothus* hybrids, with stiff arching shoots. It flowers in spring, when the whole plant can become a sheet of blue. It is a tough evergreen shrub, which flourishes when growing in full sun and exposed to the strongest winds. *C. impressus* is similar but produces smaller sticky leaves and has a more upright growth habit; 'Puget Blue' is a fine clone.
Cultivation Easily grown in well-drained soil and full exposure to the wind.
Height to 9m (30ft); spread to 6m (20ft). USZ 8–11, surviving -12°C (10°F) of overnight frost. Tolerant of summer drought. ◑

Above *Colletia ulicina* flowering at Kew

Above *Elaeagnus angustifolia* (Russian olive)

Above *Photinia arbutifolia* growing wild in Santa Barbara Botanic Garden, California

Colletia (Rhamnaceae)

The genus *Colletia* has five species of very spiny, almost leafless shrubs, found wild in eastern South America. The two species commonly grown, *C. paradoxa* and *C. hystrix*, have thick, stiff, green spines and small, white or pale pink flowers. Both are good for coastal gardens.

Colletia ulicina
This shrub has gorse-like growth (hence the specific name) and tubular, bright pink flowers. It comes from Chile and forms a stiff shrub, flowering very freely in spring. It thrives at Kew, but is at present rare in cultivation; when widely available it will become a very popular garden plant.
Cultivation Grow in fertile, well-drained soil, on a bank or sloping site.
Height to 2m (6½ft); spread to 3m (10ft).
USZ 8–11, surviving -12°C (10°F) of overnight frost. Tolerant of summer drought. ◗

Elaeagnus (Eleagnaceae)

The genus *Elaeagnus* contains around 40 species, some evergreen, some deciduous, found in North America and from eastern Europe across Asia to Japan. Most have silvery scales on the leaves, particularly on the underside. Many produce deliciously scented, small flowers, followed by small edible fruit. The evergreen species are excellent for hedging; they will grow in partial shade and tolerate salt wind.

Elaeagnus angustifolia
RUSSIAN OLIVE
This is one of the most drought-resistant and hardiest of small trees, often cultivated as a hedge but also making a lovely small specimen tree. The silvery, willow-like leaves are deciduous. Yellowish green flowers, which are greyish outside and have a most exotic perfume, appear in late spring. The fruit is dry and floury, but eaten in central Asia, where it grows wild.
Cultivation Thrives in really tough desert conditions, such as mainly dry, saline soil.
Height to 9m (30ft); spread to 6m (20ft).
USZ 7–11, surviving -17°C (2°F) and less of overnight frost. Tolerant of summer drought. ◖

Photinia (Rosaceae)

Photinia is a genus of around 60 species of evergreen and deciduous trees and shrubs. Many plants now included in *Photinia* were formerly called *Heteromeles* or *Stranvaesia*. Some species have bright red young leaves.

Photinia arbutifolia
This evergreen shrub or small tree has shallowly toothed, elliptic–oblong leaves and loose panicles of small, creamy white flowers, in late summer. The fruits develop through the winter into red berries, which are conspicuous in early spring growing wild on dry hills in California.
Cultivation Easily grown in dry rocky soil.
Height to 9m (30ft); spread to 6m (20ft).
USZ 8–11, surviving -12°C (10°F) of overnight frost. Tolerant of summer drought. ◖

Rhaphiolepis (Rosaceae)

This is a small genus of around nine species of evergreen shrubs from east and southeast Asia. Many are very tough and used as low hedges or ground cover in difficult climates such as Texas.

Rhaphiolepis umbellata
This stiff evergreen shrub, from China and Japan, has white flowers followed by small black fruit. It often grows wild on the coast.
Cultivation Easily grown in any soil.
Height to 1m (3ft); spread to 3m (10ft).
USZ 8–11, surviving -12°C (10°F) of overnight frost. Tolerant of summer drought. ◖

Above *Rhaphiolepis umbellata*

Pea Family Flowering Shrubs

Caesalpinia (Leguminosae)

Caesalpinia comprises around 150 species of evergreen and deciduous trees, shrubs, and climbers from tropical parts of America and Africa. Their habitat is usually savannah but can be open mountain sides. Some, such as *C. gilliesii*, are not only very ornamental but also have medicinal uses. Also useful in the warm garden are *C. mexicana*, with its yellow flowers, and *C. pulcherrima*, with its clusters of orange or red flowers throughout summer. *C. pulcherrima* in particular is invaluable as a fast-growing, screening plant.

Caesalpinia gilliesii
BIRD OF PARADISE BUSH

A fast-growing, evergreen shrub or small tree native to South America and deciduous when temperatures are low. It has finely divided ferny leaves and racemes of yellow, red-stamened flowers, from spring to late summer.

Cultivation Grow in light, well-drained soil, in full sun. Best kept rather dry in winter to avoid waterlogging; will normally resprout if cut to the ground by frost. *Height to 3m (10ft); spread to 2m (6½ft). USZ 9–11, surviving -6.5°C (20°F) of overnight frost. Requires occasional heavy watering in summer.* ◑

Above *Calliandra californica*

Calliandra (Leguminosae)

This genus contains around 200 species of evergreen trees, shrubs, and perennials, some of which are similar in appearance to *Acacia* (mimosa). They originate in tropical and subtropical America, India, Madagascar, and west Africa. In addition to *C. californica*, a number of other species are good for dry gardens, and bear a variety of flower colours from white to crimson. *C. emarginata* is tall, with pink or red flowers, while low-growing, spreading *C. eriophylla* has pinkish purple flowers. *C. surinamensis*, with its white or pale lilac flowers, seems to be particularly drought tolerant, and *C. tweedii*, with its scarlet flowers, can be clipped as a hedge.

Calliandra californica
This spreading shrub, from north Mexico and Baja California, has feathery green foliage. The fluffy, bottlebrush-like, crimson flowers, which attract hummingbirds, are borne most of the year.

Cultivation Good in dry sandy soil in a desert garden, but a small amount of water in summer will keep it flowering longer. *Height and spread to 1m (3ft). USZ 10–11, surviving -1°C (30°F) of overnight frost. Tolerant of summer drought.* ◑

Coronilla (Leguminosae)

This genus comprises around 20 species of evergreen shrubs and perennials, which originate in Europe, Africa, and Asia. The name *Coronilla* is from the Latin, meaning a little crown, alluding to the appearance of the flower umbels.

Above *Caesalpinia gilliesii* (bird of paradise bush)

Above *Senna corymbosa*

Above *Coronilla valentina* in Nice, France

Cultivation Grow in well-drained, sandy soil in full sun.
Height and spread to 3m (10ft). USZ 10–11, surviving -1°C (30°F) or less of overnight frost. Tolerant of summer drought. ◑

Senna (Leguminosae)

Senna contains around 350 species of evergreen and deciduous trees, shrubs, and climbers, distributed throughout the tropical regions of Africa, Australia, and South America. They have five-petalled flowers and pinnate leaves with ovate leaflets. Other shrubby species useful for the warm garden include the smaller *S. artemisioides*, with its feathery grey leaves and yellow flowers, and *S. tomentosa*, with its upright clusters of yellow flowers. For more tree-like *Senna* species *see* p.55.

Senna corymbosa (syn. *Cassia corymbosa*) This spreading evergreen shrub, native of Argentina and Uruguay, has naturalized in parts of southern USA. The leaves are dark green. Yellow flowers are borne in rounded clusters from spring to autumn.
Cultivation Does well in any well-drained soil. Occasional heavy watering encourages flowering. Prune drastically after flowering.
Height to 3m (10ft); spread to 2m (6½ft). USZ 9–11, surviving -6.5 °C (20°F) of overnight frost. Tolerant of summer drought. ●

Coronilla valentina
Native to the Mediterranean region, this shrub produces vetch-like foliage and scented, golden yellow flowers, during early spring. 'Citrina' bears pale yellow flowers, while 'Variegata' has cream-variegated leaves.
Cultivation Easy to grow, and tolerant of most soils. Can be grown on the coast.
Height and spread to 2m (6½ft). USZ 9–11, surviving -6.5°C (20°F) of overnight frost. Tolerant of moderate summer drought. ◑

Petalostylis
(Leguminosae/Caesalpinoideae)

The genus *Petalostylis* contains two species of evergreen shrubs, from the arid regions of Western Australia.

Petalostylis labicheoides
This rounded shrub, from sandy and rocky places near Perth, produces pinnate leaves, 2cm (¾in) across, and orange-yellow flowers, that are 4cm (1½in) across, in spring.

Above *Petalostylis labicheoides* near Perth, Western Australia

Pea-flowered Shrubs & Milkwort

Chorizema (Leguminosae)

Chorizema consists of around 20 species of evergreen shrubs and climbers originating in Australia, but with some species naturalized in California. These beautiful plants have long been valued both as garden plants and as florists' flowers. The numerous brightly coloured blooms give rise to the common name of flame peas.

Chorizema ilicifolium
HOLLY FLAME PEA

This free-flowering, dense shrub or sometimes scrambler has long thin shoots. It is a native of Western Australia. The leaves are bristly and holly-like, and the spikes of orange, yellow, and purplish flowers are borne in early spring.
Cultivation Best in well-drained, peaty, sandy soil, in full sun or partial shade. Mulch the roots to prevent them drying out. Prune lightly after flowering.
Height and spread to 3m (10ft). USZ 10–11, surviving -1°C (30°F) of frost. Tolerant of summer drought for short periods only. ◗

Clianthus (Leguminosae)

This genus of only one species of evergreen shrubs originates in New Zealand; plants are long-lived but rare in the wild. Another spectacular species, previously known as *C. formosus* (Sturt's desert pea), has been moved to *Swainsona*.

Clianthus puniceus
LOBSTER CLAW, KAKA BEAK

This spreading shrub has dark green, pinnate leaves and hanging clusters of

Above *Chorizema ilicifolium* (holly flame pea)

greenish white, pink, or red flowers, from winter through to spring. Various naturally occurring colour forms have been given fancy names, such as 'Red Admiral', under which they are sold commercially.
Cultivation Grow in any fertile soil in full sun. Prune in early summer after flowering to maintain a good shape.
Height to 3m (10ft); spread to 2m (6½ft). USZ 9–11, surviving -6.5°C (20°F) of overnight frost. Tolerant of summer drought. ●

Lupinus (Leguminosae)

The genus *Lupinus* comprises around 200 species of evergreen shrubs, annuals, and perennials from northern Africa, North and South America, and southern Europe.

Many species are cultivated commercially for green manure, agricultural fodder, and their edible seeds. *L. arboreus* is another evergreen shrub that is good in coastal districts. It has silky greyish green leaves and usually yellow but sometimes lilac or blue flowers.

Lupinus albifrons
This native of California is a lax, rounded shrub with silky, silvery haired leaves and spikes of blue or purplish flowers from late spring to summer.
Cultivation Does best on well-drained soil in full sun. Good in coastal sites.
Height to 1.5m (5ft); spread to 2m (6½ft). USZ 9–11, surviving -3°C (27°F) of overnight frost. Tolerant of summer drought. ◗

Podalyria (Leguminosae)

This genus of around 22 evergreen shrubby species is from South Africa. All have pea-like flowers, usually pinkish. Most species grow in the fynbos, and flower particularly well after a fire.

Podalyria cordata
This upright shrub, from the Cape area of South Africa, has dark green, downy leaves folded upwards from the mid-rib. The bright pink flowers appear in late spring.
Cultivation Best in well-drained, peaty, sandy soil in full sun. Good for planting in coastal gardens.

Left *Clianthus puniceus* (lobster claw) in Devon

Above *Lupinus albifrons*

Above *Podalyria cordata*

Above *Polygala virgata* (Cape purple broom)

Height and spread to 1m (3ft). USZ 9–11, surviving -6.5°C (20°F) of overnight frost. Tolerant of summer drought, but needs water when young. ◐

Polygala (Polygalaceae)
MILKWORT

Polygala is a widely distributed genus of some 500 species, from trees and shrubs to creeping herbs. They are natives in mainly temperate areas, from Scotland to South Africa, east to China and Australia. In addition to P. virgata, other evergreen shrubs that are good for warm gardens include P. x dalmaisiana, P. fruticosa, and P. myrtifolia, all with purple flowers.

Above *Polygala virgata* (Cape purple broom) at Prince Alfreds Pass above Knysna, South Africa

Polygala virgata
CAPE PURPLE BROOM
An upright or arching, semi-evergreen shrub, native of South Africa, with narrow leaves and racemes of reddish purple, pea-like flowers from spring onwards.
Cultivation Grow in fertile, well-drained soil in sun or semi-shade. Keep dry in winter. Is good in coastal conditions.
Height 2m (6½ft) or more; spread to 1.5m (5ft). USZ 9–11, surviving -6.5°C (20°F) of overnight frost occasionally. Tolerant of summer drought. ◐

Sutherlandia (Leguminosae)

The genus *Sutherlandia* comprises three species of evergreen shrubs with bladder-

like fruits and bird-pollinated, red flowers. They originate from dry areas of South Africa, and have naturalized in east Africa, South America, and New Zealand.

Sutherlandia montana
This shrub produces soft greyish, pinnate leaves, 10cm (4in) long, and red, pea-like flowers, to 3.5cm (1½in) long, in late spring, followed by whitish, papery, transparent seed pods. It is a native of the Drakensberg in Natal, South Africa.
Cultivation Easily grown in very dry, well-drained soil. Best in full sun. Can be pruned lightly after flowering to maintain a bushy shape.
Height and spread to 1.5m (5ft). USZ 9–11, surviving -6.5°C (20°F) of frost if dry at the roots. Tolerant of summer drought. ◑

Left *Sutherlandia montana*

Euphorbias

Euphorbia (Euphorbiaceae)

Euphorbia is a variable genus with about 2,000 species of evergreen, semi-evergreen, and deciduous trees, shrubs, annual, biennial, or perennial herbs, distributed almost throughout the world in a wide variety of habitats. The milky sap in the stems is often toxic if ingested, and can cause an allergic skin reaction.

Euphorbia bravoana
This shrub, bearing a few succulent branches, is native of northeast Gomera, in the Canary Islands, where it grows in rocky places. The narrow, greyish white leaves, 10–12cm (4–5in) are the perfect foil for the dark purplish red inflorescences.
Cultivation Good on well-drained, dry soil in full sun.
Height and spread to 1m (3ft). USZ 10–11, surviving -1°C (30°F) of frost for short periods only if dry. Tolerant of summer drought. ◗

Euphorbia milii
CROWN OF THORNS
This scrambling or creeping, deciduous shrub, native of Madagascar, has spiny succulent stems, ovate–elliptic or lance-

Above *Euphorbia bravoana*

shaped, bright green leaves, 10–25cm (4–10in) long, and scarlet bracts year-round.
Cultivation Grow in well-drained, dry soil in full sun.
Height to 1m (3ft); spread to 2m (6½ft). USZ 10–11, surviving -1°C (30°F) of frost for short periods. Tolerant of summer drought. ◑

Euphorbia x pasteurii
This spreading evergreen shrub is a hybrid of *E. mellifera* and *E. stygiana*. It is fast

Above *Euphorbia milii* (crown of thorns)

growing, with branched succulent stems bearing narrow, lance-shaped, dark green leaves. Old leaves are bright red throughout winter. The honey-scented, brown inflorescences are borne in spring.
Cultivation Grow in well-drained, dry soil in full sun. May be cut to the ground by sharp frost, but will usually recover.
Height to 2m (6½ft); spread to 2.4m (8ft). USZ 9–11, surviving -6.5°C (20°F) of frost for short periods. Tolerant of summer drought. ◗

Below *Euphorbia bravoana* in Tenerife

Jatropha (Euphorbiaceae)

A genus of around 175 species of evergreen and deciduous shrubs, herbs, and occasionally trees, originating from tropical and warm areas of Africa and North America. They mostly have fleshy stems and lobed or divided leaves.

Jatropha multifida
CORAL PLANT, PHYSIC NUT
This deciduous shrub or small tree, from tropical America, has finely dissected leaves, which are greyish white on the underside.

Upright branched clusters, 20cm (8in) across, of bright scarlet flowers are borne in spring and summer. All parts of this plant are very poisonous.
Cultivation Grow in well-drained soil in sun or partial shade, with a dry period once the leaves have fallen in winter.
Height to 7m (23ft); spread to 5m (16ft). USZ 10–11, surviving -1°C (30°F) of frost for short periods. Needs water in summer. ◗

Ricinocarpus (Euphorbiaceae)

The genus *Ricinocarpus* comprises 16 species of woody evergreen shrubs, mainly from east and south Australia.

Ricinocarpus tuberculatus
This spreading, heath-like shrub, native of Western Australia, has pin-shaped leaves and masses of white starry flowers in spring.
Cultivation Grow in acid sandy soil.
Height and spread to 2.4m (8ft). USZ 9–11, surviving -6.5°C (20°F) of overnight frost. Tolerant of summer drought. ◗

Ricinus (Euphorbiaceae)

Ricinus has one species of evergreen shrubs from northeastern Africa to western Asia.

Ricinus communis
CASTOR OIL PLANT
This deadly poisonous, fast-growing shrub, from eastern Africa and the southeastern Mediterranean, is often grown as an annual. The leaves, 30cm (1ft) across, have wide lobes. The flowers are insignificant, the male separate from and below the female. The fruits (*see* back cover) are covered in soft spikes and are reddish when young.
Cultivation Easily grown in any soil.
Height to 4m (13ft); spread to 2m (6½ft). USZ10–11, needing a minimum of -1°C (30°F) overnight. Needs water in summer. ◗◗

Above *Ricinocarpus tuberculatus*

Left *Jatropha multifida* (coral plant)

Fuchsia & Related Plants

Fuchsia (Onagraceae)

This genus contains more than 100 species of deciduous and evergreen shrubs, climbers, epiphytes, or small trees, most species originating in South and Central America, with some occurring in New Zealand. In addition to the species, some of which can become very tall, there are numerous smaller garden hybrids and cultivars. Many of these are particularly well suited to growing in containers. Most fuchsias do best in only partial sun, and require protection from drying winds and generous watering in hot dry weather in order to replicate the humid conditions they enjoy in the wild. This effort is repaid by the masses of showy flowers in shades of white, pink, orange, red, and purple. 'Gartenmeister Bonstedt', a hybrid derived from *F. triphylla* (from the West Indies), is popular in warmer gardens, as it has a long flowering season and is generally tolerant of

Above *Fuchsia denticulata*

Above *Fuchsia* 'Checkerboard'

hot conditions. It has pendent clusters of long, orange, tubular flowers, but will not stand any frost.

Fuchsia boliviana
This evergreen shrub or small tree, from South America, produces velvety green leaves and clusters of tubular crimson flowers at the end of the stems, in summer. Var. *alba* has white flowers.
Cultivation Suitable for a cool, moist corner in partial shade. Fertile, moisture-retentive soil and protection from strong drying winds are helpful, too.
Height to 6m (20ft); spread to 2m (6½ft), but usually less in gardens. USZ 10–11, surviving -1°C (30°F) of frost. Needs water in summer. ●

Fuchsia 'Checkerboard'
This deciduous shrub has a trailing pendulous habit and ovate green leaves. Reddish pink-and-white, tubular flowers are borne from summer to winter.
Cultivation Grow in fertile, humus-rich soil in partial shade and away from drying winds. Feed freely in summer.
Height and spread to 60cm (2ft). USZ 10–11, surviving -1°C (30°F) of overnight frost occasionally. Water freely in summer. ●

Fuchsia denticulata
This partially climbing, evergreen shrub or small tree can grow very tall in its natural

Left *Fuchsia boliviana*

habitat in South America, but is usually much smaller in gardens. The tubular red flowers are rather similar to those of *F. boliviana* but are carried on shorter stems, in summer and autumn.

Cultivation Grow in moist soil, in a partially shaded, sheltered place.
Height to 10m (33ft) (in cultivation); spread to 6m (20ft) but usually much less. USZ 11, needing minimum of 4.5°C (40°F) overnight. Requires summer watering. ◗

Fuchsia fulgens

This tuberous-rooted, deciduous shrub from Mexico has soft red stems and broad, bluish green leaves. The tubular flowers are pale orange/scarlet, tipped with green, and appear in late summer. There are several variants of this species, including 'Rubra Grandiflora', with its longer, bright red flowers tipped with white.

Cultivation Does well in rich, moist but well-drained soil in warm, sunny, humid conditions. Can be left dry in winter.
Height to 1m (3ft); spread to 60cm (2ft). USZ 11, needing minimum of 4.5°C (40°F) overnight. Requires summer watering. ◗

Heterocentron (Melastomataceae)

This genus of around 25 species of ground-covering evergreen subshrubs and perennials originates in Central and South America. Some can be aggressive weeds.

Heterocentron elegans

This creeping, mat-forming subshrub is a native of Central and South America. The numerous bright magenta or mauve, flat

Below *Fuchsia fulgens* 'Rubra Grandiflora'

flowers are produced in late summer, when they make a dramatic display.

Cultivation Best in moist soil in shade in a hot dry climate, or in a sunny position in humid areas.
Height to 10cm (4 in); spread to 1m (3ft). USZ 10–11, surviving -1°C (30°F) or more of overnight frost. Requires summer watering. ◗

Tibouchina (Melastomataceae)

A genus containing around 250 species of evergreen shrubs, subshrubs, and herbs, occasionally, from tropical South America.

Tibouchina urvilleana
(syn. *T. semidecandra*)
This slender upright shrub is a native of Brazil. The leaves are soft green, with marked longitudinal ribs. The round, flat, or saucer-shaped, rich purple flowers, to 10cm (4in) across, are borne in spring and may continue to appear for several months in favourable conditions.

Cultivation Needs fertile, moist, preferably slightly acid soil and shelter from winds. Prune after flowering. Good in pots or tubs.
Height and spread to 3m (10ft). USZ 10–11, mature plants surviving -1°C (30°F) of overnight frost occasionally. Needs summer watering. ●

Above *Heterocentron elegans*

Above *Tibouchina urvilleana*

The Myrtle Family

Acca (Myrtaceae)

Acca is a genus of six species of evergreen shrubs and small trees, with guava-like fruit. They are native of South America.

Acca sellowiana (syn. *Feijoa sellowiana*)
PINEAPPLE GUAVA
This evergreen shrub is a native of South America. It has dark green leaves, with white felt on the underside, and solitary flowers, 4cm (1½in) across, with bosses of conspicuous red stamens, in summer. The red-tinged, green, egg-shaped fruit, 5cm (2in) long, is edible, and has a pleasant aroma. There are several cultivars available commercially, including 'Variegata', with its leaves edged creamy white, and 'Mammoth', which has larger fruits.

Cultivation Does best in moderately fertile, well-drained soil, with protection from cold drying winds. Good for coastal areas, as it will tolerate salt-laden winds. Makes a dense hedge if clipped.
Height to 3m (10ft); spread to 2m (6½ft). USZ 8–11, surviving -12°C (10°F) of frost when dormant. Tolerant of summer drought. ◐

Chamaelaucium (Myrtaceae)

Chamaelaucium comprises 21 species of evergreen shrubs, all from southwest Australia. The flowers of most species have waxy petals, hence the common name: wax flower. When each flower is fully open, the shining top of the ovary is exposed. *Chamaelaucium* is grown for the cut-flower trade in semi-desert areas, such as Israel.

Above *Chamaelaucium uncinatum* 'University' (geraldton wax)

Chamaelaucium uncinatum
GERALDTON WAX
This tough upright shrub, native of Western Australia, has narrow leaves and clusters of cup-shaped flowers in a variety of colours ranging from white through pink to mauve, purple, or red from late winter through to early spring. *C. uncinatum* has been planted to combat soil erosion, and is also grown as a cut flower plant in dry areas. It has a number of cultivars, such as 'University', which bears vivid red flowers and is a popular garden plant in Australia and elsewhere.
Cultivation Does well in full or partial sun in sandy gravelly soil. Can be pruned immediately after flowering.
Height and spread to 5m (16ft). USZ 10–11, surviving -1°C (30°F) or more for short periods. Tolerant of summer drought. ◐

Leptospermum (Myrtaceae)

The genus *Leptospermum* contains 79 species of evergreen shrubs and trees, the majority of which originate in Australia. The leaves have been used as a tea substitute, hence the common name.

Leptospermum lanigerum
WOOLLY TEA TREE
This evergreen shrub, from Tasmania and southeast Australia, produces downy stems, greyish green leaves, and small white flowers, in spring. 'Silver Sheen' is later-flowering, with more silvery leaves.

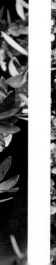

Left *Leptospermum scoparium* 'Kiwi'
Far Left *Leptospermum lanigerum*

Below *Myrtus communis*

Cultivation Best in moist, well-drained soil in sun or light shade. Light pruning after flowering will help keep the bush neat. *Height and spread to 2m (6½ft). USZ 8–11, surviving -12°C (10°F) of frost. Tolerant of summer drought once established.* ◑

Leptospermum scoparium
NEW ZEALAND TEA TREE, MANUKA
This fast-growing. evergreen shrub or small tree is a native of Australia (including Tasmania) and New Zealand. It has very narrow, dark green leaves and masses of white, pink, or red flowers, from late spring to summer. 'Kiwi' is a popular dwarf form; it bears red flowers and purple leaves.
Cultivation Grow in well-drained, acid, sandy soil. Prune after flowering to maintain a good shape.
Height and spread to 2m (6½ft). USZ 9–11, surviving -6.5°C (20°F) of overnight frost for short periods only. Tolerant of summer drought once established. ◑

Myrtus (Myrtaceae)
MYRTLE

This genus of two species of aromatic evergreen shrubs or trees is from the Mediterranean region and northern Africa. The South American species previously found under *Myrtus* have been transferred to *Luma* and other genera.

Myrtus communis
This evergreen shrub, native of the Mediterranean region and western Asia, has dark green leaves, which are aromatic when crushed. The white flowers with masses of stamens, in summer, are followed by purple berries. Subsp. *tarentina* is more compact, with narrower leaves and white berries.
Cultivation Grow in well-drained soil in full sun. Water sparingly in the growing season. Can be clipped to form a hedge.
Height and spread to 4m (13ft). USZ 8–11, surviving -12°C (10°F) of overnight frost. Tolerant of summer drought. ◑

Rhodomyrtus (Myrtaceae)

This genus comprises 11 species of evergreen shrubs and trees from China, southeast Asia, and Australia.

Rhodomyrtus tomentosa
This evergreen shrub or small tree is a native of China and southeast Asia. It has leathery, green, oval leaves, around 7.5cm (3in) long, downy on the underside. Pink, saucer-shaped flowers, around 5cm (2in) across, are borne in early summer.
Cultivation Best in deep, lime-free soil in a sheltered place.
Height to 4m (13ft); spread to 2m (6½ft). USZ 10–11, surviving -1°C (30°F) of occasional overnight frost. Tolerant of summer drought. ◑

Above *Rhodomyrtus tomentosa* growing wild on The Peak in Hong Kong

Bottlebrushes

Callistemon (Myrtaceae)
BOTTLEBRUSH

Callistemon is a native genus of Australia, with around 30 species of woody evergreen shrubs and small trees, commonly known as bottlebrushes because of the appearance of their flower spikes. Many species make good garden plants, as they have striking flowers (usually red or pink), and are tough, tolerant of most soils, and can be grown by the coast. Numerous cultivars are also available, often with flower colours such as pink, mauve, and purple, and occasionally white.

Callistemon pallidus
LEMON BOTTLEBRUSH
This shrub from southeast Australia and Tasmania has numerous branches and narrowly oblong leaves. The flowers are pale yellow, with conspicuous, cream to greenish yellow stamens, in late spring and summer. There are many cultivars,

Above *Callistemon pallidus* (lemon bottlebrush)

including 'Australflora Candle Glow', a low-growing, spreading form popular as a ground-cover plant.
Cultivation Grows in most soils, even those that are waterlogged, in full sun or partial shade. Useful as a windbreak, and can be planted on the coast. Prune after flowering to promote blooms in the following season.
Height and spread 4m (13ft) or more. USZ 9–11, surviving -6.5°C (20°F) of overnight frost. Tolerant of summer drought. ◗

Callistemon viminalis
WEEPING BOTTLEBRUSH
This shrub or small bushy tree, from southeast Australia, has weeping branches, covered with silky hairs when young. The leaves are linear to lance-shaped. The bright red flowers appear in summer, sometimes also at other times of year. There are many named forms available commercially, some of which are more drought tolerant than the species. The names of these cultivars are confused, but it is worth looking out for one of the best forms, known as 'Hen Camp Creek' or 'Luster Creek', which makes a large shrub to 4m (13ft) high and wide, and has red flowers in spring.
Cultivation Grows in most soils, although it is not as tough as *C. pallidus*, disliking exposure to strong winds.

Left *Callistemon viminalis* (weeping bottlebrush)
Opposite page *Melaleuca coccinea*

Height to 7m (23ft); spread to 5m (16ft). USZ 9–11, surviving -6.5°C (20°F) of overnight frost. Requires summer watering. ◑

Calothamnus (Myrtaceae)

The genus *Calothamnus* is a native of Western Australia and consists of 38 species of woody evergreen shrubs.

Calothamnus gilesii
GILES' NET BUSH

A tough hardy shrub from southwest Australia named after the 19th-century explorer Ernest Giles. It has strange, needle-like leaves with a sharp point, and clusters of bright red flowers with brush-like stamens, in spring and summer.
Cultivation Flourishes in most well-drained soils in full sun. Pruning will help to keep this shrub under control.
Height and spread to 4m (13ft). USZ 9–11, surviving -6.5°C (20°F) of overnight frost occasionally. Tolerant of summer drought. ◑

Kunzea (Myrtaceae)

The genus *Kunzea* is native mainly in South Australia, with 42 species there; one species is from New Zealand. Varieties range in habit from low, spreading, ground-covering plants to tall evergreen shrubs. They differ from the very similar *Leptospermum* in having the style sunk into a cup.

Below *Calothamnus gilesii* (Giles' net bush)

Kunzea baxteri
This spreading evergreen shrub, native of southwest Australia, was named after William Baxter, the British gardener who collected it in 1823–30. It has dark greyish green leaves and bright scarlet bottlebrushes, which appear near the branch tips in spring.
Cultivation Grows in well-drained soil in full sun.
Height and spread to 3m (10ft). USZ 10–11, surviving -1°C (30°F) of frost or more occasionally. Tolerant of summer drought. ◑

Melaleuca (Myrtaceae)

Melaleuca is the second largest genus in the Myrtaceae, with around 170 species of

Below *Kunzea baxteri*

evergreen shrubs and trees, mostly native of Australia. They are invaluable to gardeners for their showy flowers and tolerance of different soil types.

Melaleuca coccinea
This erect bushy shrub, from southwest Australia, has stiff, narrow leaves and spikes of bright red, bottlebrush-like flowers, in spring. Subsp. *coccinea* has narrow to broadly ovate leaves, 6–8mm (¼–⅓in) long, while subsp. *eximea* has linear ones, 8–20mm (⅓–¾in) long.
Cultivation Grows in well-drained soil in full sun.
Height and spread to 2m (6½ft). USZ 10–11, surviving -1°C (30°F) of frost or more occasionally. Tolerant of summer drought. ◑

Capers & Rues

Capparis (Capparidaceae)

The genus *Capparis* comprises 250 species of evergreen shrubs, small trees, and climbers widely distributed throughout tropical and subtropical regions worldwide.

Capparis spinosa
CAPER
This scrambling spiny shrub is a native of southern Europe east to Asia. The fleshy grey leaves set off to advantage the beautiful white flowers, with prominent pink stamens, which are borne in summer. The flowers open in the morning and fade during the day; the young buds are pickled to make the capers commonly used in cooking. Var. *nummularia*, from Australia, flowers all year round.
Cultivation Grow in well-drained soil in full sun. Is suitable for garden planting in coastal districts.
Height and spread to 1.5m (5ft). USZ 10–11, surviving -1°C (30°F) of overnight frost. Tolerant of summer drought. ◑

Choisya (Rutaceae)

This genus of around nine species of evergreen shrubs originates from the southwestern states of the USA and Mexico. *C. ternata*, often known as Mexican orange, is suitable for temperate climates, being hardier than those shown here.

Above *Capparis spinosa* (caper) photographed in the early morning in Turkey

Choisya arizonica
This shrub bears aromatic, palmate, green leaves, with narrow leaflets, and clusters of scented white flowers, measuring 2cm (¾in) across, in the spring months. It is a native of Arizona.
Cultivation Grow in fertile, well-drained soil in full sun. May be cut to the ground by frost, but will generally grow again during spring.

Height and spread to 1m (3ft). USZ 10–11, surviving -1°C (30°F) of overnight frost occasionally. Tolerant of summer drought. ◑

Choisya 'Aztec Pearl'
This beautiful hybrid of *C. arizonica* and *C. ternata* has the narrow leaflets that are characteristic of *C. arizonica* and the hardiness and larger, fragrant, white flowers, 3cm (1¼in) across, of *C. ternata*.

Above *Choisya arizonica*

Above *Choisya* 'Aztec Pearl'

Above *Correa* 'Mannii'

The pale pink flower buds are produced from spring until early summer.
Cultivation Grow in fertile, well-drained soil in full sun.
Height and spread 2m (6½ft) or more. USZ 10–11, surviving -1°C (30°F) of frost occasionally. Tolerant of summer drought. ◑◑

Correa (Rutaceae)

The genus *Correa* contains around 11 species of small evergreen shrubs, native of southeast Australia and Tasmania. Several species, with attractive tubular flowers in shades of green, pink, or red, are grown in gardens, and there are a number of cultivars available commercially. *C. alba*, with its small white flowers, is good for coastal planting because it is salt- and drought-tolerant. 'Dusky Bells' has beautiful, pinkish red flowers.

Correa 'Mannii' (syn. *C.* 'Harrisii')
This spreading shrub is probably a hybrid between *C. pulchella* and *C. reflexa*. It is an old cultivar, known since the 19th century and so well proven as a garden plant. It is valued for its striking flowers, 3.5cm (1½in) long, red on the outside and pink inside, which are carried throughout winter.
Cultivation Grows in well-drained, rather poor soil with limestone added. Tolerates full sun and partial shade.
Height and spread to 3m (10ft). USZ 9–11, surviving -6.5°C (20°F) of overnight frost. Tolerant of summer drought. ◑

Murraya (Rutaceae)

This genus comprises four or five species of spineless evergreen shrubs and trees and is a native of Asia, from India and China southwards to Australia.

Murraya paniculata
ORANGE JESSAMINE, BURMESE BOX
This slow-growing, large shrub sometimes makes a small tree. The crown of dark green, leathery leaves sets off to perfection the tight clusters of waxy white flowers, which are borne in flushes throughout the year. These are heavily scented, similar to jasmine or orange blossom, and are used in perfumery and for cosmetics. The orange-red berries develop soon after flowering.
Cultivation Grows in well-drained soil in partial shade. Good in containers, or clipped as a formal hedge. Dislikes disturbance to its root system. Flowering can be stimulated by watering.
Height to 7m (23ft); spread 5m (16ft) or more. USZ 10–11, surviving -1°C (30°F) of overnight frost. Tolerant of summer drought. ◑◑

Above The showy fruit of *Murraya paniculata* (orange jessamine)

97

Cistus, Daphne, & Relatives

Cistus (Cistaceae)

The genus *Cistus* contains around 20 species of evergreen or semi-evergreen shrubs from the Mediterranean region. Most tolerate salt-laden winds. These beautiful plants are invaluable in hot dry areas, and if a selection of different ones is planted, the gardener is rewarded with a succession of flowers from early to late summer. *C. × purpureus* is a hybrid between the two species shown here. It has reddish purple or white flowers, with deep red blotches on the petal bases.

Cistus crispus

This evergreen rounded shrub, a native of the western Mediterranean area, has pale green, downy, wrinkled, ovate leaves. The clusters of deep pinkish crimson flowers, 4cm (1½in) across, are produced at the ends of the branches in early summer.
Cultivation Grow in well-drained soil in full sun.
Height to 60m (2ft); spread to 1m (3ft).

Above *Cistus crispus*

Above A spotted form of *Cistus ladanifer* (gum cistus)

USZ 9–11, surviving at least -6.5°C (20°F) of overnight frost. Tolerant of summer drought. ◑

Cistus ladanifer

GUM CISTUS

This evergreen shrub has aromatic, very sticky branches and smooth, tongue-shaped, dark green leaves, which are white and downy on the underside. The single white flowers, 10cm (4in) across, often have purple blotches at the base of the petals, and are carried on the end of short branches in early summer. It is a native of southwest Europe to northern Africa.
Cultivation Grow in well-drained soil in full sun.
Height to 2m (6½ft); spread 1m (3ft) or more.
USZ 9–11, surviving at least -6.5°C (20°F) of overnight frost. Tolerant of summer drought. ◑

Dais (Thymelaceae)

The genus *Dais* comprises two species of deciduous shrubs, which are natives of South Africa and Madagascar. They have

Left *Cistus ladanifer* (gum cistus)

Below *Dais cotinifolia*

Below *Daphne bholua* 'Jacqueline Postill'

tough fibres under the bark, and these are used to make thread or string.

Dais cotinifolia

This large shrub, or sometimes small tree, is from South Africa and Madagascar. It has a rounded crown of shiny, dark green, narrowly ovate leaves, 8cm (3in) long. The umbels, 5cm (2in) across, of scented, pale pink, starry flowers are borne in summer.
Cultivation Grow in well-drained soil in full sun. Water during the growing season. Can be grown in a large container.
Height to 3m (10ft); spread to 2m (6½ft).
USZ 9–11, mature plants surviving -6.5°C (20°F) of frost. Tolerant of summer drought. ◑

Daphne (Thymelaceae)

The genus *Daphne* has around 50 species of small evergreen and deciduous shrubs. These attractive plants are native of Europe and northern Africa, and parts of subtropical and temperate Asia. They have wonderfully fragrant flowers, mostly in winter and early spring. Many species prefer cool conditions, and it can be a challenge to provide this in a really hot dry garden.

Daphne bholua

This evergreen or deciduous, upright shrub, from the Himalayas, has white,

strongly scented flowers, 1.5cm (½in) across, from early winter to early spring. 'Jacqueline Postill' is evergreen and has deep pink flowers. 'Gurkha' is deciduous, hardier, and bears purplish rose flowers.
Cultivation Grow in slightly acid, rich, moist but well-drained soil, in partial shade. Do not allow soil to dry out. Keep the base of the plant shaded, and apply a mulch to avoid disturbing the roots.
Height to 2m (6½ft); spread to 1m (3ft).
USZ 9–11, surviving -6.5°C (20°F) of overnight frost. Needs water in summer. ●

Halimium (Cistaceae)

This genus with around 12 species of evergreen shrubs and subshrubs originates from southwest Europe, northern Africa, and the Mediterranean region. Hybrids between *Halimium* and *Cistus* are given the name x *Halimiocistus*.

Halimium lasianthum

This upright bushy shrub, from Portugal and Spain, has greyish downy stems and leaves. The golden, *Cistus*-like flowers, with a dark red blotch at the base of each petal, appear in summer. Other forms include 'Concolor', which lacks the basal spot of colour, and 'Sandling', which has conspicuous maroon basal blotches.
Cultivation Grow in well-drained soil in full sun.
Height to 1m (3ft); spread to 4m (13ft).
USZ 8–11, surviving -12°C (10°F) of overnight frost provided that the plant is not waterlogged. Tolerant of summer drought. ◑

Above *Halimium lasianthum*

Mallows

Abutilon (Malvaceae)

This variable genus of more than 100 species of evergreen and semi-deciduous shrubs, trees, annuals, and perennials originates in tropical and subtropical areas of Africa, America, Asia, and Australia. The shrubby species and hybrids are often grown as conservatory plants in cooler climates.

Abutilon 'Nabob'
This is one of a large group of hybrids, probably the result of a cross between *A. darwinii* and *A. striatum,* but possibly also involving *A. pictum.* These striking evergreen and semi-deciduous shrubs have bell-shaped flowers in colours ranging from white, yellow, and orange to red. 'Nabob' has dark green leaves and very dark red flowers in summer. Other good forms include 'Canary Bird', with bright yellow flowers, and 'Louis Marignac', a 19th-century form with pale pink flowers.
Cultivation Grow in fertile, well-drained soil, with protection from very strong winds. Prune in late winter.
Height to 2m (6½ft); spread to 1m (3ft). USZ 9–11, surviving -6.5°C (20°F) of overnight frost for short periods only. Requires water in summer. ◗

Alyogyne (Malvaceae)

The genus *Alyogyne* comprises around four species of evergreen shrubs from Australia and is similar in appearance to *Hibiscus* (in which genus they were previously placed). All species are popular for their freely produced flowers in winter.

Alyogyne huegelii
This fast-growing, spreading shrub, native of southwest Australia, has bright green leaves and flowers in a range of colours from white and yellow through to mauve and purple. There are a number of forms, of which 'Mood Indigo' bears indigo-blue flowers, and 'Santa Cruz' has beautiful, delicate silvery, bluish mauve flowers.
Cultivation Grow in well-drained soil in sun or partial shade. Prune regularly to control straggly growth. Protect from wind.
Height and spread to 2m (6½ft). USZ 9–11, surviving -6.5°C (20°F) of overnight frost. Tolerant of summer drought. ◗

Fremontodendron (Sterculiaceae)

This genus with three species of evergreen shrubs and trees is from North America. Less hardy than *F. californicum* is *F. mexicanum* with its larger flowers, over a longer season. Vigorous 'California Glory', a hybrid between the two species, combines the hardiness of *F. californicum* with the larger flowers of the other parent.

Fremontodendron californicum
FLANNEL BUSH
This upright shrub or small tree, from Arizona, California, and Mexico, has a

Above *Alyogyne huegelii* 'Santa Cruz'

rounded crown and long branches bearing leathery leaves, which are dark green on the upper side and paler beneath. The lemon-yellow flowers, to 8cm (3in) across, are produced from spring to summer.
Cultivation Grow in poor, well-drained soil in full sun. The roots are shallow, so avoid disturbing them if possible; stake the plant when young. Do not water between spring and autumn.
Height to 4m (13ft); spread to 3m (10ft). USZ 8–11, surviving -12°C (10°F) of frost. Extremely tolerant of summer drought. ◗

Hibiscus (Malvaceae)

The genus *Hibiscus* has around 220 species of evergreen and deciduous shrubs, trees,

Above *Abutilon* 'Nabob'

Above *Hibiscus rosa-sinensis*

Above *Fremontodendron californicum* (flannel bush) in California

perennials, and annuals, which are native of the tropical, subtropical, and warm-temperate regions of the world.

Hibiscus rosa-sinensis
Probably originating in tropical Asia, this evergreen shrub or small tree bears very large and beautiful, but individually short-lived, flat, red flowers, 12–25cm (5–10in) across, throughout summer. There are hundreds of cultivars available, with flower colours ranging from red, pink, orange, and yellow to white.
Cultivation Grow in a sunny sheltered spot in well-drained soil, as a hedge or screening plant. Can be grown in a large container. Prune at once after flowering.
Height and spread to 3m (10ft). USZ 10 –11, surviving -1°C (30°F) of overnight frost. Requires water in summer. ◗

Malvaviscus (Malvaceae)

This genus contains three species of evergreen shrubs, from Central and South America. All produce striking, bell-shaped flowers and sticky seeds.

Malvaviscus penduliflorus
WAX MALLOW
This variable, much-branched shrub, from Mexico to Peru and Brazil, has bright red, pendulous flowers, 2.5–5cm (1–2in) long, with conspicuous stamens, in summer. The flowers never open further than is shown in the photograph. The light green, heart-shaped leaves are thin and soft.
Cultivation Grow in fertile soil in full sun. Keep almost dry in winter.
Height and spread to around 2m (6½ft). USZ 10–11, surviving -1°C (30°F) of overnight frost. Requires plenty of water in summer. ◗

Above *Malvaviscus penduliflorus* (wax mallow)

Camellias & Heaths

Camellia (Theaceae)

This is a genus with around 200 species of evergreen shrubs and trees, originating from south China and the Himalayan region east to China and Japan and south to Indonesia. They are popular in warm-temperate gardens for their wonderfully attractive flowers and lustrous, dark green foliage. There are literally thousands of named *Camellia* hybrids and cultivars, in a range of shapes and sizes. Although these plants prefer wetter summers, there are some species and varieties that will do well in the hotter drier conditions under discussion in this book. Camellias usually grows best in partial shade, yet in all except the hottest areas it can thrive in full sun provided the roots are kept moist and shaded. Mulch them if possible. All Camellias dislike chalky soils, and if necessary they can be container-grown in ericaceous potting compost.

Above *Camellia granthamiana* in Hong Kong

Above *Camellia reticulata* 'Howard Asper'

Camellia granthamiana
This large shrub or small tree is a native of Hong Kong. It produces leathery leaves and single white flowers, 12–14cm (5–5½in) across, with a single boss of yellow stamens, from late autumn onwards.
Cultivation Grow in fertile, well-drained, neutral or slightly acid soil in partial shade. Dislikes waterlogging intensely.
Height to 3m (10ft); spread 2m (6½ft) or more. USZ 10–11, surviving -1°C (30°F) of overnight frost. Requires water in summer. ◗

Camellia japonica
This tough shrub or small tree, from Japan, produces single red flowers, 7cm (3in) across, from late winter to spring. 'Rubescens Major' has formal, double, crimson flowers.
Cultivation Grow in fertile, neutral or slightly acid soil in partial shade.
Height to 8m (25ft); spread to 6m (20ft). USZ 7–11, surviving -17°C (2°F) of overnight frost. Requires water in summer. ◗

Camellia reticulata
This loose, rather untidy shrub is a native of western China. It has dark green, narrow

Above *Camellia japonica* 'Rubescens Major'

leaves and single or double, rose-pink flowers, 10–15cm (4–6in) across, in spring. 'Howard Asper' is a fast-growing hybrid between *C. reticulata* 'Damanao' and *C. japonica* 'Coronation'. It has semi-double, pink flowers, up to 18cm (7in) across.
Cultivation Likes neutral or slightly acid soil in partial shade.
Height to 8m (25ft); spread to 5m (16ft). USZ 9–11, surviving -6.5°C (20°F) of overnight frost. Requires water in summer. ◗

Epacris (Epacridaceae)

The genus *Epacris* comprises around 40 species of heath-like, evergreen shrubs from Australia, New Caledonia, and New Zealand. Most species have showy spikes of brightly coloured flowers throughout the summer.

Epacris impressa
This rather straggly shrub, from southern Australia (it is the national emblem of Victoria) and Tasmania, carries spikes of tubular, red, pink, or white flowers in summer. Many named forms are short-lived.
Cultivation Grow in well-drained soil in partial shade, or in full sun provided that the roots are shaded and kept moist. Good in a container. A bushier habit can be encouraged by pruning after flowering.
Height to 2m (6½ft); spread to 1m (3ft), often less. USZ 9–11, surviving -6.5°C (20°F) of frost unless waterlogged. Well-established plants tolerate drought for short periods. ◗

Erica (Ericaceae)

This variable genus comprises more than 700 evergreen shrubs, subshrubs, and small trees, collectively known as heaths and heathers. Most species originate in South Africa, but others are from elsewhere in Africa as well as Madagascar, Europe, and parts of the Middle East.

Erica arborea
TREE HEATH
This robust, upright, slow-growing shrub, or small tree, is a native of southern Europe, Madeira, and the Canaries east to southern Tanzania. It has narrow leaves and racemes of slightly scented, greyish white, bell-shaped flowers in winter and spring.
Cultivation Grows in most well-drained soils in full sun.
Height and spread to 5m (16ft). USZ 9–11 surviving -6.5°C (20°F) of overnight frost occasionally. Tolerant of summer drought. ◗◗

Erica cerinthoides
This native shrub of South Africa has narrow leaves and compact spikes of tubular flowers, produced in shades of red, pink, or white from winter to spring and occasionally throughout the year.
Cultivation In the wild this species is regularly burnt by forest fires; to replicate this in the garden, prune regularly and apply a light mulch of bonfire ash.
Height to 30cm (1ft); spread to 50cm (20in). USZ 9–11, surviving -6.5°C (20°F) of overnight frost. Tolerant of summer drought. ◗

Above *Epacris impressa*

Above *Erica cerinthoides*

Rhododendrons

Rhododendron (Ericaceae)

The genus *Rhododendron* contains around 850 species of evergreen and deciduous shrubs and trees, which are native of China, Europe, the Himalayas, and southeast Asia. They are immensely popular in gardens for their flowers, in a wide range of shapes and colours, and for their scent, in some tender species. Some types have enormous leaves, and others produce beautiful bark. There are thousands of hybrids and cultivars available commercially, many of which are suitable only for cool-temperate gardens; those derived from one of the species occurring naturally in a warmer climate are possibilities for hotter gardens. Hybrids worth considering include: 'Cilpinense' with light pink flowers; 'Countess of Haddington' with white scented flowers; 'Princess Frederica' with apricot flowers; and 'Saffron Queen' with yellow-spotted flowers.

Azaleas, which can be deciduous or evergreen, are also part of the genus *Rhododendron*. These develop into neatly shaped, compact plants in gardens, or can be grown in containers.

With very few exceptions, neither rhododendrons nor azaleas tolerate chalky soil, nor do they like being watered with alkaline or saline water.

Rhododendron crassifolium
This evergreen shrub from Borneo bears strongly ribbed, elliptic, dark green leaves and pink, red, orange, or apricot-coloured, open bell-shaped flowers in summer.
Cultivation Grow in well-drained but moisture-retentive, leafy, acid soil, in semi-

Above *Rhododendron crassifolium* in the Temperate House at Kew

shade, and a sheltered position.
Height to 4m (13ft); spread to 2m (6½ft). USZ 11, needing a minimum of 4.5°C (40°F). Requires rainwater in summer. ●

Rhododendron 'Fragrantissimum'
This lax evergreen shrub is a cross between *R. edgeworthii* and *R. formosum*, both species from the Himalayas. The narrowly ovate, bright green leaves are scaly beneath. Fragrant, widely funnel-shaped, pinkish white flowers, each with a yellowish tinge in the throat, are borne in late spring.

Cultivation Grow in well-drained but moisture-retentive, acid soil in partial shade. Can be kept smaller and more bushy by cutting back when young.
Height and spread 3m (10ft) or less. USZ 9–11, surviving -6.5°C (20°F) of overnight frost. Requires rainwater in summer. ●

Rhododendron jasminiflorum
This evergreen shrub, native of Malaysia, has scented, white, long-tubed flowers, sometimes tinged pink in the throat, in winter and early spring. The ovate, dark green leaves are scaly beneath.

Above *Rhododendron* 'Fragrantissimum', South Devon
Right *Rhododendron* 'Fragrantissimum'

Above *Rhododendron veitchianum*

pink to crimson. In warm gardens these thrive in dappled shade.
Cultivation Grow in well-drained but moisture-retentive, acid soil in partial shade. *Height to 3m (10ft); spread to 2m (6½ft). USZ 10–11, surviving -1°C (30°F) of overnight frost or less. Requires rainwater in summer.* ●

Rhododendron veitchianum
This spreading evergreen shrub is a native of Burma, Laos, and Thailand, where it is sometimes found growing epiphytically on trees. It has dark green, elliptic leaves and scented, white, frilled, funnel-shaped flowers, in spring and summer. It is named after the English nursery of Veitch, for whom it was collected in the wild by the 19th-century plant collector Thomas Lobb.
Cultivation Grow in well-drained but moisture-retentive, acid soil in shade. *Height and spread to 2m (6½ft). USZ 10–11, surviving -1°C (30°F) of frost for short periods only. Needs rainwater in summer.* ●

Cultivation Grow in well-drained but moisture-retentive, leafy, acid soil, with a bark and leaf mulch, in partial shade. *Height to 2m (6½ft); spread to 1m (3ft). USZ 11, needing a minimum of 4.5°C (40°F). Requires rainwater in summer.* ●

Rhododendron simsii
This spreading evergreen shrub is from southern China, including Hong Kong and Taiwan, to Burma, and Thailand. It has shoots covered with dense brown hairs, elliptic, dark green leaves, and red, pink, or white, spotted, funnel-shaped flowers, in spring. Var. *mesembrinum* has given rise to a popular group of so-called Indian azaleas, often sold by florists as pot plants. These have dark green leaves and flowers in a wide variety of colours from white and

Above *Rhododendron jasminiflorum* at Kew
Right *Rhododendron simsii* growing wild in Hong Kong

Phlox & Philadelphus Families

Cantua (Polemoniaceae)

Cantua consists of six species of evergreen shrubs and trees, which are native of Bolivia, northern Chile, Ecuador, and Peru.

Cantua buxifolia
SACRED FLOWER OF THE INCAS

This loose evergreen shrub comes from Bolivia, northern Chile, and Peru. The slender arching branches are clothed with box-like leaves, and weighed down during the spring by clusters of crimson and orange, tubular flowers, measuring 8cm (3in) long. These attract hummingbirds to the garden. Although this shrub is largely evergreen, it is normal for some leaves to fall in winter.

Cultivation Grow in fertile, well-drained soil in full sun or partial shade. Keep rather dry if possible in winter. Water as the plant comes into growth and in hot weather.

Height to 2.4m (8ft); spread to 1m (3ft). USZ 10–11, surviving -1°C (30°F) of overnight frost. Requires summer watering. ◗

Carpenteria (Philadelphaceae)

The genus *Carpenteria* has only one species. It is an evergreen shrub from California.

Carpenteria californica
TREE-ANEMONE

This upright shrub has light brown, peeling bark and single, white, slightly scented flowers, 6–7cm (2½–3in) across, with a central boss of yellow stamens, produced all summer. The narrowly ovate leaves are dark green. 'Elizabeth' has a more compact habit, while 'Bodnant' and larger-flowered 'Ladhams' Variety' can be grown in USZ 8.

Cultivation Grow in well-drained soil in partial shade. Apply a mulch, and avoid disturbing the roots once planted.

Above *Cantua buxifolia* (sacred flower of the Incas)

Height to 2.4m (8ft); spread to 2m (6½ft). USZ 9–11, surviving -6.5°C (20°F) of overnight frost. Requires a little water in summer. ◗

Leptodactylon (Polemoniaceae)

The genus *Leptodactylon* consists of 12 species of evergreen shrubs, subshrubs, and perennials, which are native of western North America.

Leptodactylon californicum
PRICKLY PHLOX

Bristly and upright, this shrub bears phlox-like, white, pink, or lilac flowers from early spring to early summer. The green leaves

Above *Leptodactylon californicum* (prickly phlox)
Left *Carpenteria californica* (tree-anemone)

Above *Loeselia mexicana* growing wild near Guadalajara in central Mexico

have 5–9 lobes, with each segment 1.2cm (½in) long. It grows wild in dry rocky places in the foothills of southern California.
Cultivation Grow in very well-drained, light, fertile soils. Avoid disturbing the roots once they are established.
Height and spread to 60cm (2ft). USZ 10–11, surviving -1°C (30°F) or less of overnight frost. Tolerant of summer drought. ◑

Loeselia (Polemoniaceae)

The genus *Loeselia* contains nine species of evergreen subshrubs. They are native from North America south to northern South America. Most have blue or red flowers.

Loeselia mexicana
This stiffly upright subshrub is a native of Mexico. The bristly, spine-tipped, green leaves are narrowly lance-shaped. Masses of tubular red flowers, around 5cm (2in) long, with protruding style and stamens and brimming with sticky nectar, are produced from late summer to autumn.
Cultivation Good in dry rocky soil in sunny conditions, especially in late summer because this species is prone to mould in damp weather. Prune hard in spring to encourage strong shoots in summer.
Height to 1.5m (5ft); spread to 60cm (2ft). USZ 9–11, surviving -6.5°C (20°F) of overnight frost. Tolerant of drought, but needs some water in early summer. ◑

Philadelphus (Philadelphaceae)

Philadelphus contains 60 species of deciduous and evergreen shrubs or small trees. They are native of North America south to Mexico, eastern Europe and the Caucasus, the Himalayas, and China east to Japan. Several species from Mexico are suitable for warm dry gardens: for example, *P. maculatus*, a twiggy upright shrub with masses of small, sweetly scented, starry or cup-shaped, white flowers, tinged purple inside at the base. 'Beauclerk', 'Belle Etoile', and 'Sybille', all with white flowers and purple basal blotches, are worth trying in partial shade, provided their roots are shaded and they are watered in summer.

Philadelphus mexicanus
MOCK ORANGE
This climbing or sprawling, evergreen shrub is a native of Mexico. It produces long stems and ovate green leaves with shallow teeth. The scented, white, nodding flowers, pink at the base on the inside, are borne in spring and early summer. 'Rose Syringa' has white flowers with a purple stain in the centre; it is an old cultivar, one of the parents of 'Sybille' (*see* above).
Cultivation Grow in fertile, well-drained soil in partial shade. Do not allow to dry out.
Height to 5m (16ft); spread to 2.4m (8ft). USZ 9–11, surviving -6.5°C (20°F) of overnight frost. Requires water in summer. ●

Left *Philadelphus mexicanus* 'Rose Syringa'
Far Left *Loeselia mexicana*

107

Lavender, *Phlomis*, & Rosemary

Above *Lavandula pedunculata* growing wild near Zaragoza in Spain

Lavandula (Labiatae)
LAVENDER

The genus *Lavandula* contains 39 species of aromatic evergreen shrubs native of the Mediterranean region, the Canary Islands, and from northern Africa to Somalia and India. *Lavandula* is ubiquitous in the dry hills and coastal maquis of the Mediterranean, and is ideally suited to cultivation in dry gardens. All species can be used as hedges.

Lavandula dentata
FRINGED LAVENDER

This loose, spreading shrub, with a strong scent, is from the Iberian Peninsula, northern Africa, southwest Asia, and the southwestern Arabian Peninsula. It has upright branches and long stems, clothed at the base with greyish green, rounded-toothed, narrow leaves. The flowerheads have pale blue bracts and tiny, pale blue flowers, and are borne from spring to summer.
Cultivation Grow in light, well-drained soil in full sun. Dislikes humid conditions, as the soft foliage will become mouldy.

Height and spread to 1m (3ft). USZ 10–11, surviving -1°C (30°F) of overnight frost. Moderately tolerant of summer drought. ◐

Lavandula pedunculata
This spreading aromatic shrub, which emanates from central Spain and Portugal, is similar to *L. stoechas*, from which it differs chiefly in its long flower stalks and bracts. There are several subspecies, of which the best known is probably subsp.

pedunculata, endemic to the Iberian Peninsula. An upright shrub, it has narrow, greyish green leaves and long violet-pink apical bracts from early spring to summer. 'Papillon' (butterfly lavender) has violet bracts.
Cultivation Grow in well-drained soil in full sun or dappled shade.
Height and spread to 75cm (2½ft). USZ 10–11, surviving -1°C (30°F) of overnight frost. Tolerant of summer drought. ◑

Right *Lavandula dentata* (fringed lavender)
Far Right *Lavandula stoechas* 'Marshwood'

108

Below *Rosmarinus officinalis* 'Corsican Blue'

Below *Phlomis purpurea* growing wild near Ronda in Spain

Lavandula stoechas
FRENCH LAVENDER

This spreading aromatic shrub from the Mediterranean produces large apical bracts. It has been cultivated for centuries for its therapeutic and disinfectant properties and is highly ornamental, flowering from early spring to summer. The narrow leaves are greyish. 'Marshwood' is the result of a cross between *L. stoechas, L. pedunculata,* and *L. viridis,* and is a robust plant. It has a pungent aroma (inherited from *L. viridis*) and papery, pinkish mauve bracts.
Cultivation Grow in well-drained soil in full sun. Annual trimming is advisable.
Height to 1m (3ft); spread to 75cm (2½ft). USZ 10–11, surviving -1°C (30°F) of overnight frost. Tolerant of summer drought. ◑

Phlomis (Labiatae)

The genus *Phlomis* comprises around 100 species of aromatic evergreen shrubs and herbaceous perennials, which are native of the Mediterranean east to China. *See* p.12 for *P. fruticosa* (Jerusalem sage).

Phlomis purpurea
This shrub from Spain and Portugal has felted stems and felted, grey, ovate to lance-shaped leaves. The downy, pinkish purple, two-lipped flowers appear in summer.
Cultivation Grow in poor, dry, sandy soil in full sun.
Height and spread to 60cm (2ft). USZ 9–11, surviving -6.5°C (20°F) of overnight frost. Very tolerant of summer drought. ◑

Rosmarinus (Labiatae)
ROSEMARY

The genus *Rosmarinus* contains two species of evergreen aromatic shrubs, from the Mediterranean region.

Rosmarinus officinalis
This Mediterranean shrub is well known as a culinary herb and garden plant. It has narrow green leaves, almost white below, and two-lipped flowers ranging from pale to dark blue, occasionally pink or white, mainly in spring and autumn. There are many varieties and cultivars, some upright, which can be used as a hedge, others prostrate, which are good planted on low walls. Darker blue-flowered 'Corsican Blue' is prostrate and particularly free-flowering.
Cultivation Grow in well-drained soil in a sunny position.
Height and spread around 1m (3ft). USZ 9–11, surviving -6.5°C (20°F) of overnight frost. Tolerant of summer drought. ◑

Trichostema (Labiatae)

The genus *Trichostema* contains 16 species of aromatic, evergreen, small shrubs and herbs, which are native of North America.

Trichostema lanatum
WOOLY BLUE CURLS

This rosemary-like shrub, from California, has narrow green leaves, which are grey beneath, and whorled racemes of two-lipped, blue flowers, with protruding stamens, in late spring to summer. It deserves to be better known outside the USA.
Cultivation Grow in very well-drained soil in full sun.
Height and spread to 1m (3ft). USZ 9–11, surviving -6.5°C (20°F) of overnight frost. Tolerant of summer drought. ◑

Above *Trichostema lanatum* in California

Sages & Related Shrubs

Colquhounia (Labiatae)

The genus *Colquhounia* comprises around three species of semi-evergreen shrubs. They are native of the foothills of the Himalayas from northern India east to southwest China.

Colquhounia coccinea
This upright shrub, from the Himalayas, has soft green leaves, white-felted on the underside. Red or pinkish red flowers, with orange throats, are borne in autumn.
Cultivation Grow in well-drained soil in full sun.

Height to 3m (10ft); spread to 1m (3ft). USZ 9–11, surviving -6.5°C (20°F) of overnight frost. Needs water in summer. ◗

Plectranthus (Labiatae)

Plectranthus is a variable genus with around 200 species of evergreen shrubs, subshrubs, perennials, and annuals, native of Africa, Asia, Australia, and the Pacific Islands. It includes some species formerly in *Coleus*.

Plectranthus argentatus
This spreading shrub, from Australia, has silvery hairy leaves and branches. The

Above *Colquhounia coccinea*

spikes of pale bluish white, two-lipped flowers are produced in summer.
Cultivation Grow in fertile, well-drained soil in dappled shade. Keep rather dry in winter; water in the growing season.
Height to 1m (3ft); spread to 60cm (2ft). USZ 10–11, surviving -1°C (30°F) of overnight frost. Requires water in summer. ◗

Prostanthera (Labiatae)

The genus *Prostanthera* contains around 100 species of evergreen shrubs or small trees, which are native of Australia.

Prostanthera rotundifolia
MINT BUSH
This rounded aromatic shrub, from western and southern Australia and Tasmania, has dark green, almost round leaves. The purple, or sometimes pink, five-lobed flowers are produced freely during the spring. There are numeroud naturally occurring forms and hybrids, including

Above *Prostanthera rotundifolia* (mint bush)
Left *Plectranthus argentatus*

Above *Salvia candelabrum* with *Centranthus*

commonly grown as a culinary herb. Other good shrubby species for warm gardens include: *S. clevelandii* (California blue sage) with wrinkled, grey-green leaves and spikes of lavender-blue flowers, in late summer; *S. elegans* (pineapple sage) with softly hairy leaves (which, when crushed, smell similar to pineapple) and red flowers, from spring to autumn; *S. fruticosa* with greyish green leaves and spikes of pink or lilac flowers, in summer; *S. fulgens* (cardinal sage) with bright red flowers in summer; and *S. leucophylla* (purple sage) with grey, downy leaves and light purple flowers, in autumn.

Salvia candelabrum

An upright evergreen subshrub with softly hairy leaves and long stems, which are woody at the base. The whorls of two-lipped, blue flowers, flecked with white, are borne in summer. It is a native of Spain.
Cultivation Grow in well-drained soil in full sun.
Height and spread to 1m (3ft). USZ 9–11, surviving -6.5°C (20°F) of overnight frost. Tolerant of summer drought. ◑

Salvia darcyi

This upright, much-branched, heavily aromatic, evergreen subshrub is from Mexico. It has softly hairy, green leaves and whorls of two-lipped, scarlet flowers, from late summer to autumn.
Cultivation Grow in well-drained soil in full sun, with shelter from strong winds.
Height and spread to 2m (6½ft). USZ 9–11, surviving 6.5°C (20°F) of overnight frost. Tolerant of summer drought. ◐

'Rosea', which has greyish green leaves and pink flowers.
Cultivation Grow in well-drained soil in partial shade and sheltered from wind. Prune after flowering to keep a bushy shape.
Height to 3m (10ft); spread to 2m (6½ft). USZ 9–11, surviving -6.5°C (20°F) of overnight frost. Tolerant of summer drought. ◑

Salvia (Labiatae)

This variable genus has around 900 species of deciduous and evergreen subshrubs, perennials, biennials, and annuals, originating from most regions of the world, but particularly from Central and South America and Turkey. (For perennial species *see* pp.190–1.) Nearly all species have aromatic leaves, and are not only highly ornamental but also, in some cases, grown for culinary and medicinal purposes (from the Latin *salveo* = "I heal"). *S. officinalis* is

Above *Salvia candelabrum*

Above *Salvia darcyi*

111

Acanthus, Monkey Flower, & Related Shrubs

Acanthus (Acanthaceae)

Acanthus contains around 30 species of evergreen shrubs and perennials from the Mediterranean region and Africa to southern Asia; they have long been cultivated for their handsome foliage. The shrubby species are found throughout central and east Africa, extending to southern Asia. They are generally very bristly, spreading plants, with holly-like leaves and upright spikes of red, blue, mauve, or white flowers. For the well-known perennial species *A. mollis* and *A. spinosus* see pp.188–9.

Acanthus sennii
This spreading shrub is from Ethiopia, where it is now very rare. Fortunately it is well established in cultivation, with a very long flowering period in winter and spring. The spikes of pink or red flowers have long, spine-tipped bracts. The prickly leaves, 15–20cm (6–8in) long, are deeply dissected.
Cultivation Grow in well-drained soil.
Height to 2m (6½ft); spread to 1m (3ft). USZ 10–11, surviving −1°C (30°F) of overnight frost. Tolerant of drought. ◑

Chilopsis (Bignoniaceae)

This genus contains a single species of deciduous shrubs and small trees from the

Above *Acanthus sennii* flowering in April in the Giardino Botanico Hanbury, at La Mortola, Italy

deserts of southwestern North America and Mexico. In 1964, x *Chitalpa tashkentensis* was raised in Tashkent by crossing *Chilopsis* with *Catalpa*. The result was a deciduous or evergreen, large shrub or small tree, with erect terminal racemes of pale pink flowers veined in the throat with dark purple.

Chilopsis linearis
DESERT WILLOW
This willow-like shrub or small tree has a rough shaggy bark and green, willow-like leaves. Pink, purplish, or whitish flowers, spotted and streaked with purple, are borne in summer. Var. *arcuata* has deep mauve flowers; 'Alba' carries white flowers.
Cultivation Grow in dry, well-drained soil in full sun.
Height to 3m (10ft); spread to 2m (6½ft). USZ 9–11, surviving -6.5°C (20°F) of overnight frost. Tolerant of summer heat and drought. ◑

Isoplexis (Scrophulariaceae)

Isoplexis consists of three or four species of evergreen shrubs from the Canaries and Madeira. *I. canariensis*, with spikes of reddish orange flowers, and *I. isabelliana*, with narrower leaves as well as orange

flowers, are both from the Canary Islands and are also good garden plants. They may be found included in *Digitalis*.

Isoplexis sceptrum
This spreading shrub is from Madeira, where it is rare in the wild. The tops of the upright stems carry dense clusters of brownish orange, foxglove-like flowers in summer. The inversely lance-shaped to ovate, green leaves are to 25cm (10in) long.
Cultivation Grow in fertile soil in a sheltered place.
Height to 1.8m (6ft); spread to 1m (3ft). USZ 10–11, surviving -1°C (30°F) of overnight frost. Requires water all year round. ●

Mimulus (Scrophulariaceae)

Mimulus has around 150 species, chiefly perennials and annuals, but with a few evergreen shrubs, native of North and South America, Asia, and South Africa. While many of the perennial and annual *Mimulus* are known for their love of damp situations, some such as *M. bifidus* from California are invaluable for drier spots. This spreading subshrub has lemony white flowers. The named colour forms of this

Left *Chilopsis linearis* (desert willow)

species are also good, including: 'Verity Caroline' with yellow flowers; 'Verity Purissima' with pure white flowers; and 'Verity Magenta' with purplish red flowers. *M. longiflorus* makes a spreading shrub and has flowers ranging in colour from orange to apricot or white in summer; as the name suggests, the funnel-shaped flower has a longer tube than some of the other species.

Mimulus aurantiacus
BUSH MONKEY FLOWER
This fast-growing, spreading shrub, from Oregon and California, has sticky, narrow, dark green leaves and funnel-shaped, orange-yellow flowers, from spring to summer. Var. *puniceus* is an upright shrub, with brighter red or orange-red flowers, and grows to 1m (3ft) high.
Cultivation Grow in well-drained soil in full sun. Do not allow the roots to dry out. *Height to 1.3m (4ft); spread to 1m (3ft). USZ 9–11, surviving -6.5°C (20°F) of overnight frost. Requires some water in summer.* ◗

Russelia (Scrophulariaceae)

The genus *Russelia* comprises 52 species of evergreen shrubs and subshrubs, which are

Above *Mimulus aurantiacus* (bush monkey flower)

native of Central America and Cuba. Species vary considerably in habit and leaf shape: for example, *R. sarmentosa*, also from Mexico, is taller than *R. equisetiformis*, and has broader leaves.

Russelia equisetiformis
FIRECRACKER PLANT, FOUNTAIN PLANT
A scrambling subshrub from Mexico. The arching green stems bear short, scale-like,

Above *Russelia equisetiformis* (firecracker plant)

mid-green leaves, 1mm (¹⁄₂in) across, which soon fall, and long spikes with tubular red flowers, in whorls, in winter.
Cultivation Grow in well-drained soil in sun or partial shade; good on a bank or low wall. Do not allow the roots to dry out. Prune to avoid the plant becoming straggly. *Height to 1.5m (5ft); spread to 2m (6½ft). USZ 10–11, surviving -1°C (30°F) of frost. Moderately tolerant of summer drought.* ◗

Above *Isoplexis sceptrum*, with ferns and *Cupressus cashmeriana* behind, in the garden at Tresco, Isles of Scilly

Shrubs for Butterflies & Moths

Buddleja (Buddlejaceae)

Buddleja consists of around 100 species of evergreen, semi-evergreen, and deciduous shrubs and small trees in Mexico, South America, South Africa, and eastern Asia. Many species, mostly those from northern China, are hardy in zones 6 and 7, but most are suitable only for mild climates, zone 8 and above. Most species hybridize easily, and many hybrids are commonly cultivated. The individual flowers are small, but they are produced in large numbers and are sweetly honey-scented, attracting butterflies to the garden. A species can be found to flower at almost any time of year. The heavily scented *B. auriculata* from South Africa flowers in autumn; *B. asiatica,* smelling of freesias, in winter; and *B. officinalis* in spring.

Buddleja madagascariensis
This strong-growing, evergreen shrub is almost a climber. It produces green leaves, hairy beneath, and small orange flowers, in spikes 30–50cm (12–20in) long, in early spring and summer. This native of Madagascar is unusual in having fleshy berries rather than the dry fruits found in most *Buddleja* species. It is often confused with *B. x lewisiana,* which has greyish leaves and white flowers turning orange.
Cultivation Easily grown in any soil.
Height to 4m (13ft); spread to 6m (20ft). USZ 10–11, surviving -1°C (30°F) of overnight frost. Needs summer water. ●

Above *Buddleja madagascariensis* naturalized in Bermuda

Jasminum (Oleaceae)
JASMINE

This genus has around 200 species of evergreen and deciduous plants, mostly in Africa, Asia, and Australia. Many species of jasmine are climbers (*see* p.136), but some are stiff shrubs and can be used to make scented hedges. The leaves may be simple or pinnate, the flowers white or yellow, with one species (Chinese *J. beesianum*)

deep pink. The white-flowered species are mostly renowned for their rich heady scent. In general the yellow-flowered species are less scented, except for *J. subhumile.* The flowers are followed by black berries.

.

Jasminum grandiflorum
SPANISH JASMINE
This is a scrambling evergreen shrub which can be clipped to form a hedge, as is often seen in hot dry climates such as Rajasthan in India. It is a native possibly of Arabia or

Above *Jasminum grandiflorum* (Spanish jasmine)

Above *Jasminum nitidum* in Bermuda

Above *Jasminum subhumile* var. *glabricymosum* near Dali, western China

tropics. *Lantana camara* is a noxious tropical weed, spreading in disturbed areas and forming dense thickets. In south India they call it "communist weed": where you cut one down, two come up in its place.

Lantana camara cultivars

These shrubs bear clusters, 5–6cm (2–2½in) across, of flowers in shades of white, yellow orange, or red, in summer. The flowers open one colour and change after pollination, giving a two-tone effect to each head. The flowers attract butterflies to the garden. These shrubs do well in pots in colder areas. 'Patriot Dove Wings' has white and yellowish flowers, while 'Spreading Sunset' has red and orange flowers.
Cultivation Easily cultivated in any soil. Prune in spring and feed well to build up the shrub for flowering.
Height to 3m (10ft); spread to 6m (20ft). USZ 10–11, surviving -1°C (30°F) of overnight frost. Tolerant of summer drought. ◗

Above *Lantana camara* 'Patriot Dove Wings'

China. The leaves are pinnate and the white, heavily scented, five-lobed flowers, to 4cm (1½in) across, are borne in summer and autumn. The name 'de Grasse' is often connected with this species as it was used in the perfume industry in France.
Cultivation Easily grown in deep rich soil. Can be pruned in spring.
Height to 3m (10ft); spread to 2m (6½ft). USZ 9–11, surviving -6.5°C (20°F) of overnight frost. Tolerant of summer drought. ◖

Jasminum nitidum

This bushy evergreen shrub is native of the Admiralty islands, north of New Guinea, but is widely cultivated in subtropical areas, and grows well in southern California. It has shining simple leaves. Mainly in spring, pink buds open to white scented flowers, 4cm (1½in) across, with 6–11 narrow petals and stiff, thread-like calyx-lobes, which stand out at right angles from the stem.
Cultivation Easily grown in limey soil.

Height to 1.5m (5ft); spread to 3m (10ft). USZ 9–11, surviving -6.5°C (20°F) of overnight frost. Tolerant of summer drought. ◑

Jasminum subhumile var. *glabricymosum*

This evergreen shrub with arching branches is a native of western China. The yellow, scented, five-petalled flowers, 2.5cm (1in) across, are borne in spring. The leaves are usually simple, but may have three leaflets.
Cultivation Easily grown in well-drained soil and sun or light shade.
Height to 3m (10ft); spread to 4m (13ft). USZ 9–11, surviving -6.5°C (20°F) of overnight frost. Tolerant of summer drought. ◗

Lantana (Verbenaceae)
LANTANA

The genus *Lantana* has 150 species of evergreen shrubs and perennials from the

Above *Lantana camara* 'Spreading Sunset'

Nightshade & *Convolvulus* Families

Brunfelsia (Solanaceae)

The genus *Brunfelsia* consists of around 40 species of evergreen shrubs or small trees, which are all wild in central America. Some are used in traditional medicine against syphilis.

Brunfelsia americana
LADY OF THE NIGHT

This shrub or small tree is a native of the West Indies. In summer, the flowers open white and become yellow overnight; they are wonderfully scented, especially in the evening. The flowers have a long tube and are about 7cm (3in) across the petals, with a tube around the same length. A similar species, *B. undulata*, has flowers with very wavy petals and a tube more than twice as long as that of *B. americana*.

Cultivation Easily grown in fertile soil in partial shade.
Height to 5m (16ft); spread to 4m (13ft). USZ 10–11, surviving -1°C (30°F) of overnight frost. Tolerant of seasonal drought. ◖

Brunfelsia pauciflora
YESTERDAY, TODAY, AND TOMORROW

This shrub has flat flowers, 5–7cm (2–3in) across, which change colour from purple to white overnight, hence the common name. 'Macrantha' has purple flowers, 7cm (3in) across, which do not show such an abrupt colour change. Both are wild in Brazil, flowering in spring and summer.

Cultivation Easily grown in fertile soil, in shelter and with partial shade in hot areas.

Below Brunfelsia americana (lady of the night)

Height to 3m (10ft); spread to 4.5m (15ft). USZ 9–11, surviving -6.5°C (20°F) of overnight frost. Best with summer water. ●

Convolvulus (Convolvulaceae)

Convolvulus has around 100 species found throughout the world. Many of them are herbaceous climbers, but most are evergreen shrubs, some of which are exceptionally drought tolerant.

Convolvulus cneorum

This very beautiful, soft silvery shrub with pale pink flowers is a native of Italy, Sicily, and the Adriatic coast, where it grows on limestone rocks near the sea. The narrowly lance-shaped leaves are up to 5cm (2in) long, and the conical flowers, which appear in summer, are 2.5cm (1in) across.

Cultivation Easily grown in shallow rocky soil in a crevice or hot sunny position with very good drainage at the roots.
Height and spread to 50cm (1½ft). USZ 9–11, surviving -6.5°C (20°F) of overnight frost. Tolerant of summer drought. ◑

Evolvulus (Convolvulaceae)

Evolvulus contains around 102 species of evergreen subshrubs, perennials, and annuals, mainly in North, Central, and South America. It differs from *Convolvulus* in having smaller flowers and a style deeply divided into two, not a single style divided at the tip; the capsule of *Evolvulus* has four cells, of *Convolvulus* two cells.

Evolvulus pilosus

This soft subshrub has green leaves, silvery on the back, and bright blue, conical flowers, around 1.5cm (½in) across. It is

Left Brunfelsia pauciflora (yesterday, today, and tomorrow)

Below *Convolvulus cneorum*

Below *Evolvulus pilosus*

found from Dakota and Montana south to Texas and Arizona, growing wild in dry places and flowering in spring and summer. 'Blue Daze' is a commonly grown variant, with lobed flowers of deep bright blue.
Cultivation Easily grown and tolerant of poor soil. This is a very useful plant for cold dry gardens.
Height to 30cm (1ft); spread to 1m (3ft). USZ 7–11, surviving -17°C (2°F) of overnight frost. Tolerant of summer drought. ☽

Lechenaultia (Goodeniaceae)

This genus has 26 species, of which 20 are endemic to Western Australia. Most are low-growing, heath-like, evergreen shrubs, often with beautiful, brightly coloured flowers, in red, blue, and yellow. They can be grown from cuttings in summer. As the plants are often short-lived and hard to obtain, it is wise to keep a few young plants to put out each year. This genus is named after Leschenault de la Tour and when Robert Brown latinized his name he left out the "s", so that the spelling without the "s" remains correct.

Lechenaultia biloba
This popular shrub produces flowers in shades of blue and very narrow leaves. The stems spread over the ground, flowering at their tips. Each two-lipped flower is up to 2.5cm (1in) across.
Cultivation Grow in sandy, acid or neutral soil in full sun.
Height to 50cm (1½ft); spread to 1m (3ft). USZ 9–11, surviving -6.5°C (20°F) of overnight frost. Tolerant of summer drought. ☽

Right *Solanum rantonnetii* in the south of France

Solanum (Solanaceae)

Solanum contains 1,200–1,700 species of evergreen, semi-evergreen, and deciduous shrubs, trees, and climbers as well as perennials and annuals. Many are toxic, yet some parts of some species are important crops. For climbing species *see* p.142.

Solanum rantonnetii
This spreading evergreen shrub has narrowly ovate leaves and circular purple flowers, to 2.5cm (1in) across, in spring and summer. It is found wild in Argentina.
Cultivation Easily grown in good soil.
Height and spread to 2m (6½ft). USZ 9–11, surviving -6.5°C (20°F) of overnight frost. Tolerant of summer drought. ☽

Above *Lechenaultia biloba*

117

Shrubs of the Nightshade Family

Brugmansia (Solanaceae)

The genus *Brugmansia* contains five species of evergreen shrubs from the Andes in Peru and Bolivia and several hybrids, now widely cultivated in frost-free areas in the tropics and warm coastal climates. It is deciduous in cold weather. All the species were formerly called *Datura*, but all *Brugmansia* are shrubby; they also differ from *Datura* in having smooth, berry-like fruits, rather than dry and usually prickly capsules.

Brugmansia x *candida*
This strong-growing hybrid shrub, probably *B. aurea* x *B. versicolor*, originates in southern Colombia to central Ecuador, but is now widely cultivated. The sweet-scented, hanging, trumpet-shaped flowers, 23–33cm (9–13in) long, in white, yellow, or pink, are borne in summer.
Cultivation Grows in rich wet soil, in shade in hot climates. The leaves and shoot tips are killed by -1°C (30°F) of frost but should sprout up again soon afterwards. They also require a nitrogenous fertilizer in order to grow and flower well. The leaves are prone to attack by red spider mites, so should be sprayed frequently in hot weather.

Above *Brugmansia sanguinea* with *Wisteria* in a garden in California

Height to 3.5m (11½ft); spread to 4m (13ft). USZ 10–11, surviving -1°C (30°F) of frost. Needs ample water in summer. ●

Brugmansia x *insignis*
A hybrid shrub of wild origin in the Peruvian Andes, commonly cultivated in the tropics. It is probably the result of *B. suaveolens* crossed with *B. versicolor*. The usually white or pink, sweet-scented flowers, to 35cm (14in) long, have teeth and a wide recurving mouth. They are borne in summer.
Cultivation As for *B.* x *candida*.
Height to 4m (13ft); spread to 3m (10ft). USZ 10–11, surviving -1°C (30°F) of overnight frost. Needs ample water in summer. ●

Brugmansia sanguinea
This shrub is probably the hardiest of the species, being wild in the Andes from Colombia to northern Chile, at up to 3,000m (10,000ft). The long, narrow flowers are pollinated by large, long-billed hummingbirds. The flowers, 15–25cm (6–10in) long, borne during summer, are usually tomato-red with a yellow tube and have little scent. In 'Golden Queen' the flowers are all yellow.
Cultivation As for *B.* x *candida*, although it grows well in cooler conditions.
Height and spread to 10m (33ft). USZ 9–11, surviving -6.5°C (20°F) of overnight frost. Needs summer water. ●

Above *Brugmansia* x *candida*

Above *Brugmansia × insignis*

Cestrum (Solanaceae)

Cestrum consists of around 175 species of evergreen and deciduous shrubs from Mexico and South America. The flowers are small, tubular, and brightly coloured. Some species have greenish flowers, sweetly scented at night: for example, *C. parqui* (willow-leaved jessamine) and the more tropical *C. nocturnum* (night jessamine, queen of the night) from the West Indies.

Cestrum 'Newellii'
Commonly grown, this hybrid has heads of bright red flowers in winter, probably originating in Mexico. It forms a lax evergreen shrub with arching branches, and can be trained on a wall or pergola.
Cultivation Easily grown in fertile soil. Prune plants hard after flowering, and keep them rather dry in winter.
Height to 9m (30ft); spread to 6m (20ft). USZ 9–11, surviving -6.5°C (20°F) of overnight frost. Needs summer water. ◑

Iochroma (Solanaceae)

Iochroma consists of around 20 species of evergreen and deciduous shrubs and small trees from the cooler drier parts of tropical South America. The tubular hanging flowers are usually red or purple and are followed by small, tomato-like fruit. *I. australe* is the toughest species. The other cultivated species include: *I. coccineum, I. cyaneum*, crimson *I. purpureum*, and deep purple *I. grandiflorum*; these are tenderer and only suitable for the mildest climates.

Iochroma australe (syn. *Acnistus australis, Dunalia australis*)
This is a stiff shrub or small tree, which is wild in dry areas of the Andes in northern Argentina, where it often grows with giant columnar cacti. It is deciduous during winter, and in spring produces masses of purple flowers, 3–6cm (1¼–2½in) long, hanging down along the branches. It is therefore best to train the bush into an umbrella shape, encouraging long horizontal branches, which show off the trumpet-shaped flowers best.
Cultivation Easily grown in any soil. Prune after flowering.
Height to 9m (30ft); spread to 6m (20ft). USZ 9–11, surviving -6.5°C (20°F) of overnight frost. Requires late summer water. Tolerant of winter drought. ◑

Above *Cestrum* 'Newellii'

Above *Iochroma australe*

All-summer Flowering Shrubs

Catharanthus (Apocynaceae)

This genus has six species of evergreen, low-growing shrubs, five from Madagascar and one from India and Sri Lanka.

Catharanthus roseus (syn. *Vinca rosea*)
MADAGASCAR PERIWINKLE, CAYENNE JASMINE
This shrub, originally from Madagascar, produces five-petalled, pink flowers, or white with a pink eye (as shown on the back cover), around 2.5cm (1in) across. They appear all year round.
Cultivation Easily grown in any soil. *Height and spread 2m (6½ft). USZ 10–11, needing minimum of -1°C (30°F) overnight. Requires water in summer.* ◗

Gardenia (Rubiaceae)

The genus *Gardenia* contains about 250 species of evergreen shrubs and trees, wild in Africa and Asia. Double gardenias were an indispensable buttonhole for Victorian or Edwardian evening dress, as few flowers have such a heady tropical scent. They are native of China, and were long cultivated there before being brought to Europe.

Gardenia augusta 'Veitchii'
This shrub from China is a particularly large-flowered gardenia. It produces very fragrant, fully double, white flowers, 6cm (2½in) across, in summer.

Cultivation Grow in fertile acid soil. Needs humidity in summer; keep rather dry in winter.
Height and spread to 2m (6½ft). USZ 10–11, surviving -1°C (30°F) of overnight frost. Requires summer water. ◗

Luculia (Rubiaceae)

The genus *Luculia* contains around five rather similar species of evergreen and semi-evergreen shrubs and small trees, from the Himalayan region. The flowers are white or pink, sweetly scented, and appear in autumn and winter. For *L. intermedia* from Yunnan *see* p.22.

Luculia gratissima
This is one of the loveliest winter-flowering shrubs for a cool subtropical climate. The sugar-pink flowers, around 3cm (1¼in) across, are crowded in dense flat heads.
Cultivation Grow in rich acid soil. Keep cool and moist in summer, drier in winter.
Height to 5m (16ft); spread to 6m (20ft). USZ 9–11, surviving -6.5°C (20°F) of overnight frost. Needs summer water. ◗

Nerium (Apocynaceae)
OLEANDER

The genus *Nerium* contains a single variable species, *N. oleander* (*see also* p.12). The wild species has pale pink flowers and is found

Above *Gardenia augusta* 'Veitchii'

from the Cape Verde islands and Spain eastwards to Japan. In the wild it usually grows along the banks of streams and rivers or on rocky or pebbly islands, as the seedlings need water to become established.

Nerium oleander
This evergreen shrub or small tree is cultivated extensively in the Mediterranean region and in other hot dry climates, where it is planted alongside roads and in parks. In summer it bears its tubular flowers, 3–5cm (1¼–2in) long. All parts of the plant are deadly poisonous.
Cultivation Easily grown in any soil. Is drought- and heat-tolerant, particularly if the roots are deep into a water source.
Height to 6m (20ft); spread to 5m (16ft). USZ 9–11, surviving -6.5°C (20°F) of overnight frost. Tolerant of summer drought. ◖

Above *Luculia gratissima*

Above *Nerium oleander*

Pentas (Rubiaceae)

Pentas is a genus of about 40 species of low-growing, mainly evergreen shrubs and perennials, which are wild in tropical Africa, Arabia, and Madagascar.

Pentas lanceolata

This evergreen subshrub is the only species of *Pentas* in cultivation, and it originated from Arabia and East Africa. It has hairy stems and leaves that are strongly veined. The flowers, about 2cm (¾in) across, are tubular at the base, with five pointed lobes. They are carried during summer. 'Bright Pink' is one of the showier varieties cultivated in the tropics.

Cultivation Easily grown in fertile soil. Although tolerant of summer drought, it needs water to continue flowering.
Height to 2m (6½ft); spread to 3m (10ft). USZ 9–11, surviving -3°C (27°F) of overnight frost. Tolerant of summer drought. ●

Rondeletia (Rubiaceae)

Rondeletia is a genus of around 150 evergreen shrubs and small trees, mostly found wild in Central and South America. *R. amoena* has pink or red flowers with

Below *Pentas lanceolata* 'Bright Pink'

Below *Pentas lanceolata*

yellow throats, *R. cordata* has white or pink flowers, while *R. odorata* bears orange or red flowers, again with yellow throats, and rounded, deeply veined leaves.

Rondeletia roezlii

This shrub produces large heads of pale pink, tubular flowers, about 1cm (⅜in)

across, on nodding branches during late summer. The leaves are ovate and opposite. *R. roezlii* is a native of Guatemala.

Cultivation Easily grown in warm conditions and fertile soil.
Height to 3m (10ft); spread to 4m (13ft). USZ 10–11, surviving -1°C (30°F) of overnight frost. Needs summer water. ●

Below *Rondeletia roezlii* in Florida

Sun-loving Shrubs

Echium (Boraginaceae)

The genus *Echium* has around 40 species in the Mediterranean region and South Africa. Most are annuals or short-lived perennials, but in the Canary Islands and Madeira there are evergreen shrubby species as well as giant, single-stemmed, woody biennials. Several species have naturalized elsewhere, notably in South Africa, where *E. candicans* from Madeira is often seen apparently wild.

Echium nervosum
This shrub is found wild on coastal cliffs in Madeira, but widely grown elsewhere. The leaves are silvery and rather bristly. The dense spikes of pale blue flowers, with long stamens, are borne in spring and summer.
Cultivation Easily grown in well-drained, sandy soil.

Height to 1.5m (5ft); spread to 1m (3ft). USZ 9–11, surviving -6.5°C (20°F) of overnight frost. Tolerant of summer drought. ◗

Echium pininana
This giant biennial forms a basal rosette of narrow leaves in the first year, possibly the second. In the second or third spring a thick leafy stem elongates very quickly to form a tall spike carrying hundreds of small flowers, in pale blue or almost white. The whole plant then dies, and the small seeds, still attached to their papery calyces, are dispersed by the wind. This species is wild in laurel forests in La Palma, and is often seen in coastal gardens elsewhere.
Cultivation Easily grown in partial shade and shelter, in sandy soil.
Height to 4.5m (15ft); spread to 60cm (2ft). USZ 9–11, surviving -6.5°C (20°F) of overnight frost. Tolerant of summer drought. ◗

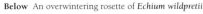

Echium wildpretii
This woody-stemmed perennial is a slightly smaller monocarpic species, forming in the first years a beautiful rosette of silver leaves and then an elongated stem bearing small, deep red flowers. It grows on La Palma and on the high volcanic slopes of Mount Teide in Tenerife; at night it is chilled and caked with frozen fog; in the day it is baked by the hot sun. This is a good plant for a high-altitude desert climate.
Cultivation Grows in poor rocky soil. Keep the rosettes dry in winter; they survive with little rainfall, even in spring.
Height to 4m (13ft); spread to 60cm (2ft). USZ 9–11, surviving -6.5°C (20°F) of overnight frost. Tolerant of summer drought. ◖

Above *Echium pininana* in the Isles of Scilly
Left *Echium nervosum* growing wild on Madeira

122

Below *Escallonia bifida*

Below *Garrya elliptica*

Escallonia (Escalloniaceae)

The genus *Escallonia* comprises 40 species from temperate South America. Many are hardy evergreen shrub and trees, with red or pink flowers, and are useful for coastal planting and hedging in moist climates.

Escallonia bifida
This evergreen shrub or small tree has shining, green, slightly sticky leaves and large heads, 20cm (8in) long, of small white flowers. The main reason to grow this plant is to attract butterflies, as its late-summer flowers are a rich source of nectar. It is wild from southern Brazil to Uruguay, growing in the mountains.
Cultivation Easily grown in any moist, preferably slightly acid soil.
Height to 5m (16ft); spread to 6m (20ft). USZ 9–11, surviving -6.5°C (20°F) of overnight frost. Best with summer water. ◗

Garrya (Garryaceae)

Garrya is a genus of 13 species of small evergreen trees or shrubs from western and central North America. It is now considered to be sufficiently isolated to merit its own family, the Garryaceae, although its DNA suggests that it is close to Solanaceae.

Garrya elliptica
This evergreen shrub is grown for its silvery catkins, which are formed in autumn and elongate in winter and early spring. It is wild in California. 'James Roof' is a male plant with catkins to 20cm (8in) long. In female plants the catkins are shorter and less showy.
Cultivation Easily grown in any soil in a sunny site. Prune in spring, as soon as the old catkins have faded; shorten each shoot, removing dead catkins and browned leaves.
Height to 3m (10ft); spread to 4m (13ft). USZ 8–11, surviving -12°C (10°F) of overnight frost. Tolerant of summer drought. ◗

Lithodora (Boraginaceae)

Lithodora, sometimes called by its earlier name *Lithospermum*, contains seven species of evergreen shrubs and subshrubs with bright blue flowers. They are wild in the Mediterranean region and western France.

Lithodora fruticosa
This spreading shrub has small bristly leaves and bright blue, trumpet-shaped flowers, 1–1.5cm (⅜–½in) long, in spring and early summer. The hardier *L. diffusa* is more sprawling, with bright blue flowers.
Cultivation Easily grown in full sun or partial shade, in acid or limestone soil.
Height to 30cm (1ft); spread to 3m (10ft). USZ 9–11, surviving -6.5°C (20°F) of overnight frost. Tolerant of summer drought. ◗

Above *Lithodora fruticosa*

The Daisy Family

Argyranthemum (Compositae)

Argyranthemum is a genus of 24 species of evergreen subshrubs, which are native to the Canary Islands and Madeira. These shrubby daisies are sometimes included in *Chrysanthemum*.

Argyranthemum gracile
This is the most graceful of the shrubby marguerites, as they are often called. It has greyish, thread-like leaves and solitary white flowers on slender arching stalks, in spring and summer. This species is a native of Tenerife. 'Chelsea Girl' is a good selection, which has particularly graceful, greyish leaves.
Cultivation Easily grown in any soil in full sun or light shade.
Height to 1.2m (4ft); spread to 2m (6½ft). USZ 10–11, surviving -1°C (30°F) of overnight frost. Tolerant of summer drought. ◗

Above *Argyranthemum gracile* growing wild, with cactuses, in Tenerife

Barnadesia (Compositae)

The genus *Barnadesia*, from South America, contains 19 species of shrubs or small trees, most of which have dark green, evergreen leaves and strong thorns. The flowers are usually pink, white, or purplish.

Barnadesia arborea
This upright or arching shrub produces box-like leaves, 1.5–3.5cm (½–1½in) long, and nodding pink flowers, to 5cm (2in) long and silkily hairy on the outside. The flowers are produced all year round. The leaves are crowded on the flowering stem. *B. arborea* is a native of Ecuador and Peru, in the Páramo and mountain woodland in the Andes, between 1,800m (6,000ft) and 5,000m (16,000ft). The form shown here, sometimes called var. *vestita* because of its velvety stem, is from the higher part of the range.
Cultivation Needs sandy soil and good drainage with full light.
Height to 5m (15ft); spread to 1m (3ft). USZ 9–11, surviving -6.5°C (20°F) of overnight frost. Tolerant of summer drought. ◗

Eupatorium (Compositae)

This genus contains around 400 species of evergreen shrubs and subshrubs and

Left *Eupatorium ligustrinum*

Below *Montanoa bipinnatifida*

Below *Barnadesia arborea* in Wales

perennials, which are natives throughout the world. It now includes the mainly shrubby genus *Ageratina*.

Eupatorium ligustrinum
This rounded shrub has dull pale purplish flowerheads, 15–25cm (6–10in) across, with a spicy scent, in autumn. It provides a late-flowering nectar source, and comes from the same areas of southern Mexico and Costa Rica where monarch butterflies overwinter. It is important in helping them to survive hibernation.
Cultivation Easily grown in any soil. *Height and spread to 6m (20ft). USZ 9–11, surviving -6.5°C (20°F) of overnight frost. Needs water in late summer.* ◑

Montanoa (Compositae)

Montanoa is a genus of around 25 species from Mexico and Central America. Most

species are tall evergreen shrubs, some are tree-like, while other species are climbers. The flowers may be white or pink.

Montanoa bipinnatifida
A dahlia-like shrub, found wild in the mountains of central Mexico. It has divided leaves and large heads of white flowers. This species is often cultivated in California and the south of France, where it is very striking when in flower in late summer.
Cultivation Plant in any soil. Grows best when given plenty of water in the growing season, less in winter and early spring. *Height to 9m (30ft); spread to 3m (10ft). USZ 9–11, surviving -6.5°C (20°F) of overnight frost. Tolerant of summer drought.* ◑

Olearia (Compositae)

The genus *Olearia* contains around 75 species of shrubs and even large trees, found

mainly in New Guinea, Australia, and New Zealand. Most are evergreen, with dark green leaves, which are silvery beneath. They are often used for shelterbelts and hedges in mild and windy climates, such as the Isles of Scilly. The daisy-like flowers are usually white, or rarely purple.

Olearia insignis (syn. Pachystegia insignis)
This is one of the lowest-growing but largest-flowered of the olearias, with its stiff, smooth, dark green, ovate leaves, felted beneath. The white flowers, to 7.5cm (3in) across, are borne in summer. This species is found wild in New Zealand, in Marlborough district, growing on rocks on the coast and in the mountains.
Cultivation Grow in well-drained, sandy soil, with some lime, and in full sun. *Height and spread to 2m (6½ft). USZ 9–11, surviving -6.5°C (20°F) of overnight frost. Needs water in summer.* ●

Phaenocoma (Compositae)

Phaenocoma is a genus of one species of *Helichrysum*-like, evergreen shrubs with pink or red everlasting flowers. It grows wild in South Africa, in the southern part of the Cape peninsula.

Phaenocoma prolifera
This lovely shrub has very small leaves and flowerheads, to 5cm (2in) across, in pink and red, during spring and summer.
Cultivation Needs sandy acid soil that is damp in spring, but drier in summer. *Height to 60cm (2ft); spread to 1m (3ft). USZ 9–11, surviving -6.5°C (20°F) of overnight frost. Tolerant of summer drought.* ◑

Above *Olearia insignis*

Above *Phaenocoma prolifera*

Climbers

CLIMBERS ARE PARTICULARLY useful for small gardens because they take up little space on the ground and can be used to "clothe" vertical surfaces. In hot dry climates, shade is one of the most important features of a garden, and here again climbers can play a key role, by covering an arch or loggia, and by providing interest, beauty, and, often, scent to a shady walk.

Above *Podranea brycei* (see p.141)

Aristolochia & Lapageria

Aristolochia (Aristolochiaceae)

Aristolochia is a genus of 120 species of mostly tropical, evergreen and deciduous climbers with a few herbaceous perennials. Its family is an ancient one, with many primitive features; the flowers, however, are very complex, having developed weird adaptations to fly pollinators and often imitating carrion. Many species are also grown as food plants for tropical butterflies such as swallowtails.

Aristolochia labiata

This tropical evergreen climber from Brazil has woody stems and heart-shaped leaves, 15cm (6in) across. The flowers, 20–30cm (8–12in) long, are borne in summer; they smell of bad fish, and attract flies, which become trapped inside, and even lay their eggs in the "prison". After pollination is completed, some of the flies may escape to visit and carry pollen to another flower.

Cultivation Grow in humus-rich soil in a warm position. Prune after flowering. *Height 10m (33ft) or more. USZ 10–11, surviving -1°C (30°F) of overnight frost. Requires water in summer, though is likely to be drought tolerant once established.* ●

Lapageria (Philesiaceae)

The genus *Lapageria* consists of one species of evergreen climber from Chile. It is named after the wife of Napoleon Bonaparte, Empress Josephine, who was born Josephine Tascher de la Pagerie in Martinique in 1763.

Above *Aristolochia labiata*

Lapageria rosea

This lovely climber is the national flower of Chile, where it grows on the edges of evergreen woods and thickets. The stems twine through the vegetation, and bear leathery ovate leaves and waxy, bell-shaped flowers, up to 7.5cm (3in) long, usually crimson but also pink and white, from late summer to autumn. 'Nash Court' carries pink flowers.

Cultivation Requires shelter, humidity, and rich, leafy or peaty soil in shade. *Height to 5m (16ft). USZ 9–11, surviving -6.5°C (20°F) of overnight frost. Tolerant of drought, but needs water in summer.* ●

Above A white form of *Lapageria rosea*
Left *Lapageria rosea* 'Nash Court'

Chilean Climbers

Bomarea (Alstromeriaceae)

The genus *Bomarea* contains around 120
species of herbaceous perennials and
climbers, found from Mexico to Argentina
and Chile, with most species in Colombia.
They have clusters of pure red, red-and-
green, pink, or yellow flowers, and are
pollinated by hummingbirds. They make
excellent climbers for frost-free areas.
Many species flower in winter and spring.

Bomarea multiflora
This is one of the most showy species, with
nodding umbels, around 23cm (9in) across,
of tubular orange flowers, around 5cm
(2in) long, almost year-round. The inner
petals are brown spotted, and the whole
flower drips with honey. The three-lobed
fruits are bright reddish orange, with a
juicy coating. *B. multiflora* grows wild in the
Andes, in Colombia and Venezuela.
Cultivation Easily grown in sandy soil in
a sunny site but with the roots in the shade.
Give ample water in the growing season.
*Height to 6m (20ft). USZ 10–11, surviving
-1°C (30°F) of overnight frost. Tolerant of
summer drought if well mulched.* ◗

Bomarea salsilla
This is one of the few *Bomarea* with pink
flowers, carried in branching heads, to
20cm (8in) across, rather than umbels, in
spring. Each tubular flower is 1–1.5cm

Above *Bomarea multiflora*

(⅜–½in) long, and is followed by dry,
brown, egg-shaped capsules of brown
seeds. It is a native of Chile.
Cultivation Easily grown in dry soil, with
water in spring; is dormant in summer.
*Height to 2m (6½ft.) USZ 10–11, surviving
-1°C (30°F) of overnight frost. Tolerant of
summer drought.* ◑

Quisqualis (Combretaceae)

The genus *Quisqualis* contains around 16
species of evergreen shrubs and climbers,
mainly from tropical Africa and Asia. The
unusual name, *Quisqualis* (Latin for "how
what"), is said to come from the Dutch

Above *Bomarea salsilla*

Above *Quisqualis indica* (Rangoon creeper) in northern Argentina

word *hoedanig*, itself a pun on the Malay name for the plant, *udani*. It indicates the variable habits of the plant, which starts life as a shrub, before becoming a climber.

Quisqualis indica
RANGOON CREEPER
This rampant climber from Burma to New Guinea can do well in cooler areas. The scented flowers are borne during summer. They open white, then turn pink, and finally on the third day become deep carmine, by which time the tube has elongated to 8–9cm (3–3½in).
Cultivation Needs a warm position in fertile soil, but is better shaded from the midday sun. A west-facing wall is ideal.
Height to 9m (30ft). USZ 10–11, surviving -1°C (30°F) of overnight frost. Requires summer water. ●

Tropaeolum (Tropaeolaceae)

The genus *Tropaeolum* consists of around 65 species from South America, mainly of

Below *Tropaeolum azureum*, with *Choisya dumosa* and *Sutherlandia montana*, in a greenhouse in Devon

Above *Tropaeolum pentaphyllum* growing in the open in southern France

herbaceous climbing or trailing plants. A few, such as *T. tuberosum*, are cultivated for their potato-like tubers. *T. majus* (nasturtium) is an annual creeper or climber with bright red flowers and leaves tasting of mustard.

Tropaeolum azureum
This delicate deciduous climber originates from the margins of the Atacamá desert in Chile, where it scrambles through low shrubs. The thin stems begin to grow in late summer from a rounded tuber. The blue flowers open in late spring and are flat, about 1.5cm (½in) across. The seeds are dry and pale brown.
Cultivation Easily grown in very dry, sandy soil. Give a little water in winter and spring; keep completely dry in summer.
Height to 2m (6½ft). USZ 10–11, surviving -1°C (30°F) of frost. Dormant in summer. ◓

Tropaeolum pentaphyllum
This deciduous climber is a native of Chile. Its thin tubers produce numerous climbing stems in spring. The red-and-green flowers, 2–3cm (¾–1¼in) across, have long spurs and are pollinated by hummingbirds in spring. The seeds have a blue fleshy coat, and are held in a persistent red calyx.
Cultivation Easily grown in dry, sandy soil, with water in winter and spring.
Height to 5m (16ft). USZ 9–11, surviving -6.5°C (20°F) of overnight frost. Dormant during summer. ◓

Winter-flowering *Clematis* & *Combretum*

Clematis (Rununculaceae)

Clematis is a mainly temperate genus of around 300 species, and includes evergreen and deciduous climbers and herbaceous perennials. The species shown here are suitable for gardens in warm climates, mainly because they flower in winter or very early spring.

Clematis cirrhosa

This Mediterranean climber is deciduous in summer, coming into leaf with autumn rain and flowering in winter and early spring. It has 1–3 shiny green leaflets. In late spring the silky fluffy seedheads can be as showy as the bell-shaped, yellow-green, cream, or freckled flowers, 4–5cm (1½–2in) long. 'Freckles' carries purple-spotted, cream flowers with a delicate scent. It is one of the most free-flowering of the cultivars and was raised from seed collected in the Balearic Islands. 'Wisley Cream' and 'Ourika Valley' (from Morocco) have unspotted, pale yellow-green flowers.

Cultivation Easily grown in fertile soil in hot summer climates, to scramble over bushes or trained against a wall.
Height to 6m (20ft). USZ 8–11, surviving -12°C (10°F) of overnight frost. Tolerant of summer drought. ◑

Above *Clematis grandiflora* in Madeira

Above *Clematis indivisa*

Above *Clematis cirrhosa* 'Freckles'

Clematis grandiflora

This evergreen clematis is native of the Highlands of Ethiopia down through central Africa as far south as Angola. The pendent, golden-yellow, bell-shaped flowers, covered with silky hairs, can reach 4.5cm (1¾in) long, in spring. They are followed by large fluffy fruit. The dark green leaves can have three or five leaflets.

Cultivation Requires fertile, well-drained soil and a warm winter climate.
Height to 9m (30ft). USZ 10–11, surviving -1°C (30°F) of overnight frost. Tolerant of summer drought. ◑

Clematis indivisa

This evergreen clematis bears neat, dark green leaves, with three leaflets, and pure white, star-shaped flowers, in early spring. Male and female flowers are found on different plants; the males are usually larger, measuring 5cm (2in) across. The fruits are fluffy. This species is a native of New Zealand, where it grows by the sea and in montane woods.

Cultivation Easily grown in moist, acid sandy soil, with in a sheltered position. *Height to 6m (20ft). USZ 10–11, surviving -1°C (30°F) of frost. Needs summer water.* ●

Clematis napaulensis

As its name suggests, this deciduous climber is a native of the foothills of the Himalayas, from Nepal to southwest China. The scented, bell-shaped flowers, to 2cm (¾in) long, appear in midwinter. They are pale greenish with purple anthers; the seeds are conspicuous, with silky styles around 5cm (2in) long. The fruits are fluffy. The leaves have three rather narrow, bright green leaflets, which drop in late summer before emerging again in autumn.
Cultivation Grow in any soil in humid, shaded, and sheltered conditions. *Height to 9m (30ft). USZ 10–11, surviving -1°C (30°F) of frost. Needs summer water.* ●

Clematis urophylla

On a plant-hunting expedition to Sichuan in western China in 1989, we were delayed at the foot of Erlang Shan, a steep, difficult pass on the road to Llasa. There were a couple more hours of daylight left, so we decided to explore a small gorge which came down to the road. There we were surprised to find a clematis with ripe seed (this was early April). When it flowered in midwinter, about three years later, it had 1–4 pure white, bell-

Below Clematis napaulensis

shaped blooms, 4.5cm (1¾in) long, in the axils of every leaf of the hanging shoots. The dark green leaves have three leaflets. The fruits are fluffy. *C. urophylla* has proved to be one of the prettiest winter-flowering climbers for a warm garden.
Cultivation Grow in any soil in partial shade and shelter from cold or drying wind. Prune hard after flowering. *Height to 3m (10ft). USZ 9–11, surviving -6.5°C (20°F) of overnight frost. Needs summer water.* ◗

Below Clematis urophylla

Combretum (Combretaceae)

The genus *Combretum* contains around 250 species of briefly deciduous shrubs and climbers from all tropical regions, except Australia. Many species have bright red flowers or coloured bracts.

Combretum paniculatum

This vigorous climbing shrub is from west Africa to Ethiopia, and south to the Transvaal, growing on hot savannah and flowering in winter or the cool, dry season. The stems have short, woody thorns and ovate leaves, to 20cm (8in) long. The red flowers have 4–5 petals and red stamens. The pink or orange fruits are four-winged.
Cultivation Needs a hot moist period in summer for growth in any soil, then a cool dry winter to initiate flowering. *Height to 9m (30ft). USZ 11, needing a minimum of 4.5°C (40°F) overnight. Tolerant of summer drought.* ◖

Above *Combretum paniculatum* flowering with *Wisteria* in early spring in Madeira

Above *Combretum paniculatum*

Climbing Pea-flowers

Hardenbergia (Leguminosae)

The genus *Hardenbergia* consists of three species of evergreen climbers, perennials, and shrubs from Australia. They may have one, three, or five leaflets.

Hardenbergia violacea
PURPLE CORAL PEA, FALSE SARSPARILLA
This tough, wiry, evergreen twining climber or shrub carries spikes of pea-like flowers in early spring. The flowers are about 1cm (⅜in) across and usually rich purplish blue, but pink and white forms are cultivated. The simple, lance-shaped leaves are 3–12cm (1¼–5in) long. *H. violacea* is native from Queensland to Tasmania, and plants from different areas have differing requirements.
Cultivation Grow in dry but preferably heavy soil. Prune hard after flowering.
Height to 3m (10ft). USZ 9–11, surviving -6.5°C (20°F) of overnight frost. Tolerant of summer drought. ◑

Above *Hardenbergia violacea*

Kennedia (Leguminosae)
CORAL-PEA

Kennedia is a genus of 16 species of evergreen scramblers, trailers, and climbers, from Australia and New Guinea. One of the species, *K. nigricans*, produces black flowers with a yellow patch on one petal.

Kennedia macrophylla
This is a strong-growing climber from Western Australia, with loose heads of orange-red, pea-like flowers, 1.3cm (½in) across, produced in spring and summer. The flowers have a black-edged, yellow spot at the base of the standard (upper)

Above *Kennedia macrophylla* in the garden at Tresco in the Isles of Scilly

petal. The leaves have three rounded leaflets, to 6cm (2½in) long.
Cultivation Easily grown in sandy soil, with moisture in spring.
Height to 3m (10ft). USZ 10–11, surviving -1°C (30°F) of overnight frost. Tolerant of summer drought. ◑

Mucuna (Leguminosae)

Mucuna consists of around 35 species of woody evergreen and deciduous climbers, mostly from the tropics in Africa, Asia, and

Left *Mucuna sempervirens*

South America. Some species such as *M. bennettii* and *M. novoguineensis*, both from New Guinea, have hanging bunches of flowers like a huge red *Wisteria*.

Mucuna sempervirens
One of the coolest-growing species of *Mucuna*, this is a native of central and eastern China and Japan, also thriving along the Mediterranean coast. This evergreen can cover large areas of scrub, forest, or even bamboos. The leaves have three leaflets, the terminal one 7–15cm (3–6in) long. The pea-like flowers, held in umbels of five or more,

Above *Wisteria floribunda* 'Multijuga' planted to cover a bridge in the Giardini di Ninfa, Italy

are 6–8cm (2½–3in) long, waxy, and evil-smelling, but rich in honey. They are borne in spring on thick branches, and followed by velvety seed pods, 40cm (16in) long.
Cultivation Easily grown in fertile leafy soil. Allow plenty of room to trail and build up a woody skeleton for flowering.
Height 12m (40ft) or more. USZ 9–11, surviving -6.5°C (20°F) of overnight frost. Needs water in summer. ●

Wisteria (Leguminosae)
WISTERIA

Wisteria consists of six species of woody deciduous climbers, natives of eastern Asia and eastern North America. Although these are hardy while dormant in winter, and usually rated zone 7 in North America, the opening buds are very susceptible to spring frosts. *Wisteria* flowers exceptionally well in warmer climates.

Wisteria floribunda
This climber is a native of southern Japan, where it grows alongside streams in the mountains. The stems twine clockwise.

The pale silvery lilac, fragrant, pea-like flowers, 2cm (¾in) across, open in succession from the top, in spring; generally they do not overlap. *W. floribunda* 'Macrobotrys' and 'Multijuga' have particularly long racemes of flowers, which can reach 1.5m (5ft) or more.
Cultivation Easily grown in any soil, with water and shade at the roots in summer. Prune in late summer, by shortening the twining shoots, and again in winter, by tidying the plant ready for spring flowering.
Height to 15m (50ft). USZ 7–11, surviving -17°C (2°F) of overnight frost. Requires water in summer. ●

Wisteria sinensis
This climber is a native of China, as far west as Hubei and eastern Sichuan. It is more often cultivated than *W. floribunda*, and has larger, bluer, fragrant flowers, 2.5cm (1in) across, in shorter, denser racemes, to 30cm (1ft) long. The stems twine anticlockwise.
Cultivation As for *W. floribunda*.
Height to 10m (33ft). USZ 7–11, surviving -17°C (2°F) of overnight frost. Requires water during summer. ●

Right A free-flowering *Wisteria sinensis* at Forde Abbey in Somerset

133

Climbing Roses

Rosa (Rosaceae)
ROSE

The genus *Rosa* contains around 150 species of deciduous and evergreen climbers and shrubs from around the northern hemisphere. Most of the modern cultivated roses, such as Hybrid Teas, are dwarf, repeat-flowering forms of wild climbers from China. The species and varieties shown here all grow best in warm climates and have 5–7 leaflets except *R. laevigata*.

Rosa banksiae
This rampant, evergreen, climbing rose has white, single or double flowers, 3–4cm (1¼–1½in) across, scented of violets, in spring. It is wild in western China, and commonly cultivated in the subtropics worldwide. Var. *normalis* bears single white flowers, while var. *banksiae*, the first variety to be brought to Europe, has double ones. 'Lutea' bears pale yellow, double flowers, and 'Lutescens' has single yellow blooms.

Cultivation Grow in any soil and a warm climate to flower well. In areas with cool summers, plant against a warm wall. *Height to 9m (30ft). USZ 8–11, surviving -12°C (10°F) of overnight frost. Tolerant of summer drought once it is established.* ◑●

Rosa gigantea
This evergreen climber, with white or pale yellow, scented, single flowers, to 12cm (5in) across, is found wild in southwestern China, Burma, and Manipur, where it flowers in spring. The ancient Chinese grew several forms of this rose, and they caused a sensation when they first came to Europe in the late 18th and early 19th centuries. The botanist Robert Fortune, who was commissioned by the Horticultural Society to collect garden plants from China, is said to have seen an orange-yellow, double rose growing over the wall of a mandarin's garden in Ningpo, and sent it back to Europe in 1845. It became known as 'Fortune's Double Yellow'.

Above *Rosa banksiae* var. *banksiae*

Cultivation Grow in any soil and a warm climate to flower well; in areas with cool summers, plant against a warm wall. *Height to 9m (30ft). USZ 9–11, surviving -6.5°C (20°F) of overnight frost. Tolerant of summer drought when established.* ●

Rosa laevigata
This strong-growing, evergreen rose produces three leaflets and single, white, fragrant flowers, 10cm (4in) across, each with a bristly stalk and hip, in spring. It is wild in China, where it climbs into trees or makes a large, arching shrub. *R. laevigata* has become naturalized in warm parts of North America.
Cultivation Grow in any soil and a warm climate to thrive and flower freely. *Height to 9m (30ft). USZ 9–11, surviving -3°C (27°F) of overnight frost. Tolerant of summer drought and heat once it is established.* ◑●

Rosa 'Lijiang Road Climber'
This lovely, pink, evergreen climber is a hybrid of *R. gigantea*, possibly with a Hybrid Perpetual. It grows in hedges along the road from Dali to Lijiang in Yunnan,

Above *Rosa laevigata* in the Villa Val-Rahmeh Exotic Botanic Garden, in Menton, France

Above *Rosa* 'Parks' Yellow Tea-scented China'

Above *Rosa gigantea* 'Fortune's Double Yellow'

and in the villages around Lijiang itself. It has proved particularly free-flowering in cultivation, especially in central Italy, where it was introduced by the rose collector Vicky Ducrot around 1995. The semi-double, scented flowers, 10cm (4in) across, are borne in spring.
Height to 9m (30ft). USZ 9–11, surviving -6.5°C (20°F) of overnight frost. Tolerant of summer drought once it is established. ◗

Rosa 'Parks' Yellow Tea-scented China'
John Parks sent this form of *R. gigantea* from China to England in 1824. It is a vigorous, deciduous or evergreen climber with scented, pale yellow, double flowers, 9–10cm (3½–4in) across, which are carried in early spring. In cold areas the buds can be killed by frost and rain.
Height to 9m (30ft). USZ 9–11, surviving -6.5°C (20°F) of frost. Tolerant of summer drought and heat once established. ◗◗

Rosa 'Senateur Lafolette'
This evergreen climber is one of the strongest-growing of all cultivated roses and is commonly planted in the south of France. It was raised by Busby, gardener to Lord Brougham at Château Eléonore in Cannes, using the wild *R. gigantea*. The scented flowers are peachy pink, to 15cm (6in) across, and loosely double from a long pointed bud. They are borne in spring.
Height to 9m (30ft). USZ 8–11, surviving -12°C (10°F) of overnight frost. Tolerant of summer drought and heat once established. ◗

Above *Rosa* 'Lijiang Road Climber' and wild *Rosa banksiae* var. *normalis* in a hedge between Dali and Lijiang, China

Above *Rosa* 'Senateur Lafolette' in Italy

135

Subtropical Climbers

Bougainvillea (Nyctaginaceae)

The genus *Bougainvillea* consists of 18 species of evergreen and deciduous climbers, shrubs, and trees, from South America, and is named after the French admiral, Louis Antoine, Comte de Bougainville (1729–1811), who circumnavigated the world. It is one of the commonest climbers for a frost-free climate. The intense colour is produced by a group of three bracts around each flower; the actual flowers are small and white.

Bougainvillea glabra

This climber is a native of Brazil, in the region of Rio de Janeiro, and is now found all over the tropics. It is evergreen in warm climates, but frost reduces it to pale grey twigs. The wild species has purple bracts, in summer, but garden varieties and hybrids bear larger bracts in colours from white to pink, orange, and yellow, and some have extra bracts so that they appear to be double flowered.

Cultivation Grow in fertile soil against a fence, pergola, or wall, where it can have plenty of space to develop. After each burst of flowering, trim plants; do any heavier pruning in early spring. Feed plants regularly, if they are to flower well.

Height to 9m (30ft). USZ 9–11, surviving -6.5°C (20°F) for short periods only. Requires water during summer. ◐◑

Above *Bougainvillea glabra*

Jasminum (Oleaceae)
JASMINE

The genus *Jasminum* contains around 200 species of evergreen and deciduous climbers and shrubs (*see also* pp.114–15). They have been valued in the Orient since ancient times for their sweet scent, which is strongest in the white-flowered species.

Jasminum polyanthum

This spring-flowering, evergreen climber was introduced from Yunnan, China, in 1897. Its masses of scented white flowers open from crimson-pink buds, which develop best in plants grown in the open. It grows well in the Mediterranean and California, as well as in London, and is sold as a pot plant. Summer-flowering *J. officinale* is similar, but has fewer flowers.

Cultivation Grow in any soil. Needs a hot sunny wall or fence to flower well, but keep the roots in shade. The long stems can be cut back after flowering.

Height to 5m (16ft). USZ 9–11, surviving -5°C (23°F) of overnight frost. Needs water and feeding in summer; also tolerates drought. ◑

Below *Jasminum polyanthum* climbing along a wall around a beautiful old jar in a garden in Madeira

Passiflora (Passifloraceae)
PASSIONFLOWER

There are around 350 species of evergreen and deciduous climbers in the genus *Passiflora* worldwide. They surprised the early Spanish travellers to America because their flowers symbolized the Passion of Christ: they have three nail-like stigmas and a thorny corona surrounded by about 12 petals. Many species are used as food plants for tropical butterflies. All species should be pruned in spring, before growth begins.

Passiflora x *exoniensis*
This beautiful evergreen climber, raised by Veitch's nursery in Exeter, combines the best of two South American species: pink *P. mollissima* and red *P. antioquiensis*. It has red flowers, in summer, followed by delicious, banana-like fruit.
Cultivation Easily grown in cool, humid shade, in rich soil.
Height to 9m (30ft). USZ 9–11, surviving -5°C (23°F) overnight. Needs water in summer. ◗

Passiflora platyloba
This evergreen climber bears strange flowers, like sea-anemones, with long bicoloured filaments. It is a native from Guatemala to Costa Rica.
Cultivation As for *P.* x *exoniensis*.
Height to 9m (30ft). USZ 9–11, surviving -3°C (27°F) of frost. Needs water in summer. ◗

Passiflora racemosa
This evergreen tropical climber, wild near Rio de Janeiro, Brazil, has long hanging racemes of red flowers throughout the year.
Cultivation Needs fertile rich soil, heat, and humidity to grow well.
Height to 9m (30ft). USZ 10–11, surviving -1°C (30°F). Needs water in summer. ◗

Above *Passiflora* x *exoniensis*

Above *Passiflora platyloba*
Left *Passiflora racemosa*

Campsis & Related Climbers

Above *Campsis grandiflora* with *Agapanthus praecox* at La Mortola, Italy

Allamanda (Apocynaceae)

Allamanda consists of around 15 species of evergreen shrubby climbers, which are from South America.

Allamanda cathartica

This strong-growing climber is a native of swampy places along the east coasts of central America from Belize to Panama. *A. cathartica* 'Hendersonii' originated in

Above *Allamanda cathartica* 'Hendersonii' at Kew

Guyana in the 1860s and has rich yellow, well-scented flowers, around 13cm (5in) across, borne throughout the year in tropical areas, and elsewhere mostly in summer. The stems and outside of the flowers tend to be maroon.
Cultivation Easily grown in any soil and warm conditions.
Height to 9m (30ft). USZ 10–11, surviving -1°C (30°F) of overnight frost. Needs ample water in summer. ◗

Campsis (Bignoniaceae)

The genus *Campsis* consists of two species of self-clinging, deciduous, woody climbers from North America and China.

Campsis grandiflora

This rampant climber produces hanging, orange, trumpet-shaped flowers, 6.5cm (2¾in) long, in summer and early autumn. The blooms are yellowish on the outside of the tube. The wood is pale brown, and the leaves are pinnate. *C. grandiflora* is wild in southeastern China, from north of Shanghai to as far south as Hainan Island.
Cultivation Easily grown in any soil, provided there is sufficient summer heat.

Height to 12m (40ft). USZ 9–11, surviving -6.5°C (20°F) of overnight frost. Tolerant of summer drought when established. ◗◗

Clytostoma (Bignoniaceae)

Clytostoma contains around 8 species of evergreen climbers from South America. Each leaf has two leaflets ending in a tendril.

Clytostoma callistegioides

This free-flowering climber is a native of southern Brazil and northern Argentina. The leaflets are 7.5–10cm (3–4in) long. Bluish mauve flowers, 6–9cm (2½–3½in) long, generally pale with darker veins, are borne in spring. The fruits are very spiny.
Cultivation Flowers best in any soil when grown in areas with a cool dry winter and warm wet summer.
Height to 9m (30ft). USZ 10–11, surviving -1°C (30°F) of overnight frost. Requires water during summer. ◗

Distictis (Bignoniaceae)

Distictis is a genus of nine species of evergreen climbers from Mexico and the

Below *Clytostoma callistegioides*

Below *Pandorea pandorana* 'Golden Showers'

Height to 5m (16ft). USZ 10–11, surviving -1°C (30°F) of overnight frost. Tolerant of summer drought. ◑

Tecoma (Bignoniaceae)

Of 14 species of evergreen, upright, scrambling shrubs, 13 are from tropical South America and one is from South Africa. All have pinnate leaves and tubular flowers.

Tecoma capensis (syn. *Tecomaria capensis*)
CAPE HONEYSUCKLE

This scrambling shrub, from the Cape to Natal, has pinnate leaves, 12cm (5in) long, with obovate leaflets. The loose terminal inflorescences of orange-red, rarely yellow, flowers, to 5cm (2in) long, with five recurved, unequal lobes, appear in late spring and summer (*see* front cover).
Cultivation Easily grown in any soil.
Height to 3m (10ft) if supported; spread to 2m (6½ft). USZ 9–11, surviving -6.5°C (20°F) of overnight frost. Tolerant of drought. ◑◑

West Indies. They may also be found under the genus *Phaedranthus*.

Distictis buccinatoria

This climber from Mexico bears leaves with either three leaflets or a pair of leaflets and a tendril. The tubular, scarlet to purplish red flowers, 7.5–10cm (3–4in) long, have yellow bases. They are freely borne in spring and summer in warm areas.
Cultivation Easily grown in any soil and is best on a sheltered, sunny wall in cooler areas.
Height to 12m (40ft). USZ 10–11, surviving -1°C (30°F) of overnight frost. Tolerant of summer drought when established. ◑

Pandorea (Bignoniaceae)

The genus *Pandorea* has around eight species of evergreen climbers in Australia, New Guinea, and the East Indies. *P. jasminoides*, has pure white to deep pink flowers streaked with crimson.

Pandorea pandorana
WONGA-WONGA VINE

This pretty climber bears upright narrow bunches of bell-shaped flowers, 1.1cm (⅜in) long, in shades of white, cream, or yellow. The leaves are dark bluish green and pinnate with 7–13 leaflets. 'Golden Showers' has brownish gold flowers.
Cultivation Easily grown in any soil, flowering well in partial shade.

Right *Distictis buccinatoria* at La Mortola, Italy

Honeysuckles & Related Climbers

Abelia (Caprifoliaceae)

Abelia comprises around 30 species of mainly evergreen and deciduous shrubs, primarily from China and Japan, but two species are from Mexico. Most are small-leaved plants with arching branches and pinkish or white, scented flowers. The hybrid *A. × grandiflora* is excellent for a wide range of conditions, being tolerant of both heat and drought.

Abelia floribunda
This striking, evergreen, scrambling shrub, which is one of the two Mexican species, can be trained against a wall or allowed to hang down over a cliff. The rounded leaves are 4cm (1½in) long at most. The crimson or deep pink, tubular flowers, to 5.5cm (2¼in) long, are produced from early to midsummer.
Cultivation Easily grown in any soil in a warm climate. Although tolerant of drought in summer, it needs some water in mid- to late summer to make long shoots for next year's flowering. Prune as soon as blooms have finished.
Height to 3m (10ft). USZ 9–11, surviving -6.5°C (20°F) of overnight frost. Tolerant of summer drought. ◑

Lonicera (Caprifoliaceae)
HONEYSUCKLE

Lonicera is a genus of around 200 species from around the northern hemisphere to as far south as Mexico and the Philippines. Most species are deciduous or evergreen shrubs, but there are a few small trees, and a number of climbers, many of which are sweetly scented to attract moths.

Lonicera hildebrandiana
This rampant evergreen climber is a native of the subtropical forests of northern Burma and southwest China. The broadly oval, green leaves are up to 12cm (5in) long. In summer the unscented flowers, 10–15cm (4–6in) long, open white and turn yellow.
Cultivation Easily grown in leafy soil, where warmth and humidity are sufficient in summer; tolerates a dry cool winter.
Height to 9m (30ft). USZ 10–11, surviving -1°C (30°F) of overnight frost. Requires water during summer. ●

Lonicera pilosa
This rare and beautiful deciduous climber was recently introduced from central and southern Mexico. The whorls of hanging, unscented, pinkish orange flowers, 5cm

Above *Lonicera hildebrandiana*

Above *Lonicera pilosa* from Mexico

Pyrostegia (Bignoniaceae)

The genus *Pyrostegia* comprises three or four species of evergreen twining climbers found in tropical America.

Pyrostegia venusta
GOLDEN SHOWER, CHINESE CRACKER FLOWER
This spectacular creeper from Brazil is commonly cultivated in the subtropics. It has hanging chains of bright orange, tubular flowers in winter. The leaves have two leaflets, 12cm (5in) long, and a long tendril. The flowers are borne in clusters at every node on long hanging stems, often forming a curtain of orange; they are 3.5–7cm (1½–3in) long, with slightly curved tubes and small recurved lobes.
Cultivation Easily grown in any soil. Flowers best in areas with cool dry winters.
Height to 9m (30ft). USZ 10–11, surviving -1°C (30°F) of overnight frost. Tolerant of summer drought. ◗

Above *Lonicera sempervirens*

Above *Pyrostegia venusta*

Above *Podranea brycei*

(2in) long, are borne in summer; they are hairy on the outside and have a hat-like bract at the base of each whorl. The ovate, pale green leaves are 2–3cm (¾–1¼in) long.
Cultivation Easily grown in any soil in a warm position in sun or partial shade.
Height to 8m (25ft). USZ 9–11, surviving -6.5°C (20°F) of overnight frost. Tolerant of summer drought. ◖

Lonicera sempervirens
This evergreen climber grows wild in eastern North America, from Connecticut to Florida. The ovate leaves are bluish green, 3–8cm (1¼–3in) long. The bright red, tubular, unscented flowers, around 5cm (2in) long, are borne all summer and attract hummingbirds.
Cultivation Easily cultivated in any soil. Is better with summer rain, though it can tolerate hot weather.
Height to 5m (16ft). USZ 8–11, surviving -12°C (10°F) of overnight frost. Requires water during summer. ◗

Podranea (Bignoniaceae)

The genus *Podranea* consists of two closely related species of evergreen climbers from southern Africa.

Podranea brycei
This beautiful climber is now cultivated throughout the world in warm climates. It is a native of Malawi and Zimbabwe, where it grows on rocky hills, flowering through the summer. The leaves are pinnate, with 7–9 leaflets, to 4cm (1½in) long. The flowers, 8cm (3in) across, are pinkish with darker lines, and hairy inside. *P. ricosoliana*, from the eastern Cape, has darker flowers, which are not hairy throated.
Cultivation Easily grown in any soil against a sunny wall. Keep cool and dry in winter, wet in summer, for good flowers.
Height to 9m (30ft). USZ 10–11, surviving -1°C (30°F) of overnight frost. Best with summer water. ◗

Opposite *Abelia floribunda* at Tapeley Park, Devon

Solandra & Potato Vines

Above *Solandra maxima* (copa de oro)

Solandra (Solanaceae)

Solandra consists of around 10 species from Mexico and the West Indies to southeastern Brazil. All are woody evergreen climbers with night-scented, trumpet-shaped, white, yellow, or greenish flowers.

Solandra longiflora
COPA DE LECHE
This evergreen forest climber bears shining green leaves, 6–10cm (2½–4in) long, and white to yellow flowers, 23–33cm (9–13in) long, in summer. The blooms are to 7.5cm (3in) across at the mouth; the narrow part of the tube is longer than the wider upper part of the tube; and the mouth is narrower than the widest part of the tube. *S. longiflora* is a native of the West Indies, Surinam, Venezuela, and Ecuador.
Cultivation Needs rich soil and heat to grow and flower well.
Height to 25m (80ft). USZ 11, needing minimum of 4.5°C (40°F) overnight. Requires water in summer. ◗

Solandra maxima
COPA DE ORO, GOLDEN CHALICE VINE
This very vigorous climber carries yellow flowers, 16–24cm (6¼–9½in) long, with five purple stripes. It is a native of Central America, from Mexico to Colombia and Venezuela, growing up into forest trees. The waxy, dark green leaves are around 17cm (6½in) long. The flowers are up to 13cm (5in) across the mouth; the narrow part of the tube is equal to or shorter than the wider upper part, and the mouth is no narrower than the widest part of the tube.
Cultivation As for *S. longiflora*.
Height to 25m (80ft). USZ 11, needing minimum of 4.5°C (40°F). Requires water during summer. ◗

Solanum (Solanaceae)
POTATO VINE

Solanum comprises 1,200–1,700 species of evergreen, semi-evergreen, and deciduous shrubs, trees, and climbers as well as perennials and annuals; many species are important food crops, including *S. tuberosum* (potato); many more are weeds; some are grown as ornamentals. For ornamental shrub species *see* p.117. Most species have poisonous leaves and fruit.

Above *Solandra longiflora* (copa de leche)

Solanum laxum ‘Album’
(syn. *S. jasminoides* ‘Album’)
This is one of the best evergreen or deciduous climbers for a small, largely frost-free garden, and it flowers throughout the summer and into autumn. It is a native of south Brazil, northern Argentina, Uruguay, and Paraguay. The ovate to lance-shaped leaves are 7–10cm (3–4in) long and are sometimes lobed. The star-shaped flowers, which are 1.5–2.5cm (½–1in) across, are pale lilac or white. The fruits, which are seldom seen in cultivation, are black, globular, and 7–9cm (3–3½in) across.

Above *Solanum wendlandii*

Above *Solanum laxum* 'Album'

Cultivation Grow in rich soil. In hot areas *S. laxum* 'Album' is best in partial shade. *Height to 6m (20ft). USZ 9–11, surviving -6.5°C (20°F) of overnight frost. Tolerant of summer drought.* ●

Solanum wendlandii
This is the most beautiful of all solanums for a warm garden. It is a woody evergreen climber with heads, around 60cm (2ft) across, of delicate, lilac or blue, star-shaped flowers in summer. It is a native of the West Indies, central America, and northern South America, but is widely cultivated elsewhere. The male and female flowers are borne on different plants, but only the male is in cultivation, so the yellow berries are seldom seen. Each male flower is 3.5–5.5cm (1½–2¼cm) across. The lower leaves are pinnately lobed; the upper leaves are almost undivided, around 15cm (6in) long, with prickles beneath.
Cultivation Easily grown in any fertile rich soil, preferably with the roots in shade. Prune plants in spring before growth starts. *Height to 9m (30ft). USZ 9–11, surviving -3°C (27°F) of overnight frost. Tolerant of summer drought, but does best with summer rain.* ●●

Streptosolen (Solanaceae)

Streptosolen has only one species, which is a native of the Andes in Ecuador and Peru.

Streptosolen jamesonii
This loose-growing, evergreen, scrambling

Above *Solanum laxum* 'Album'

shrub bears masses of orange flowers, which appear in summer, are tubular at the base, and 2.5–3cm (1–1¼in) long. The ovate leaves are up to 5cm (2in) long.
Cultivation Easily grown in fertile soil. *Height to 9m (30ft). USZ 9–11, surviving -3°C (27°F) of overnight frost. Tolerant of drought during summer.* ◐

Above *Streptosolen jamesonii*

143

Scented Climbers

Agapetes (Ericaceae)

Agapetes is a genus of around 35 species of climbing shrubs, from the foothills of the eastern Himalayas, south to Borneo, Fiji, and Australia. Most have waxy evergreen leaves and tubular or bell-shaped flowers.

Agapetes serpens

This epiphytic shrub produces long slender shoots that clamber into the branches of trees in the mossy forests of eastern Nepal, Bhutan, and northern Assam. The leaves are around 2cm (¾in) long, on either side of a hairy stem. Bright red or, rarely, cream flowers, 2.5cm (1in) long, hang down along the stems, from late winter to spring.
Cultivation Grow in slightly acid, leafy soil, with cool shade, damp, and humidity, as in mild coastal areas or in the hills.
Height to 2m (6½ft). USZ 10–11, surviving -1°C (30°F) of overnight frost. Needs moisture and rain in summer. ●

Above *Agapetes serpens*

Lophospermum
(Scrophulariaceae)

Lophospermum consists of around three species of evergreen and deciduous shrubs and perennial climbers from the southern USA, Mexico, and Central America. All have purple or pink, tubular flowers.

Lophospermum erubescens

This sticky, soft-haired perennial climber has tuberous roots and annual stems, which climb into shrubs or can hang down over a wall. Both flower and leaf stalks can coil round a support. The heart-shaped leaves are 2–7cm (¾–3in) long and wide. The sepals are flat and green, overlapping at their margins. The flower tube is 7cm (3in) long, with five unequal pinkish lobes and a yellow throat, and 1.8–2.5cm (¾–1in) across the mouth.
Cultivation Easily grown in areas with little frost, in well-drained soil.
Height to 2m (6½ft). USZ 9–11, surviving -6.5°C (20°F) of overnight frost. Tolerant of summer drought. ◑

Maurandella (Scrophulariaceae)

The genus *Maurandella* has one species of perennial climbers. This grows wild in

Left *Lophospermum erubescens*

Above *Maurandella antirrhiniflora*

Above *Maurandya barclaiana*

rocky deserts on limestone in California from the eastern Mojave desert to Texas and to Oaxaca in Mexico, where it flowers in spring. It is often found under the genera *Maurandya* or *Asarina*.

Maurandella antirrhiniflora
This delicate climber has smooth triangular leaves, 2.5cm (1in) across, and bright purple, pinkish, or red, snapdragon-shaped flowers, 2–3cm (¾–1¼in) long, with a yellow throat; the sepals are narrow, and curve outwards. The leaves are three- or five-lobed.
Cultivation Easily grown in very well-drained soil in a dry place.
Height to 3m (10ft). USZ 9–11, surviving -6.5°C (20°F) of overnight frost. Tolerant of summer drought. ◑

Maurandya (Scrophulariaceae)

Maurandya consists of two species of perennial climbers, which are from the southern USA and Mexico.

Maurandya barclaiana
This long-lived perennial climber from Mexico scrambles through shrubs and hangs down on cliffs in dry areas. It flowers for most of the summer months. The snapdragon-shaped flowers are usually purplish blue, but may be pink or white, and are 3–4.5cm (1¼–1¾in) long. The sepals are distinctly sticky, with glandular hairs, joined only at the base. The arrowhead-shaped leaves are smooth, to 4cm (1½in) long.

Cultivation Easily grown in any soil in a dry place, such as a crevice in a wall or rock. It will also thrive in a deep pot.
Height to 2m (6½ft). USZ 9–11, surviving -6.5°C (20°F) of overnight frost. Tolerant of summer drought. ◑

Rhodochiton (Scrophulariaceae)

The genus *Rhodochiton* contains three species of perennial climbers usually grown as annuals, and native of Mexico and Guatemala. They are very beautiful and distinct, with the calyx (the fused sepals) as conspicuous as the petals.

Rhodochiton atrosanguineus
This lovely climber has been widely cultivated for years, but is rarely found in the wild, where it grows in dense cool rainforest in the mountains of Oaxaca, Mexico. It is usually grown as an annual, producing masses of hanging flowers from summer to autumn. The calyx is bright pink, 4cm (1½in) across; the petals united into a tubular black corolla, 4.5cm (1¾in) long. The leaves, 3–5cm (1¼–2in) long, are heart-shaped. Though the name is often written *atrosanguineum*, the word *chiton* ("tunic") is masculine, so "-us" is the correct ending.
Cultivation Easily grown in fertile leafy soil in cool conditions until flowering begins; then keep a little drier until autumn. Sow seed in heat in early spring.
Height to 9m (30ft). USZ 10–11, surviving -1°C (30°F) of overnight frost. Requires summer water. ●

Above *Rhodochiton atrosanguineus*

Canarina, Cobaea, & Morning Glory

Canarina (Campanulaceae)

Canarina is a genus with three species of herbaceous perennials, one native of the Canary Islands and two from tropical East Africa. All have bell-shaped flowers.

Canarina canariensis
CANARY BELLFLOWER

This climbing perennial, from Gomera, Gran Canaria, La Palma, and Tenerife, has a large tuberous root, triangular leaves with toothed edges, and reddish orange flowers, sometimes stripy, in winter.
Cultivation Grow in sandy leafy soil. Keep dry in summer; give regular small applications of water from late summer onwards, when the plant starts into growth. *Height 3m (10ft) or so. USZ 10–11, surviving -1°C (30°F) of overnight frost. Tolerant of summer drought.* ◑

Above *Canarina canariensis* (Canary bellflower)

Cobaea (Polemoniaceae)

The genus *Cobaea* has around 10 species of annual or perennial climbers, which are native of Central and South America, from Mexico to Venezuela and northern Chile. They have long branching tendrils with small hooks at the end, enabling them to clasp their support (often a tree in the wild).

Cobaea pringlei
This rampant climbing perennial, from northeast Mexico, produces fleshy roots and pinnate leaves. Masses of pale greenish yellow, trumpet-shaped flowers are borne from late summer to autumn.
Cultivation Grow in fertile, moisture-retentive soil in a sheltered place. *Height to 10m (33ft). USZ 10–11, surviving -1°C (30°F) of overnight frost. Tolerant of summer drought.* ◑

Cobaea scandens
CUP AND SAUCER VINE

This fast-growing, perennial climber, from Mexico, is often grown as an annual in gardens, as it flowers in the first year after sowing. The flowers are borne in autumn and winter and are broadly bell-shaped, and greenish white becoming purple. They have a revolting smell at first, which becomes sweeter once each flower changes colour. The leaves are pinnate. *C. scandens* is useful for clothing pergolas and pillars or

Above *Cobaea pringlei*

as a screening plant for unsightly walls. Forma *alba* has white flowers.
Cultivation Grow in moisture-retentive soil in a sheltered position in full sun. *Height to 8m (25ft). USZ 10–11, surviving -1°C (30°F) of overnight frost. Requires a little water in summer.* ◑

Ipomoea (Convolvulaceae)

This variable genus comprises around 650 species of annual or perennial climbing herbs, shrubs, and, occasionally, trees. They are native of tropical and subtropical regions of the world, with around half of all species coming from North and South America. The species shown here are grown for ornament, but many others are cultivated as food crops and for medicinal use: for example, *I. batatas* (yam, sweet potato).

Ipomoea alba
MOONFLOWER

This rampant climbing annual or perennial is native of tropical America, has naturalized throughout the tropics, and is widely grown in gardens. It has long-stalked, heart-shaped, green leaves and white, scented, trumpet-shaped flowers, to 12–15cm (5–6in) across, on a long narrow tube, opening rather flat in the early evening during summer.
Cultivation Grow in any soil. Prefers a humid atmosphere until established. Is

Above *Cobaea scandens* (cup and saucer vine)

Below *Ipomoea purpurea*

in summer. These open in the morning, and last only a day, during which they become pinker.

Cultivation Grow in any soil.
Height to 3m (10ft). USZ 9–11, surviving -6.5°C (20°F) of overnight frost. Tolerant of summer drought. ◐●

Ipomoea tricolor
MORNING GLORY

This twining or scrambling annual, from Mexico, tropical South America, and the West Indies, bears heart-shaped, soft green leaves and trumpet-shaped flowers, 8–10cm (3–4in) across, in shades of blue, in summer and autumn, opening in the morning and lasting only a day. 'Heavenly Blue' is a commonly grown selection with beautiful, electric-blue flowers.

Cultivation Grow in any soil in sun. Keep humid and warm in the growing season and dry once it starts to flower. It is often grown from seed.
Height to 3m (10ft). USZ 9–11, surviving -6.5°C (20°F) of overnight frost. Tolerant of summer drought. ●

suitable for a trellis or pergola as a screening plant.
Height to 5m (16ft). USZ 11, needing a minimum of 4.5°C (40°F). Tolerant of summer drought once established. ●

Ipomoea purpurea

This climbing annual, originating from Mexico and the West Indies but now naturalized in many countries, is sometimes considered an invasive weed. It has bristly, hairy stems, ovate green leaves, and deep purplish blue, trumpet-shaped flowers, which are 5–6cm (2–2½in) across,

Above *Ipomoea alba* (moonflower)

Above Wild *Ipomoea tricolor* (morning glory) climbing over bushes, south of Lake Chapala, in central Mexico

Dregea, Hoya, & Thunbergia

Dregea (Asclepiadaceae)

This genus contains three species of deciduous climbing shrubs originating from tropical Africa and Asia. It is now often included in the Apocynaceae.

Dregea sinensis
This deciduous climber, from western China, has heart-shaped, green leaves, which are downy on the underside, and hanging umbels of scented, white or pink flowers, in early summer.
Cultivation Grow in fertile soil in sun or partial shade.

Height to 2m (6½ft). USZ 9–11, surviving -6.5°C (20°F) of overnight frost. Requires water in summer. ◗

Hoya (Asclepiadaceae)

The genus *Hoya* comprises around 70 species of evergreen climbing and twining shrubs originating from Asia to Australia. It is now often included in the Apocynaceae.

Hoya carnosa
WAX PLANT
This fleshy evergreen climber, from southeast China and India, bears ivy-like

Above *Hoya carnosa* (wax plant)

stems and thick, dull green, ovate leaves. The heavily scented, waxy, whitish pink flowers, with red centres, are carried in dense round umbels throughout summer.
Cultivation Grow in fertile, well-drained, preferably slightly sandy soil, in partial shade. Water generously but infrequently in summer; can be left almost dry in winter.
Height to 5m (16ft). USZ 10–11, surviving -1°C (30°F) of overnight frost. Needs some water in summer. ◗

Mandevilla (Apocynaceae)

Mandevilla consists of around 115 species of deciduous or evergreen, twining climbers, whiich are native of Central and South America.

Mandevilla laxa (syn. M. suaveolens)
CHILEAN JASMINE
Despite its misleading common name, this often deciduous, twining climber is from

Above *Mandevilla laxa* (Chilean jasmine)
Left *Dregea sinensis* growing wild in Baoxing, China

Below *Thunbergia grandiflora* (Bengal clock vine) growing over a wall in the south of France

Argentina and Bolivia, not Chile. It has thin, heart-shaped, green leaves and clusters of pure white, scented flowers on short branches in the leaf axils in summer. Other good species, hybrids, and cultivars, which are much less hardy than that illustrated, include *M. boliviensis* with shiny, dark green leaves that contrast beautifully with the white, yellow-throated flowers.
Cultivation Needs rich soil, partial shade, and plenty of water. Is good for a large container, where these conditions can best be provided in a dry climate. Avoid unnecessary disturbance of the roots. Can be pruned hard in winter if necessary.
Height to 5m (16ft) but usually much less. USZ 9–11, surviving -6.5°C (20°F) of overnight frost. Requires water in summer. ◗

Thunbergia (Acanthaceae)

Thunbergia has 90 species of evergreen climbing or upright herbs and shrubs. They are probably from tropical Africa and Asia, but most species have become so widely naturalized that it is difficult to be certain of their origin.

Thunbergia grandiflora
BENGAL CLOCK VINE
This rather variable climber, probably from northern India, has heart-shaped, downy, green leaves and racemes of pale blue, bell-shaped flowers, with yellow throats, from late spring onwards. 'Alba' has white, yellow-throated flowers.
Cultivation Grow in fertile, moist but well-drained soil in partial shade. Can be grown as an annual.
Height to 5m (16ft). USZ 10–11, surviving -1°C (30°F) of overnight frost. Requires water in summer. ◗

Trachelospermum (Apocynaceae)

This genus contains around 19 species of evergreen climbing shrubs that are native of Asia east to Japan, as well as one species from southeastern North America.

Trachelospermum asiaticum
This climbing shrub, from southern Japan and Korea, bears ovate–elliptic, glossy, dark green leaves and scented, white or creamy yellow, jasmine-like flowers, 2cm (¾in)

across, in late spring. *T. jasminoides*, to 3m (10ft) high, is less tolerant of low temperatures, and has smaller, very fragrant, white flowers.
Cultivation Grow in well-drained but moisture-retentive soil in sun or partial shade, in a sheltered spot. Is good as a container plant.
Height to 10m (33ft). USZ 9–11, surviving -6.5°C (20°F) of overnight frost. Tolerant of summer drought. ◗

Above *Trachelospermum asiaticum*

The *Verbena* Family & Climbing *Mutisia*

Above *Duranta erecta* (golden dewdrop)

Duranta (Verbenaceae)

Duranta contains around 17 species of evergreen and deciduous scrambling shrubs and trees from tropical America, including the Caribbean.

Duranta erecta (syn. *D. repens*)
GOLDEN DEWDROP, PIGEON BERRY
This fast-growing, climbing shrub or small tree is from South and Central America and the Caribbean. It has slender, often arching, and sometimes spiny branches and pairs of glossy, dark green leaves. The drooping

spikes of small lilac flowers, in summer, are followed by yellow berries.
Cultivation Grow in moist soil in full sun; do not let the roots dry out. Prune often. *Height to 6m (20ft). USZ 9–11, surviving -6.5°C (20°F) of overnight frost. Requires water in summer.* ◑

Holmskioldia (Labiatae)

One species of evergreen climbing shrubs, from the subtropical Himalayas.

Holmskioldia sanguinea
CHINESE HAT PLANT
This fast-growing, scrambling shrub starts out as a low shrub, then later develops climbing stems. It has short, tubular, red flowers from summer to autumn. 'Aurea' carries bright yellow flowers.
Cultivation Grow in any soil. Prune frequently to keep this plant under control. *Height to 10m (33ft). USZ 11, needing minimum of 4.5°C (40°F) overnight. Very tolerant of summer drought.* ●

Mussaenda (Rubiaceae)

Mussaenda contains 100 species of scrambling or upright, mainly evergreen shrubs, with extraordinary, enlarged, leaf-like sepals. They are native of tropical areas of Africa and Asia. *M. erythrophylla*, from western Africa, has bright red sepals and

Above *Mutisia ilicifolia*
Left *Holmskioldia sanguinea* 'Aurea' (Chinese hat plant)

yellow, pink, or red flowers; hybrids with pink sepals have been raised.

Mussaenda pubescens

This showy shrub or climber is from China and Hong Kong, where it is common. It often remains a shrub, but in favourable conditions it develops twining shoots and becomes a climber, into trees in the wild. *M. pubescens* produces loose heads of small, star-like, yellow flowers, with pure white outer sepals enlarged and leaf-like in appearance. The flowers usually appear in spring but can continue into summer.
Cultivation Grow in fertile, well-drained soil in sun or partial shade. Needs generous amounts of water during the growing season, much less in the winter.
Height to around 2m (6½ft). USZ 10–11, surviving -1°C (30°F) of overnight frost. Requires water in summer. ◑

Mutisia (Compositae)

The genus *Mutisia* contains around 60 species of evergreen shrubs and climbers originating from South America. In addition to the species shown here, several others are grown as climbers in warm gardens. The naming of these plants is somewhat confused. Scrambling *M. acuminata* is from the mountains in Bolivia and northern Argentina. It has dark green leaves, with a tendril at the end, and showy, red, daisy-like flowers (*see* p.20).

Mutisia decurrens

This suckering climber, from Chile and Argentina, produces narrow, greyish green leaves each tipped with a tendril. The orange, vermilion, or deep yellow, daisy-like flowers appear from spring to summer.
Cultivation Grow in well-drained soil in full sun, with shade and moisture at the roots. (The best way to provide this, and to protect the plant from extreme cold if necessary, is to place large flat stones around its base.)
Height to 3m (10ft). USZ 9–11, surviving -6.5°C (20°F) of overnight frost. Tolerant of summer drought if kept moist at the root. ◐

Mutisia ilicifolia

This evergreen climbing shrub, from Chile, has greyish green, holly-like leaves, toothed

Below *Mutisia decurrens*

at the margins, and whitish on the underside, tapering to a tendril. The daisy-like flowers are pale pink or mauve, with yellow centres, and are carried on short stalks almost throughout the year.
Cultivation Grow in well-drained soil in full sun. Ensure that the roots are kept dry during winter.
Height to 3m (10ft). USZ 9–11, surviving -6.5°C (20°F) of overnight frost. Tolerant of summer drought. ●

Above *Mussaenda pubescens*

Perennials

PERENNIALS ARE ESSENTIALLY plants for areas with summer rainfall, producing stems and flowers through the warm wet months. Many, however, are capable of growing in summer-dry regions, having evolved tolerance of heat and lack of water.

Above *Hordeum jubatum* (see p. 173)

152

Heliconia & Strelitzia

Heliconia (Musaceae)

Heliconia contains around 100 species of evergreen perennials. These banana-like plants are mostly from tropical America. The flowers are small, hidden in the stiff, brightly coloured bracts, and attractive to birds, which are the main pollinators.

Heliconia rostrata
LOBSTER CLAW
One of the most spectacular heliconias, this perennial is found growing wild in the wet forests from Peru to northern Argentina. The tall, banana-like leaves have oblong blades, and the red-and-yellow, hanging inflorescence can reach 60cm (2ft) when fully extended. It is borne almost year-round or in the hot wet season.
Cultivation Needs a warm wet position in shade, and rich leafy soil.
Height to 1.2m (4ft); spread to 1m (3ft). USZ 10–11, surviving -1°C (30°F) of overnight frost. Needs water in summer. ●

Above *Heliconia rostrata* (lobster claw) in the Fairchild Botanic Garden, Florida

Above *Strelitzia nicolae*

Strelitzia (Strelitziaceae)

The genus *Strelitzia* contains five species of evergreen perennials, some tree-like, from the Cape region of South Africa to Zimbabwe. All have a stiff pointed bract or bracts, and a series of flowers, emerging in succession from them. The flowers have three narrow, petal-like sepals and an arrow-shaped pair of petals which enclose the stamens and style. They make a perch for sunbirds, which feed on the sticky nectar.

Strelitzia juncea
This perennial is found in the Cape, South Africa, in damp sandy places. The green-and-red bracts and orange-and-dark-blue flowers are borne in spring and summer. It is like *S. reginae* but has no leaf blade.
Cultivation Grow in sandy soil, and keep moist in winter and spring.
Height to 1m (3ft); spread to 1.5m (5ft). USZ 9–11, surviving -6.5°C (20°F) of overnight frost. Tolerant of summer drought. ◑

Strelitzia nicolae
This tough perennial has a stiff stem, leaves with blades 1.5m (5ft) long, and a short-stemmed inflorescence with several black bracts. The flowers are white or pale blue.
Cultivation Grow in slightly acid, well-drained, fertile soil.
Height to 10m (33ft); spread to 3m (10ft). USZ 10–11, surviving -1°C (30°F) of overnight frost. Tolerant of summer drought. ◑

Above *Strelitzia juncea* at Kirstenbosch, near Cape Town, South Africa

153

Waterlilies

Nelumbo (Nelumbonaceae)

The genus *Nelumbo* consists of two species of aquatic perennials: the Asian *N. nucifera* and the American *N. lutea*, a smaller plant with yellow flowers. Although *Nelumbo* seems superficially similar to waterlilies (which belong to the family Nymphaeaceae), DNA studies have shown it to be very isolated and in fact closest to the plane tree (*Platanus*). Both the fleshy roots and the large seeds are commonly eaten in China.

Nelumbo nucifera
This aquatic perennial is the sacred Lotus of Buddhism, and is wild from the Volga

Delta, eastwards to China and south to Australia. On emerging in spring, the plant forms foliage that floats on the water; later it produces stalked leaves like an umbrella blown inside out, about 1m (3ft) across. The flowers, around 30cm (1ft) across in some cultivars, appear in summer and are generally pink, or else white or nearly red. The flat-topped seed pods are corky, with holes for the seeds.

Cultivation Plant the rhizomes in rich mud, 25cm (10in) deep, and keep at 23–27°C (73–80°F). In cool areas these plants can be grown in large jars.
Height to 2.4m (8ft); spread infinite.
USZ 9–11, surviving -6.5°C (20°F) of frost, provided the rhizomes do not freeze. ◗

Nymphaea (Nymphaeaceae)
WATERLILY

The genus *Nymphaea* contains around 50 species of aquatic perennials throughout the world. A number of fossil waterlilies have been identified from the Cretaceous Period, around 120 million years ago, in Portugal.

Nymphaea 'American Beauty'
This strong-growing, subtropical, aquatic perennial is one of a group of hybrids raised in Missouri Botanical Garden in the 1930s and 1940s. The purplish blue flowers open during the day in summer

Below *Nelumbo nucifera*

Below *Nymphaea capensis*

and can be 25cm (10in) across. The round leaves are 30–40cm (12–16in) across.
Cultivation Needs water 60–90cm (2–3ft) deep, combined with full sun and heat in summer. Keep the roots out of frost in winter. *Height of flower stalk to 25cm (10in); spread to 2m (6½ft). USZ 9–11, surviving -6.5°C (20°F) of overnight frost.* ◖

Nymphaea capensis

This aquatic perennial is from eastern Africa, from Zanzibar south to the Cape, where it often covers large sheets of shallow lakes or seasonal pools. The pale or bright blue flowers, 15–20cm (6–8in) across, are borne in summer on short stalks. The wavy-edged leaves, 25–40cm (10–16in) across, mostly float on the surface.
Cultivation Needs water 45–60cm (18–24in) deep; does not require great heat in summer. Is easily grown from seed. *Height of flower stalk to 30cm (1ft); spread indefinite. USZ 10–11, surviving -1°C (30°F) of frost. Tolerant of summer drought.* ◖

Nymphaea lotus

This aquatic perennial is found wild from Egypt to southern Africa, and to southeast Asia, in lakes and slow-flowing rivers. The leaves, 30–50cm (12–20in) across, often have toothed or spiny edges. The white or

Below *Nymphaea* 'American Beauty' in New York

pink flowers, 15–25cm (6–10in) across, open at night, on long stalks, in summer.
Cultivation Needs water 45–75cm (18–30in) deep, and at least 20°C (68°F). *Height of flower stalk to 60cm (2ft). USZ 10–11, surviving -1°C (30°F) of frost.* ●

Victoria (Nymphaeaceae)

Victoria is a genus of two species of aquatic perennials or annuals, from backwaters and slow rivers in the Amazon basin, in Brazil, Guyana, and Surinam. The juvenile leaves

Below *Nymphaea lotus*

are flat; the mature leaves have a rim, and a pattern of stiff spiny ribs.

Victoria 'Longwood Hybrid'

This aquatic perennial is usually grown as an annual, and has leaves 2m (6½ft) across. The waterlily-like, white flowers, 30–40cm (12–16in) across, turn pink, in summer; they have a strong pineapple scent at night.
Cultivation Needs 25°C (77°F) to grow and flower properly. Plant in a heated pool or in warm summer climates. *Height to 30cm (1ft); spread to 6m (20ft). USZ 11; night minimum of 20°C (68°F).* ◖

Below *Victoria* 'Longwood Hybrid' in the Princess of Wales House at the Royal Botanic Gardens Kew

Perennials for Shallow Water

Thalia (Marantaceae)

The genus *Thalia* consists of around seven species of mostly evergreen and herbaceous, semi-aquatic perennials, from tropical and subtropical America, with one species, *T. geniculata*, possibly native in West Africa.

Thalia dealbata

This upright evergreen perennial bears rounded, bluish green leaves, to 50cm (20in) long, white and mealy beneath, on stalks to 2m (6½ft) tall. The deep purple flowers, 8mm (⅓in) long, on a tall wiry stem, appear in summer. It grows from South Carolina and Missouri to Mexico, in ditches, swampy woods, and shallow water.
Cultivation Needs rich peaty soil and warmth. Plant in a pool or large jar.
Height to 3m (10ft); spread to 6m (20ft). USZ 9–11, the roots remaining above freezing under water. ●

Below *Thalia dealbata* in the Huntington Botanical Gardens, California

Xanthosoma (Araceae)

There are many large, semi-aquatic, subtropical Araceae, which have bold leaves to provide a tropical effect in a garden. The genus *Xanthosoma*, for example, contains around 50 species of large-leaved perennials, which are native in tropical America. Most species have edible leaves and starchy corms.

Xanthosoma violaceum

This exotic-looking, semi-aquatic perennial has heart-shaped leaves, to 70cm (28in) across and purplish beneath, on bluish purple stems. The flowers are covered by a whitish spathe, about 20cm (8in) long and yellow inside. They appear in summer. It is wild in the American tropics and commonly grown elsewhere.
Cultivation Grow in a shallow pool or ditch. The corms may be stored indoors in winter, in barely damp, frost-free sand.
Height to 1.5m (5ft); spread to 2m (6½ft). USZ 11, needing a minimum of 4.5°C (40°F) overnight. ●

Zantedeschia (Araceae)

The genus *Zantedeschia* contains eight species of perennials with tuberous rhizomes, from southern Africa. Many are cultivated for their beautiful flowers, the

Left *Xanthosoma violaceum* by the Victoria pool at Kew

coloured part being a bract or spathe, which is wrapped round the small crowded flowers.

Zantedeschia aethiopica

This perennial is often called arum lily. It is a native of the Cape, South Africa, where it thrives in swamps and seasonally wet sites. The leaf blades are up to 45cm (18in) long. The spathe, to 25cm (10in) long, is usually pure white, but may have a pink-flushed throat, or in 'Green Goddess' be tipped with green. It appears in spring and summer.
Cultivation Easily grown in rich moist soil, or in shallow water. It can be dormant in summer or winter, according to climate. *Height to 1m (3ft); spread to 60cm (2ft). USZ 9–11, surviving -6.5°C (20°F) of frost. Tolerant of summer drought.* ◑●

Zantedeschia albomaculata

This species is very similar to Z. *aethiopica*, but has white-spotted leaves. It is wild in the eastern Cape and into tropical eastern Africa, growing in springs and damp rock ledges. The leaf blades are up to 40cm (16in) long. The spathe, to 15cm (6in) long, is borne in summer.
Cultivation Needs rich, damp, sandy soil. *Height to 1.2m (4ft); spread to 1m (3ft). USZ 9–11, surviving -6.5°C (20°F) of overnight frost. Needs water in summer.* ●

Zantedeschia pentlandii

This perennial, from the Transvaal, South Africa, has spotted leaves. The yellow spathe, to 12cm (5in) long, often with a purple basal blotch, appears in summer.
Cultivation Needs rich, damp, sandy soil. *Height to 60cm (2ft); spread to 30cm (1ft). USZ 9–11, surviving -6.5°C (20°F) of overnight frost. Needs water in summer.* ●

Above *Zantedeschia albomaculata*, *Helichrysum petiolaris*, and ferns by a spring on the Outeniqua Pass, South Africa

Above *Zantedeschia pentlandii*
Left *Zantedeschia aethiopica*

157

Perennials with Narrow Leaves

Above *Astelia chathamica*

Astelia (Asteliaceae)

The genus *Astelia* consists of about 25 species of large or small, sedge-like perennials, of which a few are grown for their beautiful silvery leaves. Most are natives of New Zealand, with isolated species in Réunion, Polynesia, Mauritius, Australia, and the Falkland Islands. The flowers are insignificant, the male and female ones being on different plants; the females produce berry-like fruit.

Astelia chathamica
This clump-forming perennial is found wild in wet peaty places on Chatham Island, east of New Zealand. The silvery linear leaves are 0.6–2m (2–6½ft) long, 4–10cm (1½–4in) wide, and bend over at the tip. The fruit is orange.
Cultivation Grow in peaty sandy soil. *Height to 1.5m (5ft); spread to 4m (13ft). USZ 9–11, surviving -6.5°C (20°F) of overnight frost. Needs year-round water.* ●

Astelia nervosa
This tussock-forming perennial with stiff, arching, silvery leaves is a native of New Zealand, growing in open forest and tussock grassland. The linear leaves are

Above *Astelia nervosa*

0.5–1.5m (2–5ft) long, 2–4cm (¾–1½in) wide, and do not bend over at the tips. The fruits are orange to almost red.
Cultivation Grow in peaty sandy soil. *Height to 1.5m (5ft); spread to 4m (13ft). USZ 9–11, surviving -6.5°C (20°F) of overnight frost. Needs year-round water.* ●

Phormium (Phormiaceae)
NEW ZEALAND FLAX

The genus *Phormium* contains two species of evergreen perennials, which are native to New Zealand. The strong fibres in the linear leaves were used by the Maoris for cloth, rope, and netting. Many colour forms have been selected as ornamentals. The tubular flowers are borne on erect leafless stalks.

Anigozanthus (Haemodoraceae)
KANGAROO PAW

Anigozanthus is a genus of around 12 species of perennials with tufted rhizomes, all from Western Australia. They grow in heathy sandy places that are damp in winter and spring, drier in summer.

Anigozanthus flavidus
This tufted perennial from Western Australia is one of the tallest and most easily grown *Anigozanthus*, and a parent of many garden hybrids. It has flat leaves to 1m (3ft) long and 3cm (1¼in) wide. The tubular flowers, 3–5cm (1¼–2in) long, are velvet-haired outside and split on one side, usually yellow, but sometimes red, orange, pink, or green. They appear in summer.
Cultivation Needs sun, sandy, acid soil, and water in spring. Dislikes frost. Is particularly susceptible to snail damage. *Height to 2m (6½ft); spread to 4m (13ft). USZ 10–11, surviving -1°C (30°F) of overnight frost. Tolerant of summer drought.* ◗

Above *Anigozanthus flavidus* in Sydney Harbour Botanic Garden, Australia

Phormium cookianum

This clump-forming perennial from New Zealand has soft arching leaves, usually less than 2m (6½ft) long, and hanging twisted seed pods, which are round in section. The arching flower stalk bears orange or yellow blooms, 2.5–4cm (1–1½in) long, in summer.
Cultivation Easily grown in any soil. Mulch well in dry areas.
Height to 1.5m (5ft); spread to 2m (6½ft).
USZ 9–11, surviving -3°C (27°F) of overnight
frost. Tolerant of summer drought. ●

Phormium tenax

This stiff upright perennial from New Zealand has leaves to 3m (10ft) tall and an erect flower stalk with dark red flowers, 2.5–5cm (1–2in) long, in summer. The seed pods are erect, three-sided, and straight.
Cultivation Easily grown in moist soil.
Height to 3m (10ft); spread to 2m (6½ft).
USZ 9–11, surviving -6.5°C (20°F) of frost.
Tolerates short periods of drought. ●

Above *Phormium cookianum*

Above *Wachendorfia thyrsiflora*

Wachendorfia (Haemodoraceae)

The genus *Wachendorfia* contains four species of tuberous perennials from the Cape area of South Africa. All have upright stems and yellow, orange, or brown flowers.

Wachendorfia thyrsiflora

This stiff perennial from the Cape produces pleated leaves, around 60cm (2ft) long, and spikes of star-shaped, deep yellow flowers, around 3cm (1¼in) across, with a red spot on each petal, in summer.
Cultivation Easily grown in any moist soil, preferably peaty or deep and sandy.
Height to 1.2m (4ft); spread to 1m (3ft).
USZ 10–11, surviving -1°C (30°F) of overnight
frost. Needs water in summer. ◑

Right *Phormium tenax* naturalized in Connemara in western Ireland

Agapanthus & Relatives

Above *Agapanthus praecox* subsp. *orientalis*

Above *Agapanthus inapertus* 'Graskop'

Agapanthus (Agapanthaceae)

The genus *Agapanthus* contains around nine species of evergreen and deciduous perennials from southern Africa. Some species are found in the winter-rainfall area of the Cape, others in the summer-rainfall areas of Natal and the Drakensberg. The flowers are blue, rarely white in garden forms, and may be tubular or with recurved petals, but are usually something in between. The summer-rainfall species are usually deciduous, frost-hardy, and need water in summer; the species from the winter-rainfall area are evergreen and will not tolerate hard frost.

Agapanthus inapertus 'Graskop'

This perennial is a particularly dark blue-flowered form of *A. inapertus* subsp. *pendulus*, which is wild in the summer-rainfall area of the Transvaal. The linear leaves are deciduous, 2–3cm (¾–1¼in) across. The tubular flowers, 2.5–4cm (1–1½in) long, appear in summer.
Cultivation Easily grown in any fertile rich soil in sun or light shade.
Height to 1.8m (6½ft); spread to 1m (3ft). USZ 9–11, surviving -6.5°C (20°F) of overnight frost. Needs water in summer. ◑

Agapanthus praecox subsp. *orientalis*

This evergreen perennial has long-lasting umbels of blue, half-open flowers, 4–5cm (1½–2in) long, in summer. It grows wild from the eastern Cape to western Natal, in both summer- and winter-rainfall areas. Its linear leaves are 2.5–5cm (1–2in) wide.
Cultivation Easily grown in any fertile sandy soil. Give water in spring and a deep mulch in summer-dry areas.
Height to 1m (3ft); spread to 2m (6½ft). USZ 10–11, surviving -1°C (30°F) of overnight frost. Tolerant of summer drought. ◑

Opposite page *Tradescantia pallida* wild in Mexico

Above *Alstroemeria ligtu* hybrids

Alstroemeria (Alstroemeriaceae)

Alstroemeria contains around 50 species of perennials from South America. Many have large loose heads of bright pink flowers with yellow batches and brown stripes on the upper inner pair of petals. Many of the species are difficult to tell apart, and this problem is compounded by the ease with which the species hybridize in gardens. The *ligtu* hybrids have wide heads with many small flowers. Larger-flowered named cultivars, such as the Princess Series, which were bred for the cut-flower trade, are triploid and sterile; these excellent, long-lived garden plants are available in a range of beautiful colours.

Alstroemeria ligtu hybrids
These particularly free-flowering perennials send up flowering stems from creeping fleshy roots, in summer. The narrow leaves are scattered up the stem. The flat flowers, 5–8cm (2–3in) across, are white, pink, purplish, or reddish, streaked with purple, red, or yellow.
Cultivation Easily grown in well-drained stony or rocky soil.
Height to 60cm (2ft); spread to 2m (6½ft).
USZ 9–11, surviving -6.5°C (20°F) of overnight frost. Tolerant of summer drought. ◑

Tradescantia (Commelinaceae)

Tradescantia contains around 65 species from North and South America. Some are hardy perennials from woods in the Appalachians; others are subtropical evergreens, from dry regions of Mexico, and are popular as houseplants and in subtropical gardens.

Tradescantia pallida
(syn. *Setcreasea purpurea*)
This evergreeen perennial grows wild in central Mexico, forming wide patches on shallow limestone soils. The dark purple leaves are 8–15cm (3–6in) long. Pale pink flowers, 1.5–2cm (½–¾in) across, appear in summer.
Cultivation Easily grown in frost-free areas in rocky soil, with some rain in dry summers.
Height to 40cm (16in); spread to 2m (6½ft).
USZ 10–11, surviving -1°C (30°F) of overnight frost. Tolerant of summer drought. ◑

Tradescantia sillamontana
This tuberous-rooted, evergreen perennial is wild in northern Mexico, and has woolly-haired, creeping stems, reaching 30cm (1ft) long. The overlapping leaves are 4–6cm (1½–2½in) long. Purplish pink flowers, 2cm (¾in) across, are borne in summer.
Cultivation Easily grown in frost-free areas, with some rain in dry summers.
Height to 20cm (8in); spread to 2m (6½ft).
USZ 10–11, surviving -1°C (30°F) of overnight frost. Tolerant of summer drought. ◑

Above *Tradescantia sillamontana*

Cool-growing Orchids

Above *Bletilla striata*

Above *Bletilla ochracea*

Left *Aerangis kotschyana*

Aerangis (Orchidaceae)

The genus *Aerangis* contains 35 species of evergreen epiphytic orchids, from tropical Africa and Madagascar. They have tough leathery leaves and hanging spikes of small, sweetly scented flowers.

Aerangis kotschyana
This epiphytic orchid grows on tree branches in mountains from Ethiopia and Guinea to Zaire and the Transvaal. It has long twisted spurs, to 27cm (10½in) long. The leaves, to 15cm (6in) long, are broad and blunt or slightly two-lobed at the apex. The evening-scented, white flowers, to 5cm (2in) across, appear in early summer.
Cultivation Needs alternate warm wet and cooler dry periods to flower well. In a frost-free climate plant on a branch, or on a piece of bark.
Height to 20cm (8in); spread to 15cm (6in). USZ 10–11, surviving -1°C (30°F) of overnight frost. Tolerant of summer drought. ◗

Bletilla (Orchidaceae)

Bletilla is a genus of around 10 species of deciduous terrestrial orchids, from eastern Asia, growing on rocks by rivers and on steep banks or cliffs.

Bletilla ochracea
This pale yellow-flowered orchid is a native of Hubei to southwest Sichuan, in China, growing on mossy banks, rocks, and cliffs. The linear to lance-shaped leaves, to 30cm (1ft) long, are pleated, 3–6 in a shoot and 5cm (2in) wide. The flowers, 5cm (2in) across, appear in late spring.
Cultivation Grow in loose, leafy, and sandy soil. Keep rather dry in winter.
Height and spread to 20cm (8in). USZ 9–11, surviving -6.5°C (20°F) of overnight frost. Requires water in summer. ◗

Bletilla striata
This is a commonly grown orchid from China and Japan, where it grows on rocky banks. The irregularly shaped pseudobulb produces fans of bright green leaves, to 50cm (20in) long. They are pleated, oblong to lance-shaped and 5cm (2in) wide. The bright pink and purple flowers are borne in early summer. They are 5cm (2in) across.
Cultivation Needs loose, leafy, and sandy soil. Keep dry in winter.
Height and spread to 75cm (30in). USZ 9–11, surviving -6.5°C (20°F) of overnight frost. Requires water in summer. ◗

Above *Coelogyne nitida*

Eulophia (Orchidaceae)

The genus *Eulophia* consists of around 300 species of terrestrial orchids, mainly from central and southern Africa, but with a few species in tropical America. They have subterranean pseudobulbs, flowering stems arising beside the tuft of pleated leaves, and flowers in a wide range of colours from red, to green, purple, pink, and white.

Eulophia speciosa
This orchid is one of the commonest species of *Eulophia*, and is found wild in grassland and open woodland from southwest Arabia and Ethiopia to Zimbabwe and South Africa. It produces a spike with up to 50 yellow flowers, 2.5–5cm (1–2in) across, with red streaks on the lips, in summer.
Cultivation Grow in loam soil. Keep dry and cool when dormant.
Height to 90cm (3ft); spread to 15cm (6in).
USZ 10–11, surviving -1°C (30°F) of overnight frost. Needs ample water in summer. ●

Above *Eulophia speciosa* in Malawi

Coelogyne (Orchidaceae)

The genus *Coelogyne* consists of around 150 species of epiphytic orchids, from the Himalayas to China, southeast Asia, and the Pacific Islands. Most have pseudobulbs topped by a pair of evergreen leaves, and spikes of flowers produced at the beginning of the growing season. The species shown here thrive in cool subtropical conditions.

Coelogyne cristata
This creeping orchid, a native of the eastern Himalayan foothills, has pairs of narrow leaves, to 30cm (1ft) long. The arching or hanging spikes of up to 10 beautiful white flowers, 8cm (3in) across, have yellow crests on the lips. They are borne in spring.
Cultivation Grow in a shallow container or on a mossy tree or rock. Needs high humidity in summer.
Height to 23cm (9in); spread to 60cm (2ft).
USZ 10–11, surviving -1°C (30°F) of overnight frost. Requires water in summer. ●

Coelogyne nitida (syn. *C. ochracea*)
This tufted orchid, from Nepal, India to northern Burma, China (Yunnan), Thailand, and Laos, produces upright pairs of narrow leaves, to 30cm (1ft) long. The erect spikes of 6 to 8 white flowers, 4cm (1½in) across, with yellow, red-edged blotches on the lips, are carried in spring.
Cultivation As for *C. cristata*.
Height to 15cm (6in); spread to 60cm (2ft).
USZ 10–11, surviving -1°C (30°F) of overnight frost. Needs water in summer. ●

Above *Coelogyne cristata*

163

Cymbidium (Orchidaceae)

This genus contains around 50 species of epiphytic, terrestrial, and lithophytic orchids, from India and the Himalayas to China, Japan, Vietnam, Malaysia, and Australia. Most grow on rocks, in scrub, or in the forks of large trees. The majority are cultivated, and thousands of hybrids have been raised as pot plants and for the cut-flower trade, as the waxy flowers are often long-lasting and many are deliciously scented. Flowering generally takes place in autumn, winter, and spring. *Cymbidium* are among the easiest orchids to grow, provided that they are watered when they become dry, and fed lightly in the growing season. Keep them almost dry and cool when dormant.

Cymbidium 'Alexanderi Album' x Sussex Dawn 'Cold Springs'

This is a modern hybrid, carrying tall arching spikes of green flowers, to 15cm (6in) across, in winter and spring.

Above *Cymbidium* 'Kiwi Sunrise'

Cultivation Easily grown in a mixture mainly of bark and rocks, with some leafmould and loam, in partial shade. *Height to 1.2m (4ft); spread to 2m (6½ft). USZ 10–11, surviving -1°C (30°F) of overnight frost. Needs intermittent summer water.* ◗

Cymbidium 'Kiwi Sunrise'

This hybrid orchid flowers in autumn and winter. It may have 12 or more flowers in an arching spike. They are delicately scented, flesh-pink, with spots and stripes on the petals, and heavy crimson spots on the lip, 7.5cm (3in) across the lower petals.
Cultivation As for *C.* 'Alexanderi Album' x Sussex Dawn 'Cold Springs'. *Height to 60cm (2ft); spread to 1m (3ft). USZ 10–11, surviving -1°C (30°F) of overnight frost. Needs intermittent summer water.* ◗

Above *Cymbidium* old cultivar
Left *Cymbidium* old cultivar

Above *Cymbidium* 'Long John'

Above *Cymbidium* 'Alexanderi Album' x Sussex Dawn 'Cold Springs'

Cymbidium 'Long John'

This hybrid orchid has a rather crowded, erect spike of white flowers, with dark red markings on the lips, and 10cm (4in) across the lower petals, from winter to spring.
Cultivation As for *C.* 'Alexanderi Album' x Sussex Dawn 'Cold Springs'.
Height to 1m (3ft); spread to 60cm (2ft).
USZ 10–11, surviving -1°C (30°F) of overnight frost. Needs intermittent summer water. ◗

Cymbidium lowianum

This clump-forming epiphytic orchid is from northeastern India and Burma. The dark green leaves are to 75cm (30in) long. A spike of up to 25 yellowish green flowers, 7.5–10cm (3–4in) across, with a red blotch on each creamy white lip, open in spring.
Cultivation Grow mainly in bark. Needs moisture in summer, and a cool dry winter.
Height to 60cm (2ft); spread to 1m (3ft).
USZ 10–11, surviving -1°C (30°F) of overnight frost. Needs intermittent summer water. ◗

Cymbidium old cultivar

This hybrid orchid has erect or arching spikes of up to 14 flowers, 12cm (4¾in) across the lower petals. They are scented, pinkish with red lines and spots on a white lip, and open in early spring.
Cultivation As for *C.* 'Alexanderi Album' x Sussex Dawn 'Cold Springs'.
Height to 1.2m (4ft); spread to 1.5m (5ft).
USZ 10–11, surviving -1°C (30°F) of overnight frost. Needs intermittent summer water. ◗

Right *Cymbidium lowianum* near Lijiang, China

Exotic Orchids

Above *Dendrobium nobile*

Above *Dendrobium densiflorum*

Dendrobium densiflorum

This epiphytic orchid grows in the foothills of the Himalayas from Nepal to Burma, normally on tree branches. It forms a clump of narrow pseudobulbs, with 3–5 arching leaves at the apex. The flower spikes emerge from among the leaves in late spring, forming a dense, cylindrical, hanging bunch of creamy white flowers, 4–5cm (1½–2in) across, with a rich yellow lip. **Cultivation** Grow in a small pot or plant on a shady tree. Keep well misted in summer. *Height to 50cm (20in); spread to 30cm (1ft). USZ 11, needing a minimum of 4.5°C (40°F) overnight. Requires summer watering.* ◗

Barkeria (Orchidaceae)

Barkeria is a genus of around 10 species of orchids from South America, mostly from Mexico and Guatemala. They are epiphytic or grow on rocks (epilithic) up to 2,400m (8,000ft). The plants are deciduous or nearly so in winter and must then be kept cool and dry, but frost-free. *Barkeria* is related to *Epidendrum* and *Laelia*.

Barkeria lindleyana

This epiphytic orchid grows wild from Mexico to Costa Rica at up to 2,400m (8,000ft). It has a slender pseudobulb with several leaves, to 15cm (6in) long, 2–4cm (¾–1½in) wide. In early spring, the stems carry lilac flowers, to 7.5cm (3in) across, the lip with a cream centre and darker tip. **Cultivation** Grow in a small pot or pan of moss and stones, or plant on a shady ledge. *Height to 50cm (20in); spread to 20cm (8in). USZ 11, needing a minimum of 4.5°C (40°F) overnight. Requires summer watering.* ◗

Dendrobium (Orchidaceae)

This is one of the most diverse of orchid genera, with more than 900 species from India and China to Australia and New Zealand, with many species in New Guinea. Most species grow either on trees or rocks.

Above *Barkeria lindleyana*

Dendrobium nobile

This epiphytic orchid, from northeastern India to southern China, Laos, and Thailand, grows on sunny rocks and trees. It has cane-like stems with overlapping leaves, and in early spring flowers in groups of 2–4 at each node. The flowers are sweetly scented, around 7.5cm (3in) across, usually pink, white, and purple, but occasionally pure white.

Cultivation Grow in compost of bark, moss, and stones in a small pot. Keep cool and dry except in summer.

Height to 50cm (20in); spread to 60cm (2ft). USZ 10–11, surviving -1°C (30°F) of overnight frost. Needs ample summer water. ◗

Laelia (Orchidaceae)

Laelia consists of around 50 species of epiphytic and epilithic orchids, from Mexico to Peru, Brazil, and the West Indies. Many species grow on rocks, as well as on trees; they have one or two tough, rather fleshy leaves on fairly thin, stiff pseudobulbs.

Laelia anceps

This upright, epiphytic and epilithic orchid has a somewhat creeping rhizome. It is found wild on the eastern side of the mountains in southern Mexico, growing on trees and rocks and flowering in autumn. The flowers, to 10cm (4in) across, are pale pink, with deeper flushes, and a crimson lip. The thick leathery leaves are 15–23cm (6–9in) long and 3–4cm (1¼–1½in) wide.

Cultivation Needs plenty of light and air, and is best grown in a basket, hanging in a tree, or on a wall. Water regularly in summer, letting compost dry out between waterings; keep drier and cooler in winter.

Height to 80cm (32in); spread to 30cm (1ft). USZ 11, needing a minimum of 4.5°C (40°F). Requires intermittent water in summer. ◗

Phaius (Orchidaceae)

This genus contains 30 species of terrestrial orchids with large pleated leaves and upright spikes of flowers. They are found wild from Africa and India to Indonesia, New Guinea, and the Pacific islands.

Phaius tankervilleae

This is one of the largest orchid plants, with clumps of pleated, elliptic to lance-shaped leaves and spikes of 10–20 pink, white, and purple flowers, 10–13cm (4–5in) across, in early summer. The leaves are up to 1m (3ft) tall and 20cm (8in) broad. *P. tankervilleae* is found wild from northern India and China to Indonesia and Australia, growing in forests in the hills.

Cultivation Needs shade, shelter, and leafy soil, with high humidity during the growing season.

Height to 9m (30ft); spread to 6m (20ft). USZ 11, needing a minimum of 4.5°C (40°F) overnight. Requires water in summer. ◗

Above *Laelia anceps*

Below *Phaius tankervilleae* at Kew

Canna & Hedychium

Above *Canna* 'Assault' with *Argyranthemum*, used for summer bedding at Kew

Above *Canna indica* (Indian shot)

Canna (Cannaceae)

The genus *Canna* contains around 50 species of rhizomatous perennials, all native of the American tropics and subtropics. Many are found apparently wild in other tropical areas, but they are escapees from cultivation. Many hybrids and cultivars are grown with variegated leaves and pink, red, yellow, orange, or striped flowers.

Canna 'Assault'
This fine perennial has greyish, broadly lance-shaped leaves, to 30cm (12in) long, and purple stems. The red flowers, 7.5cm (3in) long, are borne in summer.
Cultivation Grow in warmth and rich soil. Keep dry while dormant.
Height to 1m (3ft); spread to 60cm (2ft). USZ 10–11, surviving -1°C (30°F) of overnight frost. Needs summer water. ●

Canna indica
INDIAN SHOT
This perennial is recognized by its bright green, broadly lance-shaped leaves and bright red flowers, to 6.5cm (2¾in) long, in summer. The flowers have the three narrow, petal-like staminodes, which curl back. The seed capsules contains masses of black, shot-like seeds. The leaves are up to 50cm (20in) long. The plant is probably a native of Mexico and has naturalized in Africa, India, and China, among other frost-free areas.
Cultivation Easily grown in warm, rich soil, that is wet in summer, drier in winter.
Height to 1.7m (5½ft); spread to 1m (3ft). USZ 10–11, surviving -1°C (30°F) of overnight frost. Needs water in summer. ●

Canna iridiflora
This perennial has greyish green, banana-like leaves and deep pink, hanging flowers,

Below *Canna iridiflora*

Below *Hedychium coccineum*

to 12cm (4¾in) long, in summer. The petal-like staminodes are joined into a tube at the base. The ovate leaves are to 1m (3ft) long. *C. iridiflora* is a native of Peru.
Cultivation Easily grown in deep, rich soil. In cold areas store roots away from frost.
Height to 3m (10ft); spread to 2m (6½ft). USZ 10–11, surviving -1°C (30°F) of overnight frost. Needs ample water in summer. ◗

Hedychium (Zingiberaceae)
GINGER LILY

Hedychium contains around 40 species of rhizomatous perennials in eastern Asia, from India and the Himalayas to China, with aromatic roots that provide ginger. They are widely grown and naturalized elsewhere, for instance in South America. The stems have overlapping leaves and leaf sheaths. The flowers are mostly scented and consist of a tubular corolla with three narrow petals, three petal-like staminodes (the lower forming a wide lip), and a long slender anther. Some species from the Himalayas survive in frosty areas if well protected with a deep mulch.

Hedychium chrysoleucum
This clump-forming perennial, from northeastern India to southeastern China, has pointed leaves, to 40cm (16in) long, and rounded heads of scented, pale yellow flowers, which meausure 8cm (3in) long, with deep yellow stains on the lip, in the summer.

Cultivation Grow in very wet soil, with as much nitrogen as possible in summer.
Height to 3m (10ft); spread to 6m (20ft). USZ 10–11, surviving -1°C (30°F) of overnight frost. Tolerant of summer drought. ◗

Hedychium coccineum
Dramtic cylindrical heads of red, orange, or salmon-pink scented flowers, to 6cm (2⅖in) long, with long protruding stamens, are produced in late summer and autumn, at the top of the year's shoots. It is native of India and Nepal to Burma, in the foothills. The leaves, 30–40cm (12–16in) long, are pointed.

Cultivation Needs leafy, fertile, warm soil.
Height to 1.5m (5ft); spread to 2m (6½ft). USZ 9–11, surviving -6.5°C (20°F) of overnight frost. Requires water in summer. ◗

Hedychium gardnerianum
Sweetly scented yellow flowers, to 6cm (2⅖in) long, a two-lobed lip, and long stamens, in summer. Leaves are 30–35cm (12–14in) long.
Cultivation Grow in fertile leafy soil in partial shade. Apply liquid feed in summer.
Height to 2m (6½ft); spread to 1m (3ft). USZ 10–11, surviving -1°C (30°F) of overnight frost. Needs water in summer. ◗

Above *Hedychium chrysoleucum*

Above *Hedychium gardnerianum*

Bromeliads

Above *Billbergia nutans*

Billbergia (Bromeliaceae)

Billbergia contains around 2,400 species, all but one of which (in Western Africa) are found wild in America. It includes more than 50 species of mainly epiphytic evergreen perennials, and comprises many popular houseplants and pineapples.

Billbergia nutans
This hardy bromeliad forms large clumps of stiff narrow leaves, 30–70cm (12–28in) long. The arching spikes with pink bracts and blue-and-green flowers, 2.5cm (1in) long, are produced in summer. The petals are twisted. It is a native of South America.

Cultivation Easily grown in any dry shallow soil, preferably in shade.
Height to 60cm (2ft); spread to 1.2m (4ft). USZ 10–11, surviving -1°C (30°F) of overnight frost. Tolerant of summer drought. ◑

Bromelia (Bromeliaceae)

The genus *Bromelia* contains around 48 species of mainly terrestrial perennials, from tropical and subtropical South America.

Bromelia balansae
This suckering bromeliad has bright red leaves and a cluster of small flowers at the apex of the stem, in summer. It is a native of countries from Colombia to Argentina and Paraguay, where it grows in very dry areas. The green leaves, to 1.5m (5ft) long, 3cm (1¼in) wide, turn red at flowering to attract pollinating birds. The petals are crimson, edged with white.

Cultivation Is suitable for any dry soil in a dry garden, but needs plenty of space.
Height to 1m (3ft); spread 3m (10ft) or more. USZ 10–11, surviving -1°C (30°F) of overnight frost. Tolerant of summer drought. ◑

Neoregelia (Bromeliaceae)

The genus *Neoregelia* consists of around 70 species of epiphytic and terrestrial perennials, which are natives of eastern Brazil. *Neoregelia* can be grown in a tree or in a small container.

Neoregelia carolinae
This epiphytic bromeliad is a typical "tank" plant. The leaves are about 40cm (16in) long, 3cm (1¼in) wide, green at first, the central ones becoming red at flowering time. The blooms are very small, in a dense clump in the centre. 'Flandria' has white-edged leaves.

Cultivation Needs little soil, but should be anchored to a branch or put in a pot of bark. Grow in warmth and humidity, especially in summer.
Height to 1m (3ft); spread to 80cm (32in). USZ 11, with a minimum of 4.5°C (40°F) overnight. Requires summer water. ●

Tillandsia (Bromeliaceae)

Tillandsia is a genus of around 400 species from throughout the Americas. Most are epiphytic; many are "airplants", that is plants that are anchored on trees, or even on telephone wires, and trap their water and nutrients in cells on the leaves; they need warm conditions to grow well. The lichen-like airplant *T. usneoides* (Spanish moss) is common in southeastern North America. Some species also produce large, blue-purple flowers.

Above *Bromelia balansae*

Above *Neoregelia carolinae* 'Flandria'

Below *Tillandsia aeranthos*

Below *Tillandsia prodigiosa* growing on a tree in Mexico

Below *Tillandsia cyanea*

Tillandsia aeranthos

This airplant is wild from Brazil and Argentina to Uruguay, growing on trees. The flowering stems are usually horizontal or hang down, and bear tubular, bright pink bracts and deep blue flowers, in summer. The leaves are about 15cm (6in) long, tapering to a long point.
Cultivation Hang in a partially shaded place in summer. Mist occasionally if the weather is dry. Keep drier in winter.
Height to 25cm (10in); spread to 30cm (1ft). USZ 10–11, surviving -1°C (30°F) of overnight frost. Tolerant of summer drought. ◗

Tillandsia cyanea

This epiphytic bromeliad is a "tank" plant and holds water in the expanded bases of its narrow leaves, to 30cm (1ft) long. It grows wild on trees in Ecuador and Peru. The flattened, bright magenta-pink flower spike, 15cm (6in) long, has overlapping bracts, and the big, purplish blue flowers emerge in succession in summer, from between the bracts.
Cultivation Grow in a small pot, or tie on to a tree in frost-free areas.
Height to 20cm (8in), spread to 30cm (1ft). USZ 10–11, surviving -1°C (30°F) of overnight frost. Needs intermittent summer water. ●

Tillandsia prodigiosa

This tufted epiphytic bromeliad has a long hanging inflorescence with well-spaced, red bracts, around 15cm (6in) long. It is a native of Mexico, where it grows on trees in cloud forests, as shown in the photograph above. The broadly linear leaves are around 50cm (20in) long. The flower spike can be 1–2m (3–6½ft) long, with blue and green flowers, around 5cm (2in) long, in summer.

Right *Vrieseia splendens* with ferns and other bromeliads

Cultivation Is best grown on a tree branch or in a hanging basket, because of its long hanging inflorescence. Mist well in hot weather.
Height to 30cm (1ft); spread to 60cm (2ft). USZ 10–11, surviving -1°C (30°F) of overnight frost. Needs water in summer. ●

Vrieseia (Bromeliaceae)

Vriesia is a genus of around 250 species of mainly epiphytic perennials, which are natives of central and South America and the West Indies.

Vrieseia splendens

This epiphytic or terrestrial bromeliad, from tropical South America, is a "tank" plant with banded rosetted leaves, 30–40cm (12–16in) long, and red flattened spikes of small yellow flowers, in summer.
Cultivation As for *N. carolinae.*
Height to 1m (3ft); spread to 30cm (1ft). USZ 11, needing a minimum of 4.5°C (40°F) overnight. Requires water in summer. ●

Grasses

Cyperus (Cyperaceae)

The genus *Cyperus* has around 300 species of annual or perennial rhizomatous herbs (sedges), from tropical areas of the world. There are many ornamental species, under a confusing array of names, but, in addition to those shown here, it is worth seeking out *C. involucratus*, from Africa, which produces elegant, slender, green bracts; alternatively, try its cream-variegated form.

Cyperus glomeratus

This annual or perennial, from Central and southeastern Europe, has narrow leaves and stiffly upright stems with dense clusters of green bracts and brownish flowers, in summer.
Cultivation Grow in fertile moist soil in sun or partial shade.
Height to 1m (3ft); spread to 60cm (2ft). USZ 8–11, surviving -12°C (10°F) of overnight frost. Requires water in summer. ◗

Cyperus papyrus

PAPYRUS

This aquatic perennial is from central Africa north to Egypt, and has also naturalized in Sicily. It is very attractive when used as an "architectural" plant. The graceful arching stems arise from short stout rhizomes. The inflorescence is produced in summer and comprises an umbrella-shaped cluster of hanging threadlike branches. Pith from the stems was the source of papyrus, which was used instead of paper in ancient times.

Above *Cyperus papyrus* (papyrus) in a pool at La Mortola, Italy

Above *Cyperus glomeratus*

Above *Miscanthus sinensis* in Hong Kong

Cultivation Grow in shallow water, as a marginal plant for pools, or in fertile, moist soil in full sun or partial shade. Is best culivated in a sheltered place to avoid damage to the stems.
Height to 3m (10ft); spread to 2m (6½ft). USZ 11, needing a minimum of 4.5°C (40°F) overnight. Requires water in summer. ◗

Hordeum (Graminae)

The genus *Hordeum* contains around 20 species of annual or perennial grasses, which are natives of Europe and North America. Many species are grown for their ornamental flowerheads, and some have been developed as food crops.

Hordeum jubatum
FOXTAIL BARLEY
This perennial grass, from North America and northeastern Asia, has long, strap-like leaves and flowers carried in nodding, pale green to purple-tinged, dense, soft, bristly spikes, in summer.
Cultivation Grow in light, slightly moist but well-drained soil, in full sun.
Height and spread to 60cm (2ft). USZ 7–11, surviving -17°C (2°F) of overnight frost. Reasonably tolerant of summer drought. ◑

Miscanthus (Graminae)

The genus *Miscanthus* contains around 20 species of grasses, which are natives of the tropical areas of southern Africa and eastern Asia. They are now cultivated as biomass and dust-free bedding for horses.

Below *Hordeum jubatum* (foxtail barley)

Miscanthus sinensis
This beautiful, clump-forming perennial grass, from China, Taiwan, and Japan, produces upright stems and long, narrow, green leaves. The drooping racemes of white or purplish spikelets are borne from late summer to autumn. There are numerous cultivars with varied foliage colours, including: 'Sarabande' with a silvery longitudinal stripe on the leaf; 'Strictus' with yellow horizontal bands; and 'Zebrinus' with white horizontal stripes.
Cultivation Grow in any reasonably fertile, deep soil in full sun or partial shade. Can become invasive.
Height to 2m (6½ft); spread around1m (3ft). USZ 7–11, surviving -17°C (2°F) of overnight frost. Requires a little moisture in summer. ◗

Stipa (Graminae)

Stipa is a varied genus with around 300 species of mainly perennial grasses, from Europe and southern Asia. *S. pulcherrima* is smaller and tougher than *S. gigantea* and produces spikelets with long, silky, hairy awns during summer.

Stipa gigantea
GIANT FEATHER GRASS
This clump-forming perennial grass, from Spain and Portugal, bears narrow arching leaves and loose clusters of creamy yellow spikelets, in spring.
Cultivation Grow in well-drained soil. Needs water until it is established.
Height to 2.4m (8ft); spread to 1m (3ft). USZ 8–11, surviving -12°C (10°F) of overnight frost. Reasonably tolerant of summer drought once established. ◑

Left *Stipa gigantea* (giant feather grass) with a background of *Cotinus coggygria*

Bamboos

Below *Chusquea culeou* behind large-leaved *Gunnera manicata*

Chimonobambusa (Graminae)

The genus *Chimonobambusa* has around 10 species of bamboos, which have invasive running rhizomes. They are natives of the Himalayas, China, and Japan.

Chimonobambusa tumidissinoda
CHINESE WALKING STICK
This spreading bamboo, from western China, has graceful green canes with conspicuous swollen nodes. The narrow leaf shoots appear in late summer. It has only recently been introduced into western gardens, where it has gained immediate popularity for its striking architectural appearance.
Cultivation Grow in fertile soil in partial shade. Warning! This is an extremely invasive plant, so cut it back regularly.
Height to 5m (16ft); spread to 10m (33ft).

USZ 8–11, surviving -12°C (10°F) of overnight frost. Tolerant of summer drought. ●

Chusquea (Graminae)

The genus *Chusquea* contains around 120 species of bamboos, from tropical and temperate parts of South America.

Chusquea culeou
This slow-growing bamboo, from Chile and Argentina, eventually forms a dense thicket, spreading by means of creeping rhizomes. It has narrow, olive-green, arching canes clothed with dense tufts of small, pale green leaves. Unlike most other bamboos, in which the canes are hollow, these have pith-filled canes, which helps to identify them. Although not a natural choice for a dry garden, *C. culeou* can be accommodated

with careful siting and is excellent for its architectural properties.
Cultivation Grow in fertile, moist soil in a sheltered position, or in a large pot.
Height and spread to 6m (20ft). USZ 8–11, surviving -12°C (10°F) of overnight frost. Requires water in summer. ●

Phyllostachys (Graminae)

The genus *Phyllostachys* contains around 55 species of bamboos, which are natives of the Himalayas east to Japan. It contains many highly ornamental species, which in turn have given rise to a number of forms, hybrids, and cultivars. These bamboos not only make attractive architectural plants but also produce wonderfully varied and patterned canes, which can be used for decorative purposes, for example as plant

Above *Phyllostachys vivax 'Aureocaulis'*

Above *Chimonobambusa tumidissinoda*

Above *Pleioblastus gramineus*

supports. Also reasonably drought tolerant is *P. aurea*, with its smooth, grey- or brown-yellow canes, and crowded nodes at the base.

Phyllostachys pubescens
This bamboo has smooth canes, 30cm (1ft) in diameter, greyish when young, and later yellowish. The leaves are 5–10cm (2–4in) long. Leafy sheaths and internodes are hairy.
Cultivation Grow in rich, moist soil, sheltered from harsh winds. Water especially when young; also feed when growing.
Height to 20m (65ft); spread to 10m (33ft). USZ 9–11, surviving –6.5°C (20°F) of overnight frost. Requires water in summer. ◑

Phyllostachys vivax
This vigorous species, from eastern China, has leaves, 15–20cm (6–8in) long, and yellow canes, to 3cm (1¼in) in diameter. 'Aureocaulis' has rich golden-yellow canes.
Cultivation As for *P. pubescens*.
Height to 5m (16ft); spread to 3m (10ft). USZ 8–11, surviving -12°C (10°F) of overnight frost. Requires water in summer. ◑

Pleioblastus (Graminae)

The genus *Pleioblastus* contains around 20 species of clump-forming or long-running bamboos, which are found wild in China

Right *Phyllostachys pubescens* with *Acanthus*, at Ninfa in Italy.

and Japan. Many were formerly included in *Arundinaria*. They tend to have slender hollow but thick-walled canes.

Pleioblastus gramineus
(syn. *Arundinaria graminea*)
This bamboo, a native of southern Japan, forms dense clumps. The linear leaves are

up to 30cm (1ft) long and around 1.2cm (½in) across. The green canes are covered in persistent leaf sheaths.
Cultivation Grow in moist, rich soil in partial shade and a sheltered position.
Height and spread to 3m (10ft). USZ 9–11, surviving -6.5°C (20°F) of overnight frost. Requires water in summer. ●

175

Stocks & Wallflowers

Anemone (Rununculaceae)

The genus *Anemone* comprises around 144 widely varying species of perennials, natives of Europe, southern and eastern Africa, America, Asia, and Sumatra.

Anemone hupehensis

This beautiful perennial, from central and western China, has slender upright stems clothed with groups of three stalked, dark green leaflets. The umbels of white, pale pink, or purplish pink flowers, with a showy central boss of golden stamens, are borne from late summer to autumn. Var. *japonica* has narrow petals, and has been crossed with *A. vitifolia* to produce a late-flowering plant and several cultivars.
Cultivation Grow in any fertile soil in sun or partial shade. Is happy in cracks in walls. Do not allow the roots to dry completely.
Height to 1m (3ft); spread to 60cm (2ft). USZ 8–11, surviving -12°C (10°F) of overnight frost. Requires water in summer. ◗

Above *Dianthus caryophyllus* 'Old Spice'

Above *Iberis gibraltarica* on the Rock of Gibraltar

Dianthus (Caryophyllaceae)

The genus *Dianthus* has around 300 species of perennial, biennial, and annual pinks and carnations, natives of Asia, Europe, North America, and northern Africa. Most garden pinks are derived from *D. plumarius*, and the carnations from *D. caryophyllus*. Most have attractive flowers, a clove-like scent, and last well in water when cut.

Dianthus caryophyllus 'Old Spice'
(syn. *D. caryophyllus* 'Old Red Clove')
CLOVE CARNATION; GILLYFLOWER
This perennial is a very old garden form of *D. caryophyllus*, from southern Europe, dating from the 16th century. It produces greyish green foliage, dark red flowers, and an exquisite scent.
Cultivation Grow in well-drained soil, in pots or on a wall, in full sun. Renew every few years, from root cuttings or by seed.
Height to 60cm (2ft); spread to 30cm (1ft). USZ 8–11, surviving -12°C (10°F) of overnight frost. Tolerant of summer drought. ◑

Erysimum (Cruciferae)

This genus contains around 200 species of annuals, biennials, and perennials, natives of Asia, California, and Europe. *E. cheiri*

(wallflower) is a common feature of ancient walls in Europe, and is the parent of many garden hybrids, which are often grown as biennials in cooler climates.

Erysimum bicolor
This much-branched shrubby perennial, from Madeira and the Canaries, has slightly scented, cream and pink flowers in winter and early spring. The leaves are green.
Cultivation Grow in moist soil in a partially shaded position.
Height to 1m (3ft); spread to 60cm (2ft). USZ 10–11, surviving -1°C (30°F) or maybe lower of overnight frost. Requires a little water in summer. ◗

Erysimum 'Bowles' Mauve'
This shrubby perennial forms a mound of greyish leaves. The cream flowers, becoming mauve, are borne from spring to summer.
Cultivation Grow in poor, well-drained soil in sun or partial shade.
Height and spread to 30cm (1ft). USZ 8–11, surviving -12°C (10°F) of overnight frost. Tolerant of summer drought. ◑

Iberis (Cruciferae)

The genus *Iberis* has around 40 species of annuals, biennials, and perennials, sometimes shrubby at the base. They are natives of the Mediterranean, especially of northern Africa, Portugal, and Spain.

Iberis gibraltarica
GIBRALTAR CANDYTUFT

This compact, evergreen, shrubby perennial, sometimes treated as an annual, is from Gibraltar and Morocco. It has fleshy leaves, slender stems, and flat heads of white, pink, or pale mauve flowers, in early spring.
Cultivation Grow in well-drained but slightly moist soil in partial shade.
Height to 30cm (1ft); spread to 60cm (2ft). USZ 9–11, surviving -6.5°C (20°F) of overnight frost. Tolerant of summer drought. ◑

Matthiola (Cruciferae)

Matthiola comprises around 55 species of annuals, biennials, or perennials, which are natives of Europe and Asia.

Matthiola incana

This shrubby perennial is from Arabia, western Europe, and the Mediterranean and has naturalized on the California coast. It has narrow, greyish green leaves and sweetly scented, pinkish white flowers in early summer. This species has been used to breed several of the cultivated annual and biennial stocks commercially available.
Cultivation Grow in well-drained, sandy soil in a sunny, sheltered place.
Height to 1m (3ft); spread to 45cm (18in). USZ 9–11, surviving -6.5°C (20°F) of overnight frost. Tolerant of summer drought. ◑

Above *Matthiola incana*

Above *Erysimum bicolor*

Above *Erysimum* 'Bowles' Mauve'

The Hollyhock Family

Alcea (Malvaceae)
HOLLYHOCK

The genus *Alcea* has around 50 species of
perennials and biennials, which are from
southeastern Europe and Asia, with some
naturalized around the Mediterranean.
Alcea rosea is found in gardens across
Europe and Asia, and has been so long in
cultivation that its exact parentage is
unknown, although it is probably a hybrid
between *A. pallida* and *A. setosa*. Forms of
this are available in a variety of colours, and
with single or double flowers, and are
commonly available from seed companies.
A. setosa is a tall perennial, with white or
pink flowers in early to midsummer, from
Crete, Cyprus, western Syria, and Turkey.
Because of the height of their flowering
stems, most hollyhocks need the support of
a stake if grown in an exposed position.

Alcea pallida
This very variable perennial is a native of
Hungary, the Balkan peninsula, and Turkey.
It has downy upright stems and thick,
shallowly lobed leaves. The white, pink, or
lilac flowers, usually with yellowish bases
to the petals, appear in summer.
Cultivation Grow in fertile, well-drained
soil in a hot dry position.
Height to 2m (6½ft); spread to 1m (3ft).
USZ 8–11, surviving –12°C (10°F) of
overnight frost. Tolerant of summer drought. ◗

Alcea rugosa
This elegant hollyhock with a stout woody
rootstock is from Armenia, the Caucasus,
Iran, Turkey, and southern Russia. The
upright bristly stems are purple spotted,

Above *Alcea rugosa*

Above *Anisodontea scabrosa*
Left *Alcea pallida* growing wild on the coast of Turkey

and the pale yellow flowers are carried
on short stalks in summer. The leaves are
rough and lobed.
Cultivation Grow in dry, well-drained soil
in full sun.
Height to 2.4m (8ft); spread to 1m (3ft).
USZ 7–11, surviving -17°C (2°F) of overnight
frost. Tolerant of summer drought. ◑

Anisodontea (Malvaceae)

The genus *Anisodontea* has around 19
species of evergreen perennials, shrubs,
and subshrubs, which are natives of South
Africa, north to Namibia and Lesotho.

Above *Sphaeralcea emoryi* in the desert near Palm Springs, California

A. capensis bears magenta flowers, while *A. × hypomadara* has larger leaves and pinkish purple flowers.

Anisodontea scabrosa

This spreading or upright, shrubby perennial is from South Africa, from the Western Cape east to Natal. It has rounded leaves and pale pink flowers, often deeper pink at the base, flowering for most of the year. The rounded, lobed, light green leaves are often sticky and scented.
Cultivation Needs well-drained soil in sun.
Height to 2m (6½ft); spread to 1m (3ft).
USZ 10–11, surviving –1°C (30°F) of
overnight frost. Tolerant of summer drought. ☽

Sphaeralcea (Malvaceae)

The genus *Sphaeralcea* contains around 60 species of perennials, which are often shrubby at the base, and sometimes creeping. They are natives of Arizona, and dry areas in the western states of North America and into south Mexico. *S. munroana* is a creeping plant, with deeply divided, greyish leaves, felted stems, and brilliant coral-pink flowers in summer.

Right *Sphaeralcea ambigua* (desert mallow) in the Anza-Borrego Desert, California

Sphaeralcea ambigua
DESERT MALLOW
This many-stemmed perennial, shrubby at the base, is from the southern USA and Mexico. It bears orange or pinkish flowers, to 3.5cm (1½in) long, in summer. The thick, toothed leaves are covered with white felt.
Cultivation Grow in dry, well-drained soil in sun. Thrives in near-desert conditions.
Height to 1.5m (5ft); spread to 1m (3ft).
USZ 9–11, surviving -6.5°C (20°F) of
overnight frost. Tolerant of summer drought. ☽

Sphaeralcea emoryi
This upright, many-stemmed perennial, from the arid regions of southwestern North America, has narrow, rather thick leaves covered with white felt. The red, orange, or pinkish flowers, to 2.5cm (1in) long, are borne throughout the summer.
Cultivation Grow in well-drained, dry soil in full sun. Thrives in very dry conditions.
Height to 1.5m (5ft); spread to 1m (3ft).
USZ 9–11, surviving -6.5°C (20°F) of
overnight frost. Tolerant of summer drought. ☽

179

Californian Perennials

Limonium (Plumbaginaceae)
SEA LAVENDER, STATICE

The genus *Limonium* comprises around 350 species of perennials, annuals, and subshrubs, distributed worldwide but found especially in salt marshes and in the arid regions of the northern hemisphere. Some 15 species of sea lavender are found only on the Canary Islands, including *L. perezii* which has become naturalized in California. This large perennial has masses of deep blue calyces and white flowers.

Limonium arborescens
This large perennial, shrubby at the base, is a native of Tenerife, where it is endangered. The leaves are ovate with a long stalk. The winged, flowering stem and branches bear clusters of striking, deep purplish blue calyces and white flowers in winter.

Above *Limonium arborescens* in the Princess of Wales House at Kew

Above *Oenothera deltoides* subsp. *deltoides* in the Californian desert

Cultivation Grow in well-drained soil. *Height to 1.8m (6ft); spread to 1m (3ft). USZ 10–11, surviving -1°C (30°F) of overnight frost. Tolerant of summer drought.* ◑

Oenothera (Onagraceae)
EVENING PRIMROSE

This genus contains around 120 species of annuals and perennials, which are natives of Mexico and parts of southern North America. Many species have naturalized in Europe and elsewhere, and all have hybridized, with a resulting confusion in the names. Most are excellent plants for hot dry gardens, thriving on neglect and drought; however, they seed freely and can become weeds. *Oenothera* flowers open in the evening, giving rise to the name "evening primrose".

Oenothera deltoides
This spreading annual or perennial is from Arizona to California and Baja California. It has a short central stem and spreading branches with greyish green, hairy leaves. The large white flowers open at dusk in spring and fade to pink. Subsp. *deltoides* is an annual, for desert areas, while subsp. *eurekensis* is a perennial for coastal regions.
Cultivation Thrives in dry sandy soil, with water in winter and spring. *Height and spread to 30cm (1ft). USZ 10–11, surviving -1°C (30°F) or lower of overnight frost. Tolerant of summer drought.*◑

Oenothera speciosa
This perennial is from western and central North America south to Mexico, and has naturalized in other parts of the USA. It has creeping underground rhizomes, from which arise stems with narrowish leaves. The white or pale pink flowers, nodding in bud, open in summer. 'Siskiyou' carries pale pink to mauve ones.

Right *Oenothera speciosa* 'Siskiyou'

180

Above *Oenothera stubbii*

Above *Osbeckia stellata* var. *yunnanensis* in China

Cultivation Grow in well-drained soil in full sun. Keep rather dry in winter. *Height and spread to 30cm (1ft). USZ 8–11, surviving -12°C (10°F) of overnight frost. Tolerant of summer drought.* ◑

Oenothera stubbii
This creeping perennial from Mexico has long rooting runners and narrow leaves. The bright yellow flowers, with exceptionally long floral tubes, open in summer. They fade to orange on hot days. **Cultivation** Grow as a ground-covering plant in well-drained soil in full sun. *Height to 10cm (4in); spread 1.8m (6ft) or more. USZ 9–11, surviving -6.5°C (20°F) of overnight frost. Tolerant of summer drought.* ◑

Osbeckia (Melastomataceae)

Osbeckia contains around 50 species of perennials, subshrubs, and evergreen shrubs, natives of Africa, Asia, and Australia.

Osbeckia stellata var. yunnanensis
This variable perennial or subshrub, from the foothills of the Himalayas, has upright stems and pinkish or purplish, four-petalled flowers, in summer and autumn. **Cultivation** Grow in well-drained but moisture-retentive, peaty soil in sun. *Height to 60cm (2ft); spread to 30cm (1ft). USZ 9–11, surviving -6.5°C (20°F) of overnight frost. Requires water in summer.* ◑

Zauschneria (Onagraceae)

The genus *Zauschneria* has around four species and as many subspecies of subshrubby perennials, which are natives of western North America.

Zauschneria californica subsp. cana
(syn. *Epilobium canum* subsp. *canum*)
CALIFORNIAN FUCHSIA
This perennial has a creeping underground rootstock and is a native of California south

to Baja California. The silky-haired leaves are narrow and dark green, and the tubular flowers are scarlet from summer to autumn. This species illustrates how hummingbird pollination can push the evolution of flowers, towards red colour, a long tube to hold ample nectar and exserted style and stamens to touch the bird's head. **Cultivation** Grow in well-drained soil in or on a wall or rock crevice. *Height to 30cm (1ft); spread to 60cm (2ft). USZ 9–11, surviving -6.5°C (20°F) of overnight frost. Tolerant of summer drought.* ◑

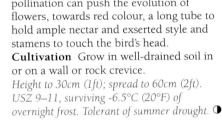

Above *Zauschneria californica* subsp. *cana* (Californian fuchsia)

Begonia & Impatiens

Begonia (Begoniaceae)

The genus *Begonia* consists of around 900 species of annuals, perennials, and subshrubs. Most are natives of subtropical and tropical regions of the Americas, but many species are also found in Asia, and a few in other parts of the world. There is great variety of form and flower in such a large genus, with some species producing fibrous roots, while others have rhizomes or tubers. As a general rule, most begonias should be watered regularly in hot, dry weather, and kept nearly dry (in the case of fibrous-rooted species) or completely dry (if tuberous-rooted) in winter, when the plants become almost dormant. Many annual species are grown for bedding in summer, but the species shown here are perennials.

Begonia boliviensis

This tuberous perennial, from Bolivia and Argentina, has upright, slightly succulent, green or purple stems and drooping branches bearing pendulous red flowers and long narrow tepals, in summer. The green leaves are elongated heart-shaped. Some trailing hybrids are excellent in hanging baskets and pots.
Cultivation Grow in moist, leafy, well-drained soil in sun or partial shade.
Height and spread to 1m (3ft). USZ 11, needing a minimum of 4.5°C (40°F) overnight. Requires water in summer. ◗

Begonia luxurians

PALM-LEAF BEGONIA
This subshrub from Brazil has fibrous roots, thick, red, fleshy stems, and dark green, palmate leaves. The upright frothy clusters of tiny white flowers are carried in summer.

Above *Begonia boliviensis* in a forest in Argentina

Cultivation Grow in fertile, rich, leafy, sandy soil, with ample water all year round.
Height to 1.5m (5ft); spread to 1m (3ft). USZ 11, needing minimum of 4.5°C (40°F) overnight. Requires water in summer. ●

Begonia minor

This fibrous-rooted subshrub, with slender, red, fleshy stems, is from originally from Jamaica but reached Europe in the 16th century. The heart-shaped, shiny, dark green leaves have wavy cream edges. Racemes of scented, pink and white flowers are borne most of the year. 'Rosea' has bright pink blooms.
Cultivation Needs sandy, humus-rich soil. Keep drier when flowering in cool weather.
Height to 2m (6½ft); spread to 1m (3ft). USZ 11, needing a minimum of 4.5°C (40°F) overnight. Requires water in summer. ●

Above *Begonia sutherlandii* in Natal, South Africa
Left *Begonia luxurians* (palm-leaf begonia)

Begonia sutherlandii

This tuberous-rooted, spreading and pendulous perennial is from South Africa, where it grows on mossy rocks and tree trunks in the forest. It has reddish fleshy stems, bright green, toothed, obliquely lance-shaped leaves, and small, apricot-coloured flowers, during late summer.
Cultivation Needs moist soil in partial shade, with the tubers kept dry in winter. *Height and spread to 75cm (2½ft). USZ 11, needing a minimum of 4.5°C (40°F) overnight. Requires water in summer.* ◗

Impatiens (Balsaminaceae)

The genus *Impatiens* contains around 850 species of annuals, perennials, and subshrubs, which are natives of most areas of the world, with the exception of South America and Australasia.

Impatiens sodenii

This robust, almost shrubby perennial, from Kenya and Tanzania, has succulent stems, dense whorls of leaves, and flat, pale pink or white flowers, 5cm (2in) across, all the year, once the plant is mature.
Cultivation Grow in fertile soil in full sun. *Height to 1.2m (4ft); spread to 60cm (2ft). USZ 10–11, just surviving -1°C (30°F) of overnight frost. Requires water in summer.* ●

Impatiens tinctoria subsp. tinctoria

This long-lived perennial is a native of eastern Africa. It has fleshy tuberous roots and succulent stems, and leaves in whorls or opposite. Scented, long-spurred, white flowers, 4cm (1½in) across, often with a red streak towards the base, appear in summer.
Cultivation Best in moist soil in dappled shade and in a sheltered position. *Height to 2m (6½ft); spread to 1m (3ft). USZ 10–11, surviving -1°C (30°F) of overnight frost. Requires water in summer.* ◗

Above *Begonia minor* 'Rosea'

Above *Impatiens sodenii*
Right *Impatiens tinctoria* subsp. *tinctoria*

Pelargoniums

Pelargonium (Geraniaceae)

The genus *Pelargonium* has around 280
species of tuberous or creeping perennials,
annuals, and succulent or wiry, evergreen
shrubs and subshrubs. Many are natives of
South Africa, but they are also found in
eastern Africa to the Arabian peninsula,
southern Turkey and northern Iraq,
Australia, and New Zealand. There are also
many cultivars, forms, and hybrids. For
more scented and wild species, *see* pp.186–7.

Pelargonium 'Blandfordianum'
This ancient hybrid subshrub, of unknown
parentage, was named after its 19th-century
English raiser, the Marquess of Blandford. It
has long thin stems and deeply cut, lobed

Above *Pelargonium* 'Captain Starlight'

Above *Pelargonium* 'Blandfordianum'

leaves, which are wonderfully scented of
rose geranium. The white, pink-marked
flowers are borne throughout the year.
Cultivation Grow in sandy soil as a bush,
if staked, or in a hanging basket.
Height and spread 1m (3ft) or more.
USZ 10–11, surviving -1°C (30°F) of overnight
frost. Tolerant of summer drought. ◑

Pelargonium 'Captain Starlight'
This subshrub is an 'Angel' pelargonium –
one of a group related to the large-flowered
'Regals' and to small-leaved *P. crispum*.
Angels flower in flushes through winter,
and have rounded, slightly scented leaves.

Some are upright and may be trained into a
bush, while others, such as the pink-and-
red-flowered 'Captain Starlight', are
spreading, so are excellent for growing over
low walls or in hanging baskets.
Cultivation Grow in well-drained soil
in a sunny position.
Height and spread to 30cm (1ft). USZ 10–11,
surviving -1°C (30°F) of overnight frost.
Tolerant of summer drought. ◑

Pelargonium 'Copthorne'
This compact, upright-growing subshrub
has aromatic, heavily lobed leaves and deep
pink flowers produced freely into winter.

Above *Pelargonium* 'Copthorne'

Above *Pelargonium* 'Moon Maiden'

Above *Pelargonium* 'Scarlet Unique' in an old cottage garden in St Martins, Isles of Scilly

Cultivation As for *P.* 'Captain Starlight'. *Height and spread to 1m (3ft). USZ 10–11, surviving -1°C (30°F) of overnight frost. Tolerant of summer drought.* ◑

Pelargonium 'Moon Maiden'

This spreading 'Angel' pelargonium (*see* left) has delicate pink flowers in summer.
Cultivation As for *P.* 'Captain Starlight'. *Height and spread to 30cm (1ft). USZ 10–11, surviving -1°C (30°F) of overnight frost. Tolerant of summer drought.* ◑

Pelargonium 'Scarlet Unique'

This subshrub has deeply divided leaves and scarlet flowers from spring to winter.
Cultivation As for *P.* 'Captain Starlight'. *Height and spread to 1m (3ft). USZ 10–11, surviving -1°C (30°F) of overnight frost. Tolerant of summer drought.* ◑

Pelargonium 'The Boar'

This spreading or clambering subshrub has well-marked, lobed, round leaves and coral-pink flowers on slender stems, in summer.
Cultivation As for *P.* 'Captain Starlight'. *Height and spread 2m (6½ft) or more. USZ 10–11, surviving -1°C (30°F) of overnight frost. Tolerant of summer drought.* ◑

Above *Pelargonium* 'The Boar' with the soft, mint-scented leaves and small flowers of *P. tomentosum* (see p. 187)

185

Geranium & Scented Pelargoniums

Geranium (Geraniaceae)

The genus *Geranium* has around 300 species of tuberous, tufted, or creeping perennials or annuals, widely distributed around the world, but with about 40 species that are native to Europe.

Geranium maderense

This spectacular perennial (sometimes biennial) is a native of Madeira, where it is common in gardens and by roadsides, but very rare in the wild. It makes a rosette-shaped plant, sending up long-stalked, deeply divided leaves. It bears masses of purplish pink flowers throughout summer.
Cultivation Grow in well-drained soil. This species makes its growth mainly in winter, at which time it requires a little regular watering.
Height to 1.5m (5ft); spread to 1m (3ft). USZ 10–11, surviving -1°C (30°F) of overnight frost. Tolerant of summer drought. ◗

Pelargonium (Geraniaceae)

For this genus of tuberous or creeping perennials, annuals, and succulent or wiry, evergreen shrubs and subshrubs *see* p.184. Many have wonderfully scented leaves.

Above *Pelargonium* 'Citriodorum'

Pelargonium acetosum

This greyish green, succulent subshrub is a native of South Africa, growing on rocky slopes in the southeastern Cape. It produces thin stems and smooth, fleshy, irregularly lobed leaves, with an acidic smell. The salmon-pink to almost white flowers have reddish lines on the upper petals, and are carried in umbels on long stiff stems throughout the year.
Cultivation Grow in dry sandy soil and desert conditions.
Height and spread to 60cm (2ft). USZ 10–11, surviving -1°C (30°F) of overnight frost. Tolerant of summer drought. ◔

Above *Pelargonium acetosum*

Pelargonium 'Citriodorum'
(syn. *P.* 'Queen of Lemons')
This attractive, free-flowering subshrub has soft, downy, lemon-scented, rounded, three-lobed leaves. The silvery mauve flowers, with darker markings on the upper two petals, are produced during late spring and summer. 'Attar of Roses' is often used as a cheaper substitute for the real thing.
Cultivation Grow in well-drained soil in a sunny position.
Height and spread 1m (3ft), or more with support. USZ 10–11, surviving -1°C (30°F) of overnight frost occasionally. Tolerant of summer drought. ◗

Above *Geranium maderense*

Above *Pelargonium tomentosum*
Opposite *Pelargonium cucullatum* subsp. *tabulare*

Pelargonium cucullatum

This shrubby perennial is from South Africa, where it is a conspicuous feature of the sea cliffs and coastal mountains of the southwestern Cape. It has been cultivated in gardens for a long time, and is one of the parents of 'Regal' pelargoniums (known in America as 'Martha Washington' or 'Lady Washington' pelargoniums), which are smaller plants but with larger flowers. *P. cucullatum* has three subspecies: subsp. *cucullatum*, with bright purplish pink flowers (there is also a white-flowered form); subsp. *strigifolium*, which has paler pink flowers and is possibly the most drought tolerant of the three; and subsp. *tabulare*, which grows on rocks by the sea, and on steep grassy slopes, and which has sweetly scented leaves and umbels of bright pinkish purple flowers in spring.

Cultivation Grow in sandy, peaty, bonfire soil. Is fast-growing and free-flowering if well watered. Good by the sea.

Height and spread to 1m (3ft). USZ 10–11, surviving -1°C (30°F) of overnight frost. Tolerant of summer drought. ◑

Pelargonium peltatum

This subshrub, from the Cape region of South Africa, has thin, spreading or climbing stems and ivy-like, rather fleshy leaves. The mauve, pale pink, or white flowers, with upper petals veined or spotted with red, are carried in umbels in spring and summer. This species is the parent of a number of ivy-leaved cultivars,

Above Ivy-leaved *Pelargonium peltatum* growing with large aloes in South Africa

such as 'L'El gante', which has white-and-pink, variegated leaves and white flowers with reddish veins.

Cultivation As for *P.* 'Citriodorum'.

Height to 1m (3ft); spread to 2m (6½ft). USZ 10–11, surviving -1°C (30°F) of overnight frost. Tolerant of summer drought. ◑

Pelargonium tomentosum

This robust, spreading, and clambering subshrub is a native of South Africa in the southwestern Cape, growing on the edges of forests. It has pale green, peppermint-scented, triangular, lobed leaves covered in soft velvety hairs, and a repeatedly branching inflorescence of small, pale pink or white flowers, in summer.

Cultivation Grow in sandy soil in partial shade, with a little moisture at the roots.

Height and spread 2m (6½ft) or more. USZ 10–11, surviving -1°C (30°F) of overnight frost. Requires water in summer. ◑

Acanthus & Related Plants

Acanthus (Acanthaceae)

The genus *Acanthus* contains 30 species of shrubs and perennials from the Mediterranean region and Africa through to southern Asia. *Acanthuses* make excellent architectural features in a garden, and their foliage was the inspiration for a number of Classical Greek and Roman designs, notably on Corinthian capitals of pillars. For shrubby species *see p.112*.

Acanthus dioscoridis

This perennial with creeping underground rhizomes is from Turkey, the Lebanon, Iraq, and Iran. In summer, the flowering stems arise from the rosettes of narrow, dark green leaves, and bear green bracts with pink or purplish flowers. Var. *perringii* has spiny lobes, while var. *brevicaulis* has stems to 20cm (8in) long.
Cultivation Grow in dry, well-drained soil in full sun.
Height and spread to 60cm (2ft). USZ 8–11, surviving -12°C (10°F) of overnight frost. Tolerant of summer drought. ◐

Acanthus hungaricus

This dense, clump-forming perennial is from Croatia and Romania south to Greece. It has dark green, deeply lobed but not

Above *Acanthus hungaricus*

spiny leaves, with only a broad midrib between the lobes. The flowering stems, which carry purplish bracts and white flowers, are borne in summer.
Cultivation Grow in dry, well-drained soil in full sun.
Height and spread to around 1m (3ft). USZ 8–11, surviving -12°C (10°F) of overnight frost. Tolerant of summer drought. ◐

Acanthus mollis
BEAR'S BREECHES

This clump-forming perennial is from southern and southwestern Europe, where it is found in rocky woods and beneath old walls. It produces handsome, dark green, lobed but not spiny leaves, which are shiny on the upper surface. The tall flowering stems carry purplish bracts and white flowers, sometimes with pinkish veins, during summer. Var. *latifolius* has broader, shallowly lobed leaves.
Cultivation Grow in well-drained soil in full sun.
Height to 2m (6½ft); spread to 1m (3ft). USZ 8–11, surviving -12°C (10°F) of overnight frost. Tolerant of summer drought. ◐

Acanthus spinosus

This perennial forming dense clumps is from the eastern Mediterranean region. The lance-shaped, green leaves are dissected to the midrib, with scattered, rather soft

Left *Acanthus dioscoridis*

Above *Acanthus mollis* (bear's breeches) on Tresco in the Isles of Scilly

Above *Acanthus spinosus*

spines. The freely produced, white flowers, with purplish bracts, appear during summer. This is probably the most drought tolerant of the *Acanthus* species illustrated here.

Cultivation Grow in well-drained soil in full sun.

Height to 1.5m (5ft); spread to 1m (3ft). USZ 8–11, surviving -12°C (10°F) of overnight frost. Tolerant of summer drought. ◗

Lobelia (Campanulaceae)

The very diverse genus *Lobelia* contains around 300 species of perennials, biennials, annuals, and shrubs, which are natives of southern Africa, tropical America, and Australia, with two species in Europe.

Lobelia tupa

This perennial, with a large tufted rootstock and numerous stems, is from Argentina and Chile. The leaves are greyish and softly hairy. The orange-red flowers, carried in long spikes in summer, are thick and fleshy.

Cultivation Grow in a sunny position, in fertile, very well-drained soil. Keep moist in summer. Is good for coastal planting.

Height to 2m (6½ft); spread to 1m (3ft). USZ 9–11, surviving -6.5°C (20°F) of overnight frost, and lower if the rootstock is protected. Requires water in summer. ◗

Rehmannia (Scrophulariaceae)

Rehmannia contains around nine species of perennials, natives of eastern Asia. Only two are commonly cultivated: *R. elata*, and the smaller hardier *R. glutinosa* from Korea and northern China, with its brick-red or pinkish flowers; it grows in walls all over the old city in Beijing. *Rehmannia angulata*, often confused with *R. elata*, has red flowers with a scarlet band on the upper lip.

Rehmannia elata

This softly hairy and glandular perennial from central China spreads by stolons. The sticky leaves are jaggedly, deeply lobed, and the purplish pink flowers, around 7.5cm (3in) long, look similar to foxgloves and appear in summer.

Cultivation Grow in well-drained soil. Keep moist in summer, dry in winter.

Height to 45cm (18in); spread to 30cm (1ft). USZ 10–11, surviving -1°C (30°F) of overnight frost. Requires water at the roots in summer. ◗

Above *Rehmannia elata*
Left *Lobelia tupa*

189

Sage, *Verbena*, & Related Plants

Heliotropium (Boraginaceae)

The genus *Heliotropium* has approximately 250 species of subshrubs, perennials, and annuals, which are found growing wild in South America, Western Australia, and Europe.

Heliotropium arborescens
CHERRY PIE, HELIOTROPE
This shrubby perennial from Chile flowers throughout most of the year. It has rather wrinkled, hairy, green leaves and masses of small, sweetly scented, white or mauve flowers, which become purple as they age. There are many named forms and hybrids, most of which are much shorter than the species, with flowers ranging from white and lilac to dark blue and purple. Good ones include: 'Chatsworth', which has purple flowers and an exceptionally good scent; and the more compact 'Lord Roberts', with violet flowers.

Above *Heliotropum arborescens* (cherry pie)

Above *Leonotis ocymifolia* (lion's tail)

Above *Hypoestes aristata* at Wisley

Cultivation Best on sandy loamy soil in partial shade. Benefits from feeding and light pruning immediately after flowering. *Height to 2m (6½ft); spread to 1m (3ft). USZ 10–11, surviving -1°C (30°F) of overnight frost. Requires water in summer.* ●

Hypoestes (Acanthaceae)

The genus *Hypoestes* has around 40 species of evergreen perennials, subshrubs, and shrubs, natives of South Africa and Arabia.

Hypoestes aristata
This perennial from South Africa produces downy, ovate, green leaves and spikes of purplish pink flowers, in winter. *Hypoestes phyllostachya* is grown for its pink-spotted foliage, hence its name "polka dot plant".
Cultivation Grow in any fertile, well-drained soil in sun or partial shade. Needs little water in winter, more in summer. *Height to 1m (3ft); spread to 60cm (2ft). USZ 10–11, surviving -1°C (30°F) of overnight frost. Requires water in summer.* ●

Leonotis (Labiatae)

Leonotis has about 15 species of perennials, annuals, and subshrubs from tropical Africa, with one species also in America and Asia.

Above *Salvia patens* 'Guanajuato'

Leonotis ocymifolia
LION'S TAIL
This upright, clump-forming perennial or subshrub, from South Africa, produces tubular, velvety, orange-red flowers from late summer to autumn. Var. *albiflora* (syn. 'Harrismith White') bears white flowers.
Cultivation Grow in reasonably fertile soil in full sun
Height to 2m (6½ft); spread to 1m (3ft). USZ 9–11, surviving -6.5°C (20°F) of overnight frost, or more if the roots are protected. Requires water in summer. ◗

Salvia (Labiatae)

This genus contains around 900 species of deciduous and evergreen subshrubs, perennials, annuals, and biennials, originating from most regions of the world, but mostly from Central and South America and Turkey. (For shrubby species *see* p.111.) In addition to that illustrated, there are many good herbaceous species, including *S. coccinea*, a spreading perennial often grown as an annual, with branching hairy stems and whorls of showy, bright red flowers, in summer; there are many cultivated varieties of this with flower colours ranging from white and pink to salmon and scarlet. *S. involucrata* is an upright perennial, with bright pink bracts and racemes of bright magenta flowers in late summer to autumn. There are several named forms, also with bright pink flowers, including 'Bethelii' and 'Hadspen'.

Salvia patens

This beautiful herbaceous perennial is from central Mexico. It has white fleshy tubers, upright stems, and the most brilliant, royal-blue flowers, 4–5cm (1½–2in) long, which are some of the largest in any *Salvia*. They are carried in summer. 'Alba' has white flowers, while 'Cambridge Blue' is very pale blue. 'Guanajuato' has particularly large flowers, 7.5cm (3in) long.
Cultivation Grow in rich moist soil in dappled shade or sun. Keep dry in winter.
Height to 2m (6½ft); spread to 1m (3ft). USZ 10–11, surviving -1°C (30°F) of overnight frost. Needs water in summer. ◗

Tweedia (Asclepiadaceae)

The genus *Tweedia*, sometimes called *Oxypetalum*, has around six species of perennials or evergreen subshrubs. All are natives of South America. They are hairy, rather succulent scrambling plants, with milky juice and tuberous roots.

Tweedia caerulea

This twining or scrambling subshrub, from southern Brazil and Uruguay, has softly hairy, elongated heart-shaped leaves and pale blue, star-shaped flowers, in summer.
Cultivation Grow in fertile, well-drained soil in full sun.
Height and spread to 80cm (32in). USZ 9–11, surviving −6.5°C (20°F) of overnight frost. Tolerant of summer drought. ◗

Verbena (Verbenaceae)

The genus *Verbena* has around 200 species of perennials, annuals, and subshrubs. Two species are natives of Europe, and the remainder grow wild in America, mostly in the south.

Verbena platensis

This perennial produces hairy leaves and sweetly scented, white, long-tubed flowers

Above *Tweedia caerulea*

in heads 5cm (2in) across, which are carried during summer. *V. platensis* grows wild in Argentina and Uruguay.
Cultivation Needs fertile soil and warmth in summer. Keep dry in winter.
Height to 20cm (8in); spread to 1m (3ft). USZ 9–11, surviving -6.5°C (20°F) of overnight frost. Needs water in summer. ◗

Above *Verbena platensis* with *Lavandula* 'Papillon'

Perennial Daisies

Coreopsis (Compositae)

Coreopsis is a genus of around 50 species. Most are hardy herbaceous perennials or annuals. All species originate in North and South America.

Coreopsis gigantea

This evergreen perennial has a bare green stem topped by a large rosette of finely divided, bright green leaves, to 20cm (8in) long, and masses of yellow flowers, 5–8cm (2–3in) across, in spring. It is wild in southern California from San Luis Obispo county south to Baja California, growing on cliffs and sandy places by the sea.
Cultivation Grows well in sandy soil in coastal areas.

Height to 3m (10ft); spread to 1.5m (5ft). USZ 10–11, surviving -1°C (30°F) of overnight frost. Tolerant of summer drought. ◗

Cosmos (Compositae)

The genus *Cosmos* contains around 25 species, which are natives of southern North America and into Central America. Many are perennial, but the most familiar is the pink-flowered annual *C. bipinnatus*, which is a native of Mexico but has now naturalized in all dryish parts of the world.

Cosmos atrosanguineus

This tuberous-rooted perennial is an unusual plant, being common in cultivation yet now unknown in the wild, and possibly

Above *Helichrysum bracteatum* 'Dargan Hill Monarch'

extinct. The stems are sprawling, and produce flat-lobed leaves. The flowers, around 4cm (1½in) across, are on long stalks, very dark crimson, and scented of chocolate. They appear in late summer.
Cultivation Easily grown in fertile soil. In frosty areas dig up the tubers in autumn and store in cold, moist sand or peat.
Height to 60cm (2ft); spread to 1m (3ft). USZ 10–11, surviving -1°C (30°F) of overnight frost. Needs water in summer. ◗

Dahlia (Compositae)

This genus comprises around 30 species of perennials and subshrubs, generally tuberous-rooted, from Mexico to Colombia. With their late flowering and diversity of colour, size, and shape, *Dahlia* have been popular since they were introduced from Mexico – where they were already grown as ornamentals – in the 18th century. Most cultivated Dahlias are hybrids, with double flowers, but a few species, such as the giant

Above *Cosmos atrosanguineus*
Left *Coreopsis gigantea* in Santa Barbara, California

Above *Osteospermum* 'Nairobi Purple'

shown here, are popular garden plants in mild areas. In frosty areas the tubers need lifting and bringing indoors during winter.

Dahlia imperialis

This shrubby perennial grows to its full height in one summer, and then produces beautiful, pale lilac-pink, nodding flowers, 10–20cm (4–8in) across, in autumn and winter. The two- or three-pinnate leaves are 60–90cm (2–3ft) long.
Cultivation Grow in fertile soil. Needs fertilizer in the growing season, and drier conditions in winter. It flowers well only in a frost-free climate, and is sometimes grown for its foliage in subtropical plantings.

Height to 9m (30ft); spread to 3m (10ft). USZ 10–11, surviving -1°C (30°F) of overnight frost. Needs ample water in summer. ◗◗

Helichrysum (Compositae)

The genus *Helichrysum* contains around 500 species of annuals, perennials, and evergreen shrubs and subshrubs, from Europe, Africa, Asia, and Australia. They have few to many rows of dry, papery, often coloured bracts, which keep their colour when dried. *H. bracteatum* and some other Australian species have often been placed in the genus *Bracteantha*, and even more recently in *Xerochrysum*.

Helichrysum bracteatum

This annual or perennial has soft silvery leaves and brightly coloured, everlasting flowers. It is a native of most of Australia, but commonly cultivated as an annual, and often escapes. Perennial or subshrubby 'Dargan Hill Monarch', and its progeny, come from the Macpherson Ranges of southeast Queensland. Their felted leaves are narrow and pointed, to 12cm (5in) long; the yellow flowers are around 9cm (3½in) across and borne in summer.
Cultivation Needs dry sandy soil, with a little water to prevent the plant from becoming soft, floppy, and prone to disease.
Height to 90cm (3ft); spread to 3m (10ft). USZ 9–11, surviving -6.5°C (20°F) of overnight frost. Tolerant of summer drought. ◗

Above *Helichrysum petiolare*

Helichrysum petiolare

This fast-growing, spreading, evergreen subshrub is a native of South Africa, from the Cape to Natal, growing in damp rocky places. The silvery grey leaves are stalked, the blade almost round, up to 3.5cm (1½in) long. The dull yellowish, sweetly scented flowers, 3mm (⅛in) across, are borne in rounded heads in summer.
Cultivation Easily grown in slightly damp soil. Plant in partial shade in hot areas.
Height to 1m (3ft); spread to 5m (16ft). USZ 9–11, surviving -6.5°C (20°F) of overnight frost. Tolerant of summer drought. ◗

Osteospermum (Compositae)

This genus of perennials, annuals, and subshrubs is described on p.217.

Osteospermum 'Nairobi Purple'
(syn. *O.* 'Tresco Purple')
This long-lived, spreading perennial has toothed leaves and dark purple flowers, 6cm (2½in) across, in spring and summer.
Cultivation Easily grown in well-drained, sandy soil in a sunny position.
Height to 30cm (1ft); spread to 1m (3ft). USZ 9–11, surviving -6.5°C (20°F) of overnight frost. Tolerant of summer drought. ◗

Above *Dahlia imperialis* flowering near Lake Chapala in Mexico in October

Tree Ferns

Blechnum (Blechnaceae)

The genus *Blechnum* contains 200 species of mainly evergreen ferns, which grow wild worldwide. Most have wide sterile fronds and narrower fertile fronds.

Blechnum gibbum
This clump-forming tree fern gradually develops a black fibrous trunk, to about 1m (3ft) tall. The pale green, arching, sterile fronds can grow up to 2m (6½ft) long, while the fertile leaves, which appear on mature plants, are erect, with narrower segments. This handsome fern is valued for its architectural form, and can be seen to advantage when grown in a container. It is a native of Fiji, New Caledonia, and the New Hebrides, where it grows in open forest and by streams.
Cultivation Grow in bark and leaves in a moist shady spot, or in a container.
Height and spread to 4m (13ft). USZ 10–11, surviving -1°C (30°F) of overnight frost. Needs summer water. ●

Cyathea (Cyatheaceae)

Cyathea is a genus of 620 species of tree ferns, found throughout the world in tropical and subtropical areas, especially on wet mountains. Most species have rather slender, scaly trunks compared with the stouter *Dicksonia*. Many of the species are sometimes allocated botanically into the genera *Alsophila* and *Sphaeopteris*.

Above *Blechnum gibbum*

Cyathea capensis
CAPE TREE FERN
This tree fern is found from the Cape peninsula northwards to eastern Africa, and it is also recorded from Brazil; it grows in moist forests and deep sheltered valleys. Eventually it can develop a tall trunk, to 25cm (10in) in diameter, and two-pinnate fronds to 2m (6½ft) long.
Cultivation Needs peaty soil, shade, moisture, and humidity.
Height to 4.5m (15ft); spread to 4m (13ft). USZ 10–11, surviving -1°C (30°F) of overnight frost. Tolerant of summer drought. ●

Cyathea medullaris
This elegant tree fern is a native of New Zealand, where it grows in humid woods.

The slender trunk is 15–20cm (6–8in) in diameter. The three-pinnate fronds, which can reach 6m (20ft) long, eventually fall, leaving triangular leaf scars.
Cultivation Needs shade, moisture, and humidity. Soil should be rich and peaty. In hot weather, mist-spray at night.
Height to 15m (50ft); spread to 12m (40ft). USZ 10–11, surviving -1°C (30°F) of overnight frost. Needs water in summer and winter. ●

Dicksonia (Dicksoniaceae)

The genus *Dicksonia* consists of around 25 species of tree ferns, from Australia, New Zealand, Polynesia, and Mexico. It is close to *Cyathea*, but has hairs rather than scales on the trunk and frond bases, and tends to have a thicker, straighter trunk.

Dicksonia antarctica
This is one of the hardiest tree ferns, found wild in southern and eastern Australia, and Tasmania. It is imported to Europe in large numbers from forest areas, and will survive as far north as Scotland in coastal gardens. It has a thick trunk, covered with the remains of old fronds. The two-pinnate fronds reach 2m (6½ft) long.
Cultivation Easily grown in wet peaty soil in a sheltered humid site. Misting and watering the trunk helps it to survive dry weather in winter or summer. Cover the crown to aid survival in frosty areas.
Height to 15m (50ft); spread to 4m (13ft). USZ 9–11, surviving -6.5°C (20°F) of overnight frost. Needs summer water. ●

Above *Cyathea capensis* (Cape tree fern)

Above *Cyathea medullaris*

Above *Dicksonia antarctica* at Trebah in Cornwall

Dicranopteris (Gleicheniaceae)

This genus has 12 species of ferns in the tropics and subtropics of eastern Asia.

Dicranopteris linearis
This rampant, climbing or scrambling fern is commonly seen growing wild across the tropics and subtropics of Asia, hanging down on roadside banks or wooded cliffs. It is particularly elegant, with long wiry stalks bearing repeatedly dividing fronds, 30–60cm (1–2ft) long, with narrowly dissected leaflets, giving a feathery effect.
Cultivation Unfortunately, this fern is not easy to establish in gardens, as it dislikes disturbance. Grow in soil containing plenty of leafmould or compost, with extra humidity until they become established. Shade young plants from direct sunlight. *Height to 1.8m (6ft); spread to 3m (10ft). Zones 10–11, surviving -1°C (30°F) of overnight frost. Needs summer water.* ●

Pteris (Pteridaceae)

Pteris is a genus with around 280 species of ferns found throughout the world, but mainly in subtropical and tropical areas. There is great diversity in frond type, but the most commonly cultivated species, *P. cretica*, has undivided or forked fronds.

Pteris wallichiana
This noble fern is a native from the Himalayas to Taiwan and Samoa. It produces tall stiff stems from a thick creeping root. The fronds are pinnate and lobed, each around 23cm (9in) long. The rootstock is thick and almost tuberous, and may be eaten by mice in winter.
Cultivation Needs space and shelter, in deep, leafy, well-drained soil, to do well. *Height to 2m (6½ft); spread to 1.2m (4ft). USZ 9–11, surviving -6.5°C (20°F) of overnight frost. Needs water in summer.* ●

Far Left *Dicranopteris linearis*
Left *Pteris wallichiana*

195

Smaller Ferns

Adiantum (Adiantaceae)
MAIDENHAIR FERN

The genus *Adiantum* contains around 200 species of the most delicate and graceful of all ferns, which are natives of subtropical and tropical areas worldwide. Most can be recognized by their fan-shaped or parallelogram-shaped leaf segments, with sporangia on the edge, covered by a flap.

Adiantum capillus-veneris
This is a very common fern worldwide in limestone areas that have little or no frost. The bright green fronds are to 50cm (20in) long, but usually around 20cm (8in), with delicate segments to 1cm (⅜in) long.
Cultivation Grow in peaty soil with lime and in a shady wall or rock crevice, ideally by a spring or with running water.
Height to 30cm (1ft); spread to 60m (2ft). USZ 10–11, surviving -1°C (30°F) of overnight frost. Needs water in summer. ●

Davallia (Davalliaceae)
HARE'S FOOT FERN

The genus *Davallia* contains around 40 species of ferns with creeping scaly rhizomes (hence the common name), which root in the surface of mossy rocks or tree branches.

Davallia canariensis
This creeping fern produces finely divided, triangular leaves from a thick rhizome, about 1cm (⅜in) in diameter. It is wild in Madeira, the Canaries, and the extreme southwest of Spain, on rocks, walls, or trees. The dark green, shining fronds, 50–80cm (20–32in) long, die in midsummer; new ones appear in autumn.
Cultivation The rhizomes need a firm substrate on which to root, with moss or shallow leafy soil.
Height to 30cm (1ft); spread to 1m (3ft). USZ 10–11, surviving -1°C (30°F) of overnight frost. Tolerant of summer drought. ◑

Dennstaedtia (Dennstaedtiaceae)

Dennstaedtia is a genus of around 70 species of ferns, mainly tropical but with temperate species in Japan, North America, Chile, and Tasmania. Some species are extensive creepers with tough rhizomes.

Dennstaedtia appendiculata
This beautiful, clump-forming fern has soft, finely divided, deciduous fronds, with a pale central stalk (rhachis) covered in white hairs. It is wild in Asia.

Above *Adiantum capillus-veneris*

Cultivation Grow in moist, leafy, acid soil with shade and shelter.
Height to 1.2m (4ft); spread to 1m (3ft). USZ 9–11, surviving -6.5°C (20°F) of overnight frost. Needs water in summer. ●

Drynaria (Polypodiaceae)
BASKET FERN

There are about 20 species of these large epiphytic ferns, mostly from tropical Asia.

Drynaria quercifolia
This fern is a native of Asia, Polynesia, and northeastern Australia, where it grows on trees in open forest. The short rhizome is covered by persistent, sterile, lobed fronds, around 30cm (1ft) long, which help to catch leaves and other debris. The main fronds arch out from the tree trunk, and are deeply divided, nearly to the mid-rib.
Cultivation Grow in a hanging basket or on a tree trunk.
Height and spread to 1.5m (5ft). USZ 11, needing minimum of 4.5°C (40°F) overnight. Needs water in summer. ●

Above *Dennstaedtia appendiculata*
Right *Davallia canariensis* on a volcanic cliff in Madeira

Platycerium (Polypodiaceae)
STAGHORN FERN

This genus contains around 18 species of epiphytic ferns, natives of the tropics. They have two kinds of fronds: those that form a flat green nest, which is pressed to the tree; and the antler-like, fertile fronds, which often spread upwards before hanging down.

Platycerium bifurcatum
This fern is a native of forests in Australia, Indonesia, and New Guinea. The fertile fronds, to 1m (3ft) long, have brown patches of sporangia beneath the tips.
Cultivation Grow in a large basket suspended in a tree. Needs some moss, bark, and soil for the roots, and foliar feed in the growing season. Keep drier in winter. *Height 1m (3ft); spread to 2m (6½ft). USZ 11, needing a minimum of 4.5°C (40°F) overnight. Needs summer water.* ●

Above *Woodwardia radicans* in a laurel forest in Tenerife

Above *Platycerium bifurcatum*

Woodwardia (Blechnaceae)

Woodwardia consists of 10 species of ferns from the northern hemisphere. It is sometimes called chain fern, because it roots at the tips of the fronds.

Woodwardia radicans
This fern has arching fronds, to 2m (6½ft) long, often coloured bronze when young. It is wild in evergreen woods in Madeira, the Canaries, southwest Spain, and Crete.
Cultivation Needs shelter, shade, and leafy soil. Is best on a moist bank under trees. *Height to 45cm (18in); spread to 2m (6½ft). USZ 10–11, surviving -1°C (30°F) of overnight frost. Needs water in summer.* ◑◑

Right *Drynaria quercifolia*

197

Bulbs

BULBS MAKE PERFECT plants for dry gardens as they can create a colourful display while in flower and disappear for the rest of the year. Some grow in desert areas and are dormant during the hottest months, while others flower during the summer rains.

Above *Gloriosa superba* 'Rothchildiana' (see p. 213)

Nerine

Nerine (Amaryllidaceae)

The genus *Nerine* contains around 30 species of perennial bulbs, which are natives of South Africa. Some species grow in the desert conditions of the Kalahari and the Great Karoo, while others occur in the damper climate of eastern southern Africa. Most of them flower in autumn.

Nerine bowdenii

This elegant, variable, clump-forming, and hardy perennial bulb is from Eastern Cape province north to Orange Free State and northern Natal in the Drakensberg. The form usually grown in Europe has green, strap-like leaves, which emerge in late winter and die down in summer to be followed by umbels of pink flowers in autumn. In var. *wellsii*, the leaves appear later, remaining green throughout summer, and the flowers, which are smaller than the species, with more wrinkled petals, appear in late summer. Other varieties have white flowers, flushed with pink, and there is also deeper pink clone.

Above *Nerine* 'Fortune'

Cultivation Needs well-drained soil in sun or partial shade. Keep drier when dormant. *Height to 75cm (30in); spread to 20cm (8in). USZ 9–11, surviving -6.5°C (20°F) of overnight frost. Tolerant of summer drought.* ◗

Nerine sarniensis
GUERNSEY LILY
Despite its name, this perennial bulb comes from the Cape region of South Africa. It has upright, strap-shaped leaves and rounded clusters of usually scarlet flowers with wavy-edged petals and conspicuous stamens in autumn. Some plants growing

Above *Nerine sarniensis* (Guernsey lily)

on the Cape peninsula have carmine to pink flowers, and this natural variation has been used to enhance the range of colours in breeding. Most of the many modern cultivated hybrids, such as 'Fortune' with its pink flowers, are derived from *N. sarniensis*. Their colours vary from purple to crimson, red, pink, and white.
Cultivation Grow in fertile, well-drained soil in sun or partial shade. Water in winter and spring. Is good for coastal conditions. *Height to 45cm (18in); spread to 15cm (6in). USZ 10–11, surviving -1°C (30°F) of overnight frost. Tolerant of summer drought.* ◗

Above *Nerine bowdenii*, with *Liriope muscari* in the foreground

Large Flowering Bulbs

Above *Clivia miniata* (kaffir lily)

Amaryllis (Amaryllidaceae)

Amaryllis has two species of perennial bulbs, which are natives of South Africa.

Amaryllis belladonna
This striking perennial bulb is from Cape province in South Africa. It has one or two stout stems per bulb, topped with heads of large, trumpet-shaped, scented, white or pink flowers, flushed pale yellow at the base, in autumn.
Cultivation Grow in fertile loamy soil in full sun. A hot, dry summer, a dressing of hot wood ash, and water in early autumn will encourage flowering.

Height to 60cm (2ft); spread to 20cm (8in). USZ 8–11, surviving -12°C (10°F) of overnight frost. Tolerant of summer drought. ◑

Clivia (Amaryllidaceae)

The genus *Clivia* contains four species of large, evergreen, stemless perennials with fleshy roots and swollen, bulb-like leaf bases. They grow wild in forests in the summer-rainfall region of South Africa.

Clivia miniata
KAFFIR LILY
This evergreen perennial with tuberous roots is from South Africa. It has clumps of dark green, strap-shaped leaves and stout stems carrying large umbels of outward-facing, bright orange, funnel-shaped flowers, from early spring to summer. Hybrids have broader leaves, thicker stems, and sometimes yellow flowers.
Cultivation Grow in leafy, well-drained, sandy soil in partial shade. Keep rather dry in winter, but water in the growing season.
Height to 75cm (2½ft); spread to 30cm (1ft). USZ 10–11, surviving -1°C (30°F) of overnight frost. Requires water in summer. ◗

Crinum (Amaryllidaceae)

The genus *Crinum* contains around 120 species of evergreen perennial bulbs, which are natives of the tropical regions of the world. *C.* x *powellii*, with its pale pink or white, trumpet-shaped flowers, is a well-known, almost hardy garden hybrid, of which *C. moorei* is one of the parents.

Crinum asiaticum
This perennial, from southeastern Asia, has a huge bulb, many broadly strap-shaped, green leaves, to 13cm (5in) across, and large umbels of around 20 spidery, white or pinkish, scented flowers, around 15cm (6in) long, throughout much of the year.
Cultivation Grow in well-drained, sandy soil. Is good for coastal districts in subtropical areas.
Height to 1.2m (4ft); spread to 2.4m (8ft). USZ 10–11, surviving -1°C (30°F) of overnight frost. Requires water in summer. ●

Crinum moorei
This perennial is from woodlands in the summer-rainfall area of the Cape and Natal in South Africa. It has a huge, long-necked bulb and broadly strap-shaped, pale green leaves. The long stiff stems bearing umbels of 5–10 trumpet-shaped, white or pink, scented flowers, with a tube to 10cm (4in) long and spreading lobes to 15cm (6in) across, are produced in summer.
Cultivation Grow in fertile, moisture-retentive soil in sun or partial shade.
Height to 1.5m (5ft); spread to 1.2m (4ft). USZ 10–11, surviving -1°C (30°F) of overnight frost. Requires water in summer. ◗

Above *Crinum asiaticum* in Bermuda

Above *Amaryllis belladonna*

Above *Crinum moorei*

Hippeastrum (Amaryllidaceae)

The genus *Hippeastrum* contains around 80 species of perennial bulbs, which are natives of Central and South America, including the West Indies; one species is also found in western Africa.

Hippeastrum 'Apple Blossom'

Numerous *Hippeastrum* hybrid cultivars such as 'Apple Blossom', with its white, pink-tinged flowers, as much as 25cm

Above *Hippeastrum* 'Apple Blossom'

(10in) across, in winter, have been raised, with flower colours in shades of white, pink, and red. They are usually sold as *Amaryllis*, particularly in the USA. Other cultivars include: 'Lemon 'n' Lime' with greenish yellow flowers, which fade to pink; 'Pamela' with smaller, intense red flowers; and those with spidery or spotted blooms.
Cultivation Plant each large bulb so that the "neck" protrudes from any fertile soil. Although most *Hippeastrums* do well in warm gardens, they usually produce a better display if they are well watered and fed while growing; once they have flowered, keep them almost dry. The exotic blooms make the extra work worthwhile.

Left *Hippeastrum* x *johnsonii*

Height to 60m (2ft); spread to 15cm (6in). USZ 10–11, just surviving -1°C (30°F) of overnight frost. Tolerant of summer drought. ◗

Hippeastrum x *johnsonii*

This perennial bulb has red flowers, around 12cm (5in) across, with white markings, in spring. It is a hybrid between the bright red *H. reginae* and *H. vittatum*, which has white flowers with a red stripe, from Brazil and Peru. It is widely grown in warm areas such as southwestern China.
Cultivation As for *H.* 'Apple Blossom'.
Height to 60cm (2ft); spread to 1m (3ft). USZ 10–11, surviving -1°C (30°F) of overnight frost. Needs watering in summer. ◗

Exotic Flowering Bulbs

Cyrtanthus (Amaryllidaceae)

The genus *Cyrtanthus* contains around 50 species of perennial bulbs, natives from South Africa northwards to Kenya. Many species are known as fire lilies, as they flower in the bare ground after a bush fire.

Cyrtanthus elatus (syn. *Vallota purpurea, V. speciosa*)

SCARBOROUGH LILY, GEORGE LILY

This perennial bulb from George in South Africa is now very rare in the wild. It has strap-shaped, shiny, green leaves, 45cm (18in) long, a strong stem, and a cluster of scarlet, rarely pink or white, flared trumpet-shaped flowers, 7–10cm (3–4in) long, in late summer and autumn.

Cultivation Grow in sandy peaty soil. *Height to 60cm (2ft); spread to 30cm (1ft). USZ 10–11, surviving -1°C (30°F) of overnight frost. Requires water in spring and summer.* ◗

Cyrtanthus falcatus

This perennial bulb is from Natal, in South Africa, where it grows on rocks by waterfalls. It has stout stems and curved, semi-horizontal, strap-shaped, green leaves, 25cm (10in) long, appearing in spring with umbels of tubular, nodding, greenish pink flowers, 7.5cm (3in) long.

Cultivation Plant bulbs on the surface of well-drained soil in sun or dappled shade. Feed well during the growing season. *Height and spread to 30cm (1ft). USZ 10–11, surviving -1°C (30°F) of overnight frost. Requires ample water in summer.* ◗

Above *Cyrtanthus falcatus*

Above *Haemanthus coccineus*

Haemanthus (Amaryllidaceae)

The genus *Haemanthus* contains around 21 species of perennial bulbs, some evergreen, from Cape province in South Africa. Some species need a wet climate.

Haemanthus coccineus

This deciduous perennial bulb, from South Africa, has waxy, pink to scarlet bracts, to 6cm (2½in) long, surrounding the mass of flowers in late summer. The leaves, barred beneath with purple, appear at the same time, or just after, the flowers and persist through much of winter, reaching 45cm (18in) long, and 15cm (6in) across.

Cultivation Needs sandy soil. Water only during the growing season. *Height and spread to 30cm (1ft). USZ 10–11, surviving -1°C (30°F) of overnight frost. Tolerant of summer drought.* ◗

Left *Cyrtanthus elatus* (Scarborough lily)

202

Above *Lycoris radiata* on banks between paddy fields near Kyoto, in Japan

Below *Lycoris radiata*

Height to 45cm (1½ft); spread to 30cm (1ft). USZ 9–11, surviving -6.5°C (20°F) of frost. Requires water most of the year. ◗

Pancratium (Amaryllidaceae)

Pancratium contains around 16 species of perennial bulbs, from southern Europe to South Africa and tropical Asia.

Pancratium canariense
This perennial bulb is from the Canaries. It has broad, greyish green leaves, which appear after the umbels of sweetly scented, white flowers, around 5cm long, in autumn. *P. maritimum* is a also lovely species for a dry garden; it flowers in summer and autumn.
Cultivation Grow in stony soil in full sun. Keep wet in winter and dry in summer.
Height to 75cm (2½ft); spread to 60cm (2ft). USZ 9–11, surviving -6.5°C (20°F) of overnight frost. Tolerant of summer drought. ◑

Lycoris (Amaryllidaceae)

The genus *Lycoris* contains around 11 species of perennial bulbs, which are natives of eastern China and Japan.

Lycoris radiata
This perennial bulb from Japan looks quite similar to a *Nerine* (*see* p.199). It has deep green leaves and umbels of bright red, spidery flowers, with narrow wavy perianth segments and stamens to 10cm (4in) long, during autumn.
Cultivation Grow in fertile soil in sun. When dormant in midsummer, keep drier. For the rest of the year, it needs regular watering in order to flourish. Does particularly well in southeastern North America.

Above *Pancratium canariense*

Onions, Hyacinths, & Related Bulbs

Above *Allium cristophii* (star of Persia)

Allium (Alliaceae)

The genus *Allium* contains around 700 species of perennials usually with bulbs and with flowering stems smelling of onion or garlic. *Alliums* are natives of Europe east to China, and are also found in North America. The edible members of the genus, such as chives, garlic, leeks, and onions, are well known. Many of the ornamental species are useful for hot dry gardens, where they can make a striking display in spring and summer.

Allium cristophii
STAR OF PERSIA
This fine perennial bulb, from Iran, Turkey, and Central Asia, has bluish green leaves, 30cm (1ft) long and 3.5cm (1½in) across. The head, 20cm (8in) across, of shining, starry, purple flowers, 3cm (1¼in) across, is borne in summer.
Cultivation Grow in well-drained, stony soil in sun. Water in winter and spring.
Height to 60cm (2ft); spread to 30cm (1ft). USZ 7–11, surviving –17°C (2°F) of overnight frost. Tolerant of summer drought. ◑

Eremurus (Asphodelaceae)
FOXTAIL LILY

The genus *Eremurus* consists of around 45 species of perennials with fleshy roots, natives of southern Europe eastwards to the western Himalayas, central Asia, and China. Most grow on dry, overgrazed steppes and mountain slopes. There are many fine *Eremurus* species eminently suited to cultivation in dry gardens.

Eremurus x *isabellinus* 'Cleopatra'
This perennial with its deep orange flowers in early summer is a 'Shelford Hybrid', with white, pink, yellow, or orange flowers. It was derived from chance hybridization between the white-flowered *E. olgae* and taller, yellow-flowered *E. stenophyllus*.
Cultivation Grow in stony, well-drained soil in sun. Water in autumn and spring.
Height 2m (6½ft) or more; spread to 30cm (1ft). USZ 7–11, surviving –17°C (2°F) of overnight frost. Tolerant of summer drought. ◑

Above *Eremurus* x *isabellinus* 'Cleopatra'

Hyacinthus (Hyacinthaceae)

The genus *Hyacinthus* contains three species of perennial bulbs, which grow wild in the eastern Mediterranean and Iran.

Hyacinthus orientalis
This perennial bulb has green leaves, around 20cm (8in) long, and 2–12 scented, pale blue, bell-like flowers, measuring around 2.5cm (1in) long and hanging from the stem in spring. It is a native of Turkey, Syria, and the Lebanon.
Cultivation Grow in well-drained, sandy soil in full sun. Keep partially shaded in summer.
Height to 20cm (8in); spread to 10cm (4in). USZ 9–11, surviving -6.5°C (20°F) of overnight frost. Tolerant of summer drought. ◑

Ornithogalum (Hyacinthaceae)

The genus *Ornithogalum* contains around 120 species of perennial bulbs, from the Mediterranean area and southern Africa.

Ornithogalum dubium
This perennial bulb is from the Cape winter-rainfall region of South Africa. It has broad, shining, green leaves, which are around 15cm (6in) long and 2.5cm (1in) across, and up to 20 orange to bright yellow or white flowers, 2–4cm (¾–1½in) across, in spring and summer, often after the leaves have begun to shrivel in the summer drought.
Cultivation Grow in well-drained, sandy soil in sun.
Height to 50cm (20in); spread to 10cm (4in). USZ 10–11, surviving -1°C (30°F) of overnight frost. Tolerant of summer drought. ◑

Above *Hyacinthus orientalis* naturalized near Grasse, in France, where it is grown for the perfume industry

Ornithogalum thyrsoides
CHINCHERINCHEE
This perennial bulb from South Africa has broad green leaves around 15cm (6in) long, 2.5cm (1in) across, and white flowers 4–5cm (1½–2in) across, often with a dark eye, in early summer. It grows in great numbers in *vleis*, places that are wet in winter and dry out in summer.
Cultivation Grow in well-drained soil in sun. Provide ample water during the growing season. In cultivation smoke treatment can help it to flower
Height to 80cm (32in); spread to 15cm (6in). USZ 10–11, surviving -1°C (30°F) of overnight frost. Tolerant of summer drought. ◑

Above *Ornithogalum dubium*

Veltheimia (Hyacinthaceae)

The genus *Veltheimia* contains two species of perennial bulbs, which are natives of South Africa. *V. capensis* is winter-growing and flowers from autumn to winter.

Veltheimia bracteata
This perennial bulb from South Africa has dark green leaves, 30cm (1ft) long and 10cm (4in) across, and a purplish-spotted or black stem. The heads of up to 60 pinkish green or pale yellow flowers, 3–4cm (1¼–1½ in) long, appear in spring.
Cultivation Grow in leafy loamy soil in shade or partial shade.
Height to 45cm (18in); spread to 30cm (1ft). USZ 10–11, surviving -1°C (30°F) of overnight frost. Needs water in summer. ◑

Above *Veltheimia bracteata*

Above *Ornithogalum thyrsoides* (chincherinchee)

Crocuses & Irises

Above *Crocus chrysanthus* 'Blue Prince'

Above *Crocus imperati* subsp. *suaveolens* in midwinter

Crocus (Iridaceae)

The genus *Crocus* contains around 85 species of perennial corms, which are natives of Europe, from Portugal eastwards to northwestern China (Xinjiang province), growing in dry stony places and flowering in autumn, winter, or spring. Many species or species groups may be recognized by the details of the papery tunic, which covers the corm.

Crocus chrysanthus

This perennial corm from Turkey and the Balkans has many cultivars or hybrids, which vary in flower colour from yellow to white and blue, variably striped on the back. The flowers, around 5cm (2in) across, open in early spring, when the sun shines. The tunics split into rings at the base of the

corm. The leaves are around 2.5mm (⅒in) across. 'Blue Prince' has steely blue flowers.
Cultivation Needs fertile sandy soil. Water in winter and spring.
Height to 5cm (2in); spread to 10cm (4in). USZ 8–11, surviving -12°C (10°F) of overnight frost. Tolerant of summer drought. ◑

Crocus imperati subsp. suaveolens

This perennial corm is a native of western Italy, from Naples to Rome. The tunics are membranous and split into parallel fibres, and the leaves are around 2.5mm (⅒in) across. The flowers, measuring around 6cm (2½in) across, are buff with dark feathering outside, lavender inside, with yellow or orange styles. They open during winter, in the sunshine.
Cultivation Needs fertile sandy soil. Water in winter and spring.
Height to 7.5cm (3in); spread to 10cm (4in). USZ 8–11, surviving -12°C (10°F) of overnight frost. Tolerant of summer drought. ◑

Iris (Iridaceae)

The genus *Iris* contains around 250 species of perennials, most with swollen rhizomes or bulbs. They are natives throughout the northern hemisphere. Some species are found in marshes and wet areas, but most

Above *Iris lutescens*, with pink *Anthyllis* on limestone in the hills above Grasse, in France

inhabit dry ground, and become dormant or semi-dormant during summer. The flowers usually have two whorls of three petals (strictly perianth segments); the outer ones (the falls) are reflexed, while the inner ones (the standards) are upright. There is also a flattened style, which covers the anthers, and may have a petaloid crest. Divide irises in early autumn, every three or four years, to retain vigour. A dressing of fertilizer and wood ash in late autumn or winter will encourage flowering.

Above *Iris germanica* 'Florentina'

Above *Iris histrio,* from the Amanus mountains, in Turkey

reddish, and bicoloured, often in the same locality. The leaves are green, to 2.5cm (1in) across. The bracts are green, sometimes brownish at the apex.
Cultivation Easily grown in dry sandy soil, preferably raised up on a bank.
Height to 35cm (14in); spread to 30cm (1ft). USZ 9–11, surviving -6.5°C (20°F) of overnight frost. Tolerant of summer drought. ◑

Iris pallida
This pale lilac-blue rhizomatous perennial is wild on the Dalmatian coast and widely cultivated. The grey-green leaves are to 4cm (1½in) across, and the bracts are white and papery. Scented, pale blue flowers, 7.5cm (3in) across, are borne in early summer.
Cultivation Needs well-drained soil.
Height to 1.2m (4ft); spread to 1m (3ft). USZ 9–11, surviving -6.5°C (20°F) of overnight frost. Tolerant of summer drought. ◑

Iris germanica 'Florentina'
This rhizomatous perennial is a white form of the common, blue-flowered *I. germanica,* an ancient garden plant of uncertain origin, but long cultivated in the Mediterranean region. The grey-green leaves are 3.5cm (1½in) across. The bracts are green and papery, and the fragrant, white, blue-flushed flowers, 10cm (4in) across, are borne in late spring. The stems have distinct lateral branches, which distinguish it from the Arabian *I. albicans,* in which the side flowers are stalkless.
Cultivation Grow in dry rocky soil.
Height to 80cm (32in); spread to 1m (3ft). USZ 8–11, surviving -12°C (10°F) of overnight frost. Tolerant of summer drought. ◑

Iris histrio
This perennial bulb is from southern Turkey, Syria, and the Lebanon. The late winter flowers are 6–7.5cm (2½–3in) across, mid- to pale blue, with dark spots and a yellow guide mark on the falls. The thin bracts are white tinged green. The green, narrow, upright leaves, 0.5cm (⅕in) across, elongate after flowering, to 60cm (2ft).
Cultivation Easily grown in sandy or well-drained, clay soil. Water in winter.
Height to 10cm (4in); spread to 12.5cm (5in). USZ 9–11, surviving -6.5°C (20°F) of overnight frost. Tolerant of summer drought. ◑

Iris lutescens
This rhizomatous perennial from southern France, northeastern Spain, and Italy grows on dry hills, flowering in late spring. In spite of its name (meaning "becoming yellow"), the flowers, 5–7.5cm (2–3in) across, can be purple, claret, yellow, white,

Above *Iris pallida*

South African Iris Family

Babiana (Iridaceae)

The genus *Babiana* contains around 65 species of perennials with corms, which are natives of southern Africa and Socotra. All have distinctly pleated leaves. The genus *Antholyza*, with its narrow, red, sunbird-pollinated flowers, is now put in *Babiana*.

Babiana vanzyliae

This perennial corm from the northwestern Cape, particularly around the Pakhuis pass and Nieuwoudtville, in South Africa, grows in fynbos and grassy places on sandstone. The scented flowers, to 5cm (2in) across, are usually yellow but sometimes mauve. The tube is as long as the petals. The flowers are produced in spring.

Cultivation Needs fertile soil, with water when in growth, in winter; keep dry during the summer. Apply fresh wood ash to encourage flowering.

Height to 12cm (5in); spread to 5cm (2in). USZ 10–11, surviving -1°C (30°F) of overnight frost. Tolerant of summer drought. ◑

Dierama (Iridaceae)

Dierama has around 44 species of perennial corms, from South Africa northwards to

Above Wild *Babiana vanzyliae* near Nieuwoudtville

Ethiopia. Most are clump-forming and have tough, flat, narrow leaves and arching stems hung with bell-shaped flowers.

Dierama floriferum

This perennial corm has pale lavender-blue flowers, 4cm (1½in) long, in early summer. It is found wild in the grasslands of central Natal, South Africa. It does not form clumps.

Cultivation Needs well-drained, heavy soil. Water mainly in spring.

Height to 1m (3ft); spread to 60cm (2ft). USZ 9–11, surviving -6.5°C (20°F) of overnight frost. Tolerant of summer drought. ◑

Above *Gladiolus callianthus*

Above *Gladiolus tristis*

Gladiolus (Iridaceae)

With more than 250 species, the genus *Gladiolus* is the largest in the Iris family. It is found from Cape province in South Africa (105 species) northwards to Europe (four species). All varieties have solid corms and leaves that may be rolled or ridged.

Gladiolus callianthus

This perennial corm has flat leaves and long-tubed, sweetly scented, white flowers, with a dark purple star in the throat. It grows wild on wet rocks from Malawi to Kenya, flowering in the rainy season. It is sometimes sold under the old name *Acidanthera murielae*.

Left *Dierama floriferum* with *Geranium robustum*

Below *Watsonia borbonica*

Cultivation Easily grown in wet peaty soil. Keep dry during the dormant season. *Height to 1m (3ft); spread to 60cm (2ft). USZ 10–11, surviving -1°C (30°F) of overnight frost. Tolerant of seasonal drought.* ◗

Gladiolus tristis

This winter-growing perennial corm lives in marshes in the Cape, South Africa, flowering in early spring. The leaves are very narrow, and cruciform in section. The stem has up to 20 pale yellow, night-scented flowers, with a curved tube and more or less equal petals, which together are 6–9cm (2½–3½in) long.
Cultivation Grow in sandy peaty soil. Needs water as well as plenty of sun and air in winter; keep dry in summer. *Height to 1.5m (5ft); spread to 15cm (6in). USZ 10–11, surviving -1°C (30°F) of overnight frost. Tolerant of summer drought.* ◗

Sparaxis (Iridaceae)

Fifteen species of perennial corms, natives of South Africa, from Western Cape to the Karroo. They are close to *Dierama*, but have deciduous leaves and usually upright flowers.

Sparaxis tricolor

This brightly coloured perennial corm has slightly arching stems bearing six orange, purple-pink, or red flowers with a yellow-and-black centre, in spring. It is found only in the Nieuwoudtville district, on the Bokkeveld, in South Africa.
Cultivation Easily grown in deep sandy soil. Keep wet in winter, dry in summer.

Height to 35cm (14in); spread to 10cm (4in). USZ 10–11, surviving -1°C (30°F) of overnight frost. Tolerant of summer drought. ◗

Watsonia (Iridaceae)

Watsonia contains 51 species of perennial corms, which are natives of South Africa, most in the winter-rainfall area of the Cape, but with several in the summer-rainfall areas in Natal. Most species are like the small-flowered *Gladiolus*, but are usually clump-forming with flat evergreen leaves and deeply divided style branches.

Watsonia borbonica

This lovely pink or sometimes white perennial corm can form large colonies on rocky hillsides in the Cape, and flowers most freely after a fire. The flowers, 7cm (3in) across, in two rows on either side of the stem, are borne in spring and summer.
Cultivation Easily grown in well-drained soil in full sun.
Height to 2m (6½ft); spread to 1m (3ft). USZ 9–11, surviving -6.5°C (20°F) of overnight frost. Tolerant of summer drought. ◗

Above *Sparaxis tricolor*

The Lily Family

Fritillaria (Liliaceae)

Fritillaria contains around 150 species from around the northern hemisphere, with the exception of eastern North America. Most species are winter-growing and have solid bulbs and nodding flowers in sombre shades of green, brown-purple, or yellow.

Fritillaria imperialis
This perennial bulb has a whorl of red, orange, or, in cultivated forms, yellow, bell-shaped flowers, to 7.5cm (3in) long, under a tuft of green bracts, in early summer. Each petal has a tear-like drop of watery nectar at its base. The shiny green leaves are to 15cm (6in) long. This species is found wild in the Zagros Mountains in Iran and in southeastern Turkey, on rocky ledges.
Cultivation Grow in fertile, sandy, chalky soil in sun. Water in winter and spring.
Height to 1.2m (4ft); spread to 30cm (1ft). USZ 7–11, surviving -17°C (2°F) of frost. Needs summer drought. ◗

Below *Fritillaria imperialis*

Above *Fritillaria persica* 'Adiyaman' with yellow *Asphodeline* in the Taurus Mountains, in Turkey

Fritillaria persica
This perennial bulb produces greyish leaves, around 6in (15cm) long, and a spike of black, grey, or greenish flowers, to 2cm (¾in), in spring. This species is wild from the Lebanon and southern Turkey to western Iran. 'Adiyaman' is a strong-growing form, which produces sturdy stems, to 1.5m (5ft) long.
Cultivation Easily grown in fertile, rich, well-drained, sandy soil in sun. Water in winter; keep dry in summer.
Height to 1.2m (4ft); spread to 60cm (2ft). USZ 8–11, surviving -12°C (10°F) of overnight frost. Tolerant of summer drought. ◗

Lilium (Liliaceae)
LILY

The genus *Lilium* has around 100 species of perennial bulbs from the northern hemisphere. Most species are summer-growing, with tall stems, many-scaled bulbs, and large flowers, often trumpet-shaped or with recurved petals (Turk's cap).

Lilium candidum
MADONNA LILY
This perennial bulb is one of the few lilies to come from a Mediterranean climate; it grows wild on rocks near the sea and in the mountains from Montenegro and Greece to Turkey and the Lebanon. The flowering stem with numerous narrow leaves emerges in early spring, with blooms opening in late spring. The sweetly scented, pure white flowers, around 15cm (6in) across, are wide-open and trumpet-shaped.
Cultivation Needs well-drained, limestone soil. Water in winter and spring.
Height to 2m (6½ft); spread to 30cm (1ft). USZ 9–11, surviving -6.5°C (20°F) of overnight frost. Tolerant of summer drought. ◗

Lilium formosanum
This elegant, subtropical perennial bulb from Taiwan is widely naturalized elsewhere in subtropical areas, for instance in Natal (South Africa) and Malawi. In late spring or at the start of the rainy season, it forms a tall stem bearing numerous very narrow leaves and up to 10 white, scented,

Above *Lilium* Oriental hybrid

Above *Lilium candidum* (madonna lily)

Above *Lilium formosanum*

trumpet-shaped flowers, around 20cm (8in) long, tapering to a long narrow base, often with a purple stripe on the back of each petal.

Cultivation Easily grown in cool tropical areas, in leafy soil in hedges and among shrubs. Keep bulbs rather dry in winter; water well in summer. It sometimes flowers within a year of sowing seed.

Height to 9m (30ft); spread to 6m (20ft). USZ 9–11, surviving -3°C (27°F) of overnight frost. Tolerant of summer drought. ◖

Lilium Oriental hybrid

This group of hybrid lilies, generally called VII group in the lily classification, has been raised from crosses between the Japanese species *L. auratum* and *L. speciosum*. The scented flowers, around 23cm (9in) across, are borne in late summer. They vary mainly in the amount of spotting and the degree of pink in the flower. 'Casa Blanca' carries pure white flowers.

Cultivation Grow in sandy, leafy soil in sun or partial shade. These summer-growing hybrids are excellent in containers, in which watering and shading can be controlled. If possible, keep them rather dry in winter.

Height to 2m (6½ft); spread to 60cm (2ft). USZ 9–11, surviving -6.5°C (20°F) of overnight frost. Needs water in summer. ◖

Tulipa (Liliaceae)

This genus has around 100 species of spring-flowering perennial bulbs, from Europe to China, growing on dry hills.

Tulipa praestans 'Fusilier'

This fine perennial bulb from central Asia has 1–5 red flowers, 12cm (5in) wide, on a hairy stem, in spring.

Cultivation Plant in autumn, about 20cm (8in) deep, in sandy soil. Water in winter; keep dry after flowering.

Height to 30cm (1ft 5in); spread to 12cm (4¾in). USZ 8–11, surviving -12°C (10°F) of overnight frost. Tolerant of summer drought. ◖

Left *Tulipa praestans* 'Fusilier'

Arum, Gloriosa, & Related Plants

Arum (Araceae)

The genus *Arum* contains 12 species of perennials with thick tubers and stalked, spear- or arrowhead-shaped leaves. They grow wild in Europe, northern Africa, and Asia as far east as Kazakhstan. The flowers are very small, crowded on to a thick stalk (the spadix), the male above the female. These sterile flowers end in hair-like points. Above the flowers is an appendix of the spadix, a smooth fleshy organ, which is purple, black, or sometimes white. The flowers and the base of the spadix are encircled in a smooth flat spathe. When the seeds are becoming ripe, the spadix withers, the stem elongates, and the shining red berries are exposed.

Arum italicum
This tuberous perennial is as attractive in leaf and fruit as it is in flower. The shining green leaves often have white veins and mid-rib or may be irregularly mottled.

Above *Arum palaestinum*

Above *Arum italicum*

Left *Dracunculus vulgaris*

The spathe is 15–40cm (6–16in) long, and is often creamy white like the spadix. *A. italicum* grows wild from southern England to the Mediterranean, and flowers during late spring.
Cultivation Easily grown in leafy soil in sun or shade.
Height and spread to 30cm (1ft). USZ 9–11, surviving -6.5°C (20°F) of overnight frost. Tolerant of summer drought. ◑

Arum palaestinum
This tuberous perennial, which is a native of Palestine, has plain green, rather broad leaves and an intense purplish black spathe and spadix, both 15–20cm (6–8in) long, which are produced in spring.
Cultivation Grow in dry stony soil in a sunny place.
Height and spread to 30cm (1ft). USZ 9–11, surviving -6.5°C (20°F) of overnight frost. Tolerant of summer drought. ◑

Dracunculus (Araceae)

Dracunculus is a genus of three species of perennials, with rounded tubers, a very large appendix to the spadix, and deeply divided leaves on top of a fleshy stem made up of overlapping leaf sheaths. The flowers smell strongly of carrion, and attract blowflies. *Dracunculus* grows wild in the Mediterranean region.

Dracunculus vulgaris
This striking tuberous perennial is found in waste places and among rocks in the Mediterranean, from Corsica to Turkey, flowering in early summer. The palmate leaves are around 35cm (14in) across, and the spadix is around 30cm (12in) long.
Cultivation Easily grown in dry, rocky, or sandy soil. Water in winter.
Height to 2m (6½ft); spread to 50cm (20in). USZ 9–11, surviving -6.5°C (20°F) of overnight frost. Tolerant of summer drought. ◑

Gloriosa (Colchicaceae)

This genus comprises one variable species, or, according to some authorities, around 30 closely related species, of scrambling tuberous perennials, which may have tendrils on the ends of the shining green leaves. The flowers vary greatly from creamy yellow to various types of stripes, to dark red, as well as in the degree of waviness of the petal margins. *Gloriosa* is found mainly in Africa, but extends to Asia. Though the species has a lily-like flower, it is more closely related to autumn-flowering *Colchicum* and, like it, is very poisonous.

Gloriosa superba

Two forms of this striking perennial with its smooth, forked tuberous root are shown here: Virescens group grows wild in Malawi and has yellow-and-red flowers, while the commonly cultivated form, usually called 'Rothschildiana', bears red-and-yellow flowers. Both have petals around 10cm (4in) long. The style is bent to one side, so that it rests in the same plane as the anthers. It flowers from summer to autumn.
Cultivation Plant in early summer in any fertile soil. Keep drier in winter.
Height to 2.4m (8ft); spread to 1m (3ft). USZ 10–11, surviving -1°C (30°F) of overnight frost. Needs water in the growing season. ◗

Sandersonia (Colchicaceae)

Sandersonia has one species of tuberous-rooted perennial, from South Africa, which is closely related to *Gloriosa*.

Sandersonia aurantiaca

This unusual tuberous perennial has scrambling stems, lance-shaped leaves, with a tapering point, and small, swollen bell-shaped, pale orange flowers, in summer. It grows wild in Natal, in South Africa, by streams and on the margins of forest.
Cultivation Plant in early summer in leafy, loamy soil. Keep drier in winter.
Height to 75cm (30in); spread to 1m (3ft). USZ 10–11, surviving -1°C (30°F) of overnight frost. Needs water in the growing season. ◗

Above *Gloriosa superba* 'Rothschildiana'

Above *Sandersonia aurantiaca*
Left *Gloriosa superba* Virescens group in Malawi

Anemone, Cyclamen, & Oxalis

Above A fine blue form of *Anemone coronaria*

Anemone (Ranunculaceae)

The genus *Anemone* comprises around 150 species from most parts of the temperate world. Many are herbaceous perennials; some, such as the familiar wood anemone, are woodland plants with fleshy rhizomes; and several species are Mediterranean plants, flowering in spring and becoming dry and dormant in summer.

Anemone blanda

This early flowering tuberous perennial is found in the mountains of Albania and Greece to Turkey and the Lebanon, where it flowers as soon as the snow has melted. Each stem has three, three-lobed bracts and a single flower, usually blue but sometimes white or pink, 4–6cm (1½–2½in) across. The basal leaves have three lobes.
Cultivation Easily grown in bare, stony, or sandy soil in sun or partial shade. *Height to 10cm (4in); spread to 7.5m (3in). USZ 8–11, surviving -12°C (10°F) of overnight frost. Tolerant of summer drought.* ◑

Anemone coronaria

This tuberous perennial is wild from Spain to Turkey and in North Africa, with the red, blue, or white flower colours tending to stay separate in the wild. The leaves are deeply and finely dissected. Stems with a ruff of finely divided bracts below the single flower, 5–9cm (2–3½in) wide, with black anthers and styles, are borne in early spring. 'De Caen' is commonly grown as a cut flower, in a variety of colours.
Cultivation As for *A. blanda*. *Height to 30cm (1ft); spread to 10cm (4in). USZ 9–11, surviving -6.5°C (20°F) of overnight frost. Tolerant of summer drought.* ◑

Anemone hortensis

This graceful tuberous perennial is wild in the south of France and Italy to Croatia,

Above *Anemone blanda* growing wild in the Taurus Mountains, in Turkey

Above *Anemone hortensis* near St Tropez, in France

Above *Cyclamen repandum* subsp. *repandum* in Italy

Above A seedling of the florists' cyclamen, *Cyclamen persicum*, at La Mortola, in northwestern Italy

growing in thin grass in dry places, often under pines. The leaves are deeply divided into three lobes. Each stem has a ruff of 3–4 simple bracts, half way up, and a single, pink-mauve flower, 5–6cm (2–2½in) wide, with black anthers and styles, in spring.
Cultivation As for *A. blanda*. Plant where competition is not too stiff.
Height to 15cm (6in); spread to 10cm (4in). USZ 9–11, surviving -6.5°C (20°F) of overnight frost. Tolerant of summer drought. ◗

Cyclamen (Primulaceae)

Cyclamen is a genus with around 22 species of perennials, which are natives from around the Black Sea, the Mediterranean, and Somalia. The plants have round and often flattened tubers, numerous heart-shaped leaves, and small flowers with reflexed petals. After blooming the flower stem of most species (not *C. persicum*) coils up to drag the developing capsule among the leaves away from grazing animals. Some species flower in spring, others in autumn.

Cyclamen persicum
This is the species from which all the florists' cyclamen were raised. In spite of its name, this tuberous perennial is a native of the Greek islands, the eastern Mediterranean coast, and the Lebanon, not Persia; it usually grows on cliff ledges or among rocks, away from grazing animals. In the wild forms the flowers are scented, pale pink or white with a red "nose", similar to those of *C. repandum*, but breeding has developed broader, less twisted petals, in a wider range of colours. They appear from late winter to early spring.
Cultivation Easily grown in rocky soil. Self-sows in rock crevices or under trees.
Height and spread to 25cm (10in). USZ 10–11, surviving -1°C (30°F) of overnight frost. Tolerant of summer drought. ◗

Cyclamen repandum
This is a Mediterranean, spring-flowering tuberous perennial. It has marbled leaves and slender petals, around 2.5cm (1in) long. Subsp. *repandum* is the deep pink, wild form from central Italy, while pale pink subsp. *peloponnesiacum*, with more spotted leaves, grows wild in oak woods near Sparta, Greece.
Cultivation. Easily grown in leafy stony soil, in shade in hot areas, and away from spring frosts in cold areas.The leaves die away in early summer.
Height to 15cm (6in); spread to 30cm (1ft). USZ 9–11, surviving -6.5°C (20°F) of frost in winter. Tolerant of summer drought. ◗

Left *Cyclamen repandum* subsp. *peloponnesiacum*

Oxalis (Oxalidaceae)

The genus *Oxalis* contains around 500 species from throughout the world, but mostly in South Africa (120 species in the Cape) and South America. Most have small bulbs, but some are annuals, and a few are succulent shrubs. Several are pernicious weeds, but nearly all are beautiful, with shining flowers and a great diversity of leaves based on a shamrock-like design.

Oxalis smithiana
This lovely perennial bulb from South Africa has three deeply divided leaflets and lilac or white flowers, around 2.5cm (1in) across, with red throats, in autumn.
Cultivation Grow in sandy soil in sun.
Height and spread to 20cm (8in). USZ 10–11, surviving -1°C (30°F) of overnight frost. Tolerant of summer drought. ◗

Above *Oxalis smithiana*

Annuals

S<small>UMMER ANNUALS ARE AN</small> excellent choice for warm gardens, as their seed germinates quickly at high temperatures, and, if well watered, the plants produce a good display of colour over a long period. Other annuals originate in arid regions, growing through the winter and flowering for a short season, in spring and early summer.

Above *Dimorphotheca pluvialis* (see p. 222)

South African Daisies

Felicia (Compositae)

The genus *Felicia* contains around 83 species of annuals, perennials, and dwarf evergreen shrubs, mostly natives of South Africa, but with some also occurring in tropical Africa and the Arabian peninsula. *F. australis* and *F. dubia* both have rich blue or mauve flowerheads.

Above *Felicia amelloides* 'Santa Cruz'

Felicia amelloides

This perennial normally grown as an annual comes from South Africa. It has elegant slender stems and light green leaves. 'Santa Cruz' is a good selection bearing light or deep blue, daisy-like flowerheads, with yellow centres, from summer to autumn.
Cultivation Grow in well-drained soil in full sun.
Height and spread to 60cm (2ft). USZ 10–11, surviving -1°C (30°F) of overnight frost. Tolerant of summer drought. ◑

Osteospermum (Compositae)

Osteospermum comprises around 70 species of annuals, perennials, shrubs and subshrubs, natives mostly of southern Africa, but with some species also in tropical Africa and on the Arabian peninsula and one species on St Helena. There are many hybrid cultivars, ranging in habit from bushy to sprawling, with flowers from white to deep purple, usually with a contrasting colour on the reverse. For perennial *Osteospermums* see p.193.

Above *Osteospermum pinnatum*

Osteospermum pinnatum

This annual from Namibia and South Africa has creeping stems and pinnate leaves. The white, yellow, or buff-orange rays that form the daisy-like flowers are dark beneath. Seed germinates after winter rains, and the plants grow in cool moist conditions, flowering in spring and early summer.
Cultivation Grow in dry sandy soil in full sun. Is tolerant of coastal conditions.
Height and spread to 30cm (1ft). USZ 10–11, surviving -1°C (30°F) of overnight frost. Tolerant of summer drought. ◑

Above *Osteospermum pinnatum* with other daisies in dry country east of Nieuwoudtville, in South Africa

American Annuals

Argemone (Papaveraceae)

This genus has around 25 species of spiny-leaved annuals, biennials, and perennials, which are mostly natives of North and Central America and the Caribbean.

Argemone pleiacantha
This annual or short-lived perennial is from Arizona and New Mexico to northern Mexico. It has prickly stems, grey prickly leaves, and white flowers with a mass of crimson stamens, from summer to early autumn. Subsp. *pleiacantha* is sometimes sold under the name 'White Lustre'.
Cultivation Grow in well-drained soil in sun. Is easy to raise from seed sown in autumn or spring.
Height to 1m (3ft); spread to 60cm (2ft). USZ 10–11, surviving -1°C (30°F) of overnight frost. Tolerant of summer drought. ◑

Above *Cleome hassleriana*

Above *Argemone pleiacantha*

Cleome (Cruciferae)

Cleome contains around 75 species of annuals, biennials, and perennials, some of which are shrubby. Most are natives of tropical America and Africa.

Cleome hassleriana (syn. *C. spinosa*)
SPIDER PLANT
This sticky aromatic annual from Argentina to southeastern Brazil is widely naturalized in the warmer parts of America. It has palmate leaves and spikes of spidery pink, mauve, or white flowers with long stamens in summer and autumn.
Cultivation Grow in fertile, well-drained soil in full sun. Sow seeds in spring and water when young; tolerates dry soil later.

Height to 2m (6½ft); spread to 1m (3ft). USZ 10–11, surviving -1°C (30°F) of overnight frost. Tolerant of summer drought. ◑

Eschscholzia (Papaveraceae)

This genus contains about 12 species of annuals, biennials, and perennials, natives of western North America and Mexico.

Eschscholzia californica
CALIFORNIA POPPY
This robust annual or perennial is from northwestern America to southern California. Its feathery leafy stems bear cup-shaped flowers in yellow and orange from early spring to autumn. There are varieties with single or double flowers, including 'Ballerina' (pink and cerise, with frilled petals) and 'Sundew' (pale cream).
Cultivation Does best in light, well-drained soil in full sun. Often self-seeds.
Height and spread to 30cm (1ft). USZ 10–11, surviving -1°C (30°F) of overnight frost. Tolerant of summer drought. ◑

Nicotiana (Solanaceae)

The genus *Nicotiana* comprises around 70 species of annuals, biennials, perennials, and evergreen shrubs, which are mostly natives of America, but with a few species in Australia and one in southern Africa.

Nicotiana alata
TOBACCO PLANT
This bushy annual or perennial from South America produces sticky stems and loose heads of strongly evening-scented, funnel-shaped, greenish white flowers, around 7.5cm (3in) long, in summer.
Cultivation Needs fertile, deep, rich, well-drained soil in sun. Often self-seeds.
Height 1m (3ft) or more; spread to 60cm (2ft). USZ 10–11, surviving -1°C (30°F) of frost. Water in summer until flowering begins. ◑

Petunia (Solanaceae)

Petunia has around 35 species of annuals, biennials, and short-lived perennials, which

Above *Eschscholzia californica* (California poppy)

Above *Platystemon californicus* (Cream Cups) and *Eschscholzia californica* (Californian poppy) near the Russian River on the coast of northwest California

are natives of South America. White petunias are generally the best scented.

Petunia integrifolia (syn. *P. violacea*)

This spreading annual or occasionally short-lived perennial is from Argentina. Its sticky stems bear funnel-shaped, single, violet flowers, 5cm (2in) across, in summer. **Cultivation** Grow in fertile soil in sun. Sow seeds in spring or early summer. *Height to 60cm (2ft); spread to 30cm (1ft). USZ 10–11, surviving -1°C (30°F) of overnight frost. Requires regular watering in summer* ◗

Petunia 'Satin and Silk'

This is one of the many garden hybrid annuals raised by breeders, in a great variety of flower colours, shapes, and sizes. It has single, funnel-shaped, pink, purple, or violet flowers, 10cm (4in) across, in summer. Most hybrids are more compact in habit than the *Petunia* species, the exception to this being Surfinias (sometimes put in *Calibrachoa*), which are trailing plants. **Cultivation** Grow in fertile soil in sun. Sow seed in heat in spring. Deadhead to prolong the flowering season. *Height and spread to 30cm (1ft). USZ 10–11, surviving -1°C (30°F) of overnight frost. Requires regular watering in summer.* ◗

Platystemon (Papaveraceae)

The genus *Platystemon* has one species, an annual from California east to Arizona.

Above *Nicotiana alata* (tobacco plant)

Platystemon californicus

CREAM CUPS

This pretty, hairy annual grows in open grassy places on the coast or along streams in drier areas inland. It produces narrow leaves and yellow or white, cup-shaped flowers, around 2cm (¾in) across, with many conspicuous stamens, in spring. The seedheads are made up of thin carpels, which break into single-seeded sections. **Cultivation** Grow in well-drained, fertile soil in sun. Sow seeds in autumn. *Height and spread to 30cm (1ft). USZ 9–11, surviving −6.5°C (20°F) of overnight frost. Requires water in summer.* ◗

Left *Petunia integrifolia* with a modern white cultivar
Far Left *Petunia* 'Satin and Silk'

219

Mediterranean Annuals

Campanula (Campanulaceae)

This genus has around 300 species of annuals, biennials, and perennials, mostly natives of western Europe, with some also in Japan and North America, and 108 species in Turkey. *C. medium* (Canterbury bells), from the Alpes Maritimes in France and Italy, is a beautiful tough biennial, which plant breeders have used to produce often more compact, less elegant plants, with double flowers. However, the original, single-flowered forms are still the best.

Campanula incurva
This stiff, usually spreading biennial is from eastern Greece. It produces greyish, hairy stems and pale blue flowers, around 5cm (2in) long, in early summer.
Cultivation Grow in a little soil in partial shade, on an old wall, where it will naturalize if allowed to seed. Deadhead to prolong the flowering season, but remember to keep a head or two for seed.
Height and spread to 45cm (18in). USZ 10–11, surviving -1°C (30°F) of overnight frost. Tolerant of summer drought if in shade. ◗

Cerinthe (Boraginaceae)

The genus *Cerinthe* contains around 10 species of annuals, biennials, and, occasionally, perennials, which are natives of Europe and the Mediterranean region.

Cerinthe major
This upright or spreading annual is from Portugal and all around the Mediterranean. It has bluish green leaves, blotched with white when young, followed by striking, dark greeny blue bracts that almost hide the tubular, yellow, reddish, or purplish flowers, around 2.5cm (1in) long, which appear in spring. 'Purpurascens' is a selection with darker blue bracts.
Cultivation Grow in light, well-drained soil in full sun or partial shade. Sow seed in autumn. Deadhead to prolong flowering.
Height and spread to 60cm (2ft). USZ 9–11, surviving -6.5°C (20°F) of overnight frost. Tolerant of summer drought. ◗

Lupinus (Leguminosae)
LUPIN

Lupinus comprises around 200 species of annuals, perennials, and evergreen shrubs, mostly native of North or South America, but with a few species in southern Europe and southwestern Asia. *L. luteus* is another good annual species, with yellow scented flowers. Most lupin seeds are poisonous if eaten.

Lupinus pilosus (syn. *L. varius* subsp. *orientalis*)
This upright annual, which is a native from Greece and Crete to Israel, produces silky-haired, greyish green leaves with oblong to inversely ovate, folded leaflets, around 5cm (2in) long. The deep blue flowers, around 1cm (⅜in) across, with a white-and-yellow or pale purple blotch, are carried in spring (*see also* p.11).
Cultivation Grow in well-drained soil in sun or partial shade. Sow seed in autumn.
Height and spread to 45cm (18in). USZ 10–11, surviving -1°C (30°F) of overnight frost. Tolerant of summer drought. ◗

Above *Cerinthe major*

Michauxia (Campanulaceae)

This genus has around seven species of biennials and monocarpic perennials, which are natives of southwestern Asia and the eastern Mediterranean.

Michauxia campanuloides
This upright biennial, from western Syria and southwestern Turkey, has bristle-haired stems and cyclamen-shaped, white or pale purple flowers, around 9cm (3½in) across, in early summer.
Cultivation Grow in dry, well-drained soil, in a rock crevice or wall, in full sun. Sow seed in spring; plants may take several years to reach flowering size, slowly building up a tuberous root.
Height to 1.5m (5ft); spread to 30cm (1ft). USZ 10–11, surviving -1°C (30°F) of overnight frost. Tolerant of summer drought. ◗

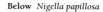
Below *Nigella papillosa*

Papaver (Papaveraceae)
POPPY

The genus *Papaver* contains around 70 species of annuals, biennials, and perennials natives of temperate areas worldwide.

Papaver rhoeas
A tough annual from Europe and northern Africa, east across Asia to northwest China. Green leaves and red flowers, with a black blotch at the base of the petals, in summer. Shirley Series is a group of strains from a wild, pale-edged mutant of *P. rhoeas*. They bear single flowers in white, pink, and salmon; 'Reverend Wilks' is one with a white centre.
Cultivation Needs well-drained, sunny soil. *Height and spread to 60cm (2ft). USZ 9–11, surviving -6.5°C (20°F) of overnight frost. Tolerant of summer drought.* ◑

Above *Lupinus pilosus* on the beach at Phaselis, in southern Turkey

Nigella (Ranunculaceae)
LOVE-IN-A-MIST

Nigella has around 22 species of annuals, native of southwestern Asia and southern Europe. *N. damascena* is the source of many cultivars, such as 'Miss Jekyll', with its semi-double, soft blue or white flowers.

Nigella papillosa (syn. *N. hispanica*)
This annual, from Portugal and Spain, has feathery green bracts and deep purplish blue flowers, around 5cm (2in) across, with masses of dark reddish stamens, in summer, followed by horned seed pods.
Cultivation Grow in fertile, well-drained soil in sun or partial shade. Sow seed in autumn or spring.
Height to 45cm (18in); spread to 30cm (1ft). USZ 9–11, surviving -6.5°C (20°F) of overnight frost. Tolerant of summer drought. ◑

Above *Papaver rhoeas* Shirley Series

Left *Michauxia campanuloides*
Far Left *Campanula incurva* on a shady wall

Annual Daisies

Cosmos (Compositae)

The genus *Cosmos* contains around 26 species of annuals and perennials, which are natives of tropical and warm areas of central and northern South America.

Cosmos sulphureus
This annual from Mexico produces divided leaves and yellow or orange flowerheads in late summer and autumn. Shorter varieties include: 'Ladybird Scarlet' with bright reddish orange flowerheads; 'Lemon Bird' with soft yellow flowerheads; and 'Sunset' with bronze-shaded, orange flowerheads.
Cultivation Grow in well-drained soil in sun. Sow seeds in early summer.

Height to 2m (6½ft); spread to 1m (3ft). USZ 10–11, surviving -1°C (30°F) of overnight frost. Tolerant of summer drought. ◑

Dimorphotheca (Compositae)

The genus *Dimorphotheca* has around 19 species of annuals, which are natives of southern and tropical Africa.

Dimorphotheca pluvialis
RAIN DAISY
This quick-growing annual is from Namibia and South Africa. It produces coarsely toothed, dark green leaves and shiny, white, daisy-like flowerheads, which are purplish and sometimes blue at the base, borne from

Above *Dimorphotheca pluvialis* (rain daisy)

late summer to autumn. 'Glistening White' is a dwarf form.
Cultivation Grow in light soil in full sun. Sow seed in late summer or early autumn. In South Africa it germinates quickly after rain (hence the name), so water after sowing, and when young. Keep dry later. *Height and spread to 40cm (16in). USZ 9–11, surviving -6.5°C (20°F) of overnight frost. Tolerant of summer drought.* ◑

Gazania (Compositae)

This genus comprises around 17 species of annuals and perennials, which are natives of tropical and South Africa.

Gazania rigida
This stemless annual, or perennial, is from South Africa. It has deeply divided leaves, which are greyish and woolly on the underside, and formed in a basal tuft. The solitary, deep orange flowerheads, with a dark blotch at the base of each petal, are borne in winter.
Cultivation Grow in well-drained soil in full sun. Sow seeds in autumn or spring.

Above *Gazania rigida* growing wild in South Africa
Left *Cosmos sulphureus* on Tequila Mountain in Mexico

Above *Gorteria diffusa* (beetle daisy) near Nieuwoudtville, South Africa

Above *Zinnia elegans*

are a few annuals, some of which are cultivated and have become naturalized in other parts of the world. All species appear to have yellow or white flowerheads, and those in the annual species have a dark centre. *U. cakilefolia* has finely divided leaves.

Ursinia calenduliflora

This annual from Namaqualand, South Africa, has finely divided leaves and solitary orange flowerheads, 2–5cm (¾–2in) across, with a dark ring at the base, from summer to autumn.
Cultivation Grow in sandy soil in full sun. Sow seed in winter, watering at first.
Height to 1m (3ft); spread to 30cm (1ft). USZ 10–11, surviving -1°C (30°F) of overnight frost. Tolerant of summer drought. ◗

Zinnia (Compositae)

Zinnia has around 11 species of annuals, perennials, and low deciduous subshrubs, natives of Central America, especially Mexico. *Z. angustifolia* has small orange flowerheads, as does the rather similar *Z. haageana*, from which has been bred 'Persian Carpet' with its large double flowerheads in mixed shades of cream, yellow, pink, red, purple, and brown.

Zinnia elegans

This stout-stemmed, upright annual, from Mexico, has bristly stems, ovate hairy leaves, and single, daisy-like flowerheads in white, pink, and orange, in summer. 'Envy' bears green flowerheads, and 'Whirligig' has striking bicoloured marks on the ray petals.
Cultivation Grow in rich, well-drained soil in full sun. Sow seed in spring, and water while becoming established.
Height to 60cm (2ft); spread to 30cm (1ft). USZ 10–11, surviving -1°C (30°F) of overnight frost. Tolerant of summer drought. ●

Height and spread to 20cm (8in). USZ 9–11, surviving -1°C (30°F) of overnight frost. Tolerant of summer drought. ◗

Gorteria (Compositae)

The genus *Gorteria* has around three species of annuals, which are natives of southern Africa, from the Cape to Namibia.

Gorteria diffusa
BEETLE DAISY
This mat-forming, sprawling annual has narrow, rolled, green leaves, which are hairy on the upper side and white-felted

underneath. The daisy-like flowerheads, around 5cm (2in) across, are yellowish orange, with realistic, shiny, black, beetle-like markings. They appear in summer.
Cultivation Grow in fertile, well-drained soil in full sun.
Height to 10cm (4in); spread to 30cm (1ft). USZ 10–11, surviving -1°C (30°F) of overnight frost. Tolerant of summer drought. ◗

Ursinia (Compositae)

This genus contains around 38 species from South Africa, with one species in Ethiopia. Most are small evergreen shrubs, but there

Right *Ursinia calenduliflora*

Cactuses & Other Succulents

SUCCULENTS INCLUDING CACTUSES have developed their fleshy stems or leaves to store water and survive dry weather in hot climates. They are the perfect plants for growing in areas where rain is unreliable or watering difficult, and most combine unusual shapes with beautiful and often wonderfully scented flowers.

Above *Echinopsis tarijensis* (see p. 243)

Agaves

Agave (Agavaceae)

The genus *Agave* consists of around 100 species of rosette-forming succulent perennials, which are natives of the Americas, with most species in Mexico. These plants spend several years building up a large rosette, until it is large enough to bloom. Although the rosette dies after flowering, it leaves suckers or produces plenty of seed. The flowers of *Agave* are generally small, yellow, brown, or greenish, with six tepals and six long stamens. Many species are grown as ornamentals, but *A. sisalana* is an important fibre plant, widely grown in semi-arid areas, and *A. tequilana* is used to make tequila.

Below *Agave attenuata* lining the edge of a cliff in the Sierra Madre Occidental, in western Mexico

Above *Agave deserti*

Agave americana

This succulent perennial is a native of Mexico and has naturalized in the Mediterranean region. It forms a huge rosette, with leaves growing to 1.5m (5ft) long. A spike, to 8m (25ft) long, with horizontal tiers of yellow flowers, measuring to 10cm (4in) long, is produced in summer. 'Mediopicta-alba' has a white stripe down the centre of each leaf; 'Marginata' has pale-edged leaves.

Right *Agave americana* 'Mediopicta-alba'

Cultivation Easily grown in any dry soil in full sun; is good also in a pot (*see* p.29). *Height to 8m (25ft); spread to 3m (10ft). USZ 9–11, if dry surviving -6.5°C (20°F) of frost. Tolerant of summer drought.* ◗

Agave attenuata

This succulent perennial is wild in Mexico, where it hangs from ledges on the cliffs. It has a prostrate trunk and fleshy glaucous rosettes of broad leaves, 50–70cm (20–28in) long. An arching inflorescence, to 3.5m (11½ft) long, of green flowers, 3.5–5cm (1½–2in) long, appears in summer. After flowering, small plants form on the stem.
Cultivation Easily grown in shallow, well-drained soil.

Height to 1.5m (5ft); spread to 3.5m (11½ft). USZ 9–11, surviving -6.5°C (20°F) of frost. Tolerant of summer drought. ◗◗

Agave deserti

This desert succulent perennial is found in southern California, Arizona, and northwestern Mexico. It forms colonies of greyish rosettes with pale-spined leaves, 15–40cm (6–16in) long. Yellowish flowers, to 5cm (2in) long, in a slender inflorescence, to 3m (10ft) long, in spring.
Cultivation Easily grown in any hot, dry, sandy soil in full sun.
Height to 5m (16ft); spread to 1m (3ft). USZ 10–11, surviving -1°C (30°F) of overnight frost. Tolerant of summer drought. ◑

Aloes

Aloe (Aloacae)

This genus of succulent perennials is invaluable for its colourful and long-lasting flowers, which have the bonus of being borne mostly in winter. There are around 350 species, and most are very drought-tolerant, as they come from dry parts of southern Africa and Arabia. Apart from being of ornamental value, a few species are effective medicines: *A. vera* contains an antibiotic juice, and is still a popular remedy for burns. Keep a plant on your kitchen windowsill and dab the sap from the juicy leaves on to any burn. Recent studies have moved *Aloe* into its own family, Aloaceae, which is close to the larger, more diverse Asphodelaceae. All *Aloe* have tubular, red, yellow, or green flowers, and produce thick sweet nectar, which attracts sunbirds as well as other honey-eating birds.

Above *Aloe mitriformis* growing wild in Vleiland, South Africa

Above *Aloe arborescens* (krantz aloe) at Le Clos du Peyronnet, Menton, in France, in January

Aloe arborescens
KRANTZ ALOE

This shrubby succulent perennial was one of the earliest *Aloes* to be cultivated, by Philip Miller in the Chelsea Physic Garden in the late 18th century, and is widespread now in gardens. In the wild in southern Africa, from Malawi and Zimbabwe as far south as Caledon in South Africa, it grows in bushland and open forest. It forms large clumps of branching stems, and the tall spikes of red or yellow flowers, 4cm (1½in) long, each on a thin stalk, are produced in midwinter. The sword-shaped, bluish green, wavy-edged leaves, 50–60cm (20–24in) long, 5–7cm (2–3in) wide, are in spreading rosettes and have short teeth.
Cultivation This is one of the most tolerant species, being drought-resistant but accepting rain at any time of year. It also survives salt winds from the sea. It grows well on dry rocks and cliffs, for instance on the Mediterranean coast. Plant it in poor rocky soil.
Height and spread to 3m (10ft). USZ 10–11, surviving -1°C (30°F) of overnight frost. Tolerant of summer drought. ☉

Aloe dichotoma
GULIVER TREE

This strange, primitive-looking, tree-like succulent perennial has a thick bare trunk at the base, branching out stiffly to form a distinctive flat top. It is native of the Cape area of South Africa, Namaqualand, and

Namibia, where it grows on north-facing slopes in hilly areas. The thick, narrowly lance-shaped, greyish green leaves, 25–35cm (10–14in) long, and 4–6cm (1½–2½in) wide, have tiny yellowish teeth on the margin. The flowers, 3.5cm (1½in) long, are bright yellow and carried on a branched inflorescence in midwinter.
Cultivation Grow in a warm, dry, sunny position in sandy soil in a desert climate. Would make a dramatic focal point in a large garden.
Height to 9m (30ft); spread to 7m (23ft). USZ 10–11, surviving -1°C (30°F) of overnight frost. Tolerant of summer drought. ☉

Aloe mitriformis

This prostrate succulent perennial is from South Africa, where it grows on rocky

Above *Aloe dichotoma* (Guliver tree) in Namaqualand in South Africa

sandstone and granite from the Bokkeveld Mountains to Kleinmond. The stems sprawl along the ground, turning upwards at the ends and sending up short, thick, fleshy, greyish, lance-shaped, usually unmarked leaves, 30cm (1ft) long, 15cm (6in) wide, with toothed margins and occasionally a stray spine on the back. The teeth are white when young, turning brownish yellow on older leaves. The inflorescence consists of several dense clusters of drooping scarlet flowers, around 7.5cm (3in) long, borne from winter to spring.

Cultivation Grow in sandy soil in a warm sunny spot.

Height to 60cm (2ft); spread to 3m (10ft). USZ 10–11, surviving -1°C (30°F) of overnight frost. Tolerant of summer drought. ◖

Aloe plicatilis

BERGAALWYN

This tree-like succulent perennial is a native of South Africa in the Cape from Tulbagh to Stellenbosch, where it grows on rocky mountain slopes. The stems are repeatedly forked. The stiff, greyish, strap-shaped leaves are around 30cm (1ft) long and 4cm (1½in) wide, almost flat, spineless,

and carried in two ranks, a feature that distinguishes this from most other common species of *Aloe*. The red-stalked flowers, around 5cm (2in) long, are borne in a simple inflorescence, which appears from spring to early summer in South Africa, and from late winter to early spring in the Mediterranean and California.

Cultivation Does well in sandy soil in a hot sunny place. Survives in climates that are cool in summer.

Height to 5m (16ft); spread to 6m (20ft). USZ 10–11, surviving -1°C (30°F) of overnight frost. Tolerant of summer drought. ◖

Aloe variegata

PARTRIDGE-BREAST ALOE

This succulent perennial grows wild in South Africa, from Namaqualand and the Western Karoo to Uniondale, where it inhabits gravelly clay desert flats. It is stemless and makes only a small rosette of very thick, stiff, sword-shaped leaves, to 35cm (14in) long and 2cm (¾in) wide, arranged in three ranks. The fleshy, dark green leaves are horizontally striped and edged with white (hence the name). Loose spikes of hanging, bright pinkish to red

Above *Aloe variegata* (partridge-breast aloe)

flowers, 3–4.5cm (1¼–1¾in) long, edged white at the throat, are produced in spring on purple stems.

Cultivation Grow in sandy soil in a warm sunny place, or in a container on a sunny windowsill.

Height to 40cm (16in); spread to 30cm (1ft). USZ 10–11, surviving -1°C (30°F) of overnight frost. Tolerant of summer drought. ◖

Above *Aloe plicatilis* (bergaalwyn) in the National Botanic Gardens, Kirstenbosch, in South Africa

Desert Bromeliads & Yuccas

Puya (Bromeliaceae)

Puya has around 170 species of succulent bromeliads, from South America. Most are found in dry valleys in the Andes, and some occur at considerable altitudes, for instance 5,000m (16,000ft) in Peru and Bolivia, in the case of the giant *P. raimondii*, whose rosettes can take 100 years to reach flowering sizes and whose inflorescence, with 8,000 flowers, reaches 11m (36ft). Most species have flowers with three thick petals, in shades of green or blackish blue, and many have the ends of the branches modified into a perch, where pollinating birds can sit as they reach the nectar. In spite of their dry mountain habitat, most species grow well in mild climates, especially if protected from excessive winter rain.

Puya berteroana
This desert succulent bromeliad is from the mountains near the coast in central Chile, and it grows well in the drier parts of coastal California. The thick stems, with 60 or more grey branches, bear rather soft, sword-shaped leaves, 1m (3ft) long and 6cm (2½in) wide. Dark greenish blue, tubular flowers, around 4cm (1½in) long, with contrasting orange anthers and a flared mouth, are carried in summer.
Cultivation Needs dry sandy soil in a hot sunny position, with some water in spring.
Height to 4m (13ft); spread to 2m (6½ft). USZ 10–11, surviving -1°C (30°F) of overnight frost. Tolerant of summer drought. ◖

Puya castellanosii
This succulent bromeliad forms large clumps of silvery, sword-shaped leaves,

Above *Puya berteroana*

1m (3ft) long and 6cm (2½in) across, with recurved thorns, and milky blue, flared, tubular flowers, 7.5cm (3in) long, on around 40 long, dark purplish branches. We found it flowering in early summer in the Andes in northern Argentina.
Cultivation As for *P. berteroniana*.
Height to 2m (6½ft); spread to 3m (10ft). USZ 10–11, surviving -1°C (30°F) of overnight frost. Tolerant of summer drought. ◖

Puya chilensis
This succulent bromeliad has green, sword-shaped leaves, around 1m (3ft) long and 6cm (2½in) across, with very strong recurved thorns. The yellow, flared, tubular flowers, around 7.5cm (3in) long, on a thick inflorescence, are borne on around 100 short green branches in summer. *P. chilensis* is found wild in central Chile.
Cultivation As for *P. berteroniana*.
Height to 5m (16ft); spread to 3m (10ft). USZ 10–11, surviving -1°C (30°F) of overnight frost. Tolerant of summer drought. ◖

Puya venusta
This succulent bromeliad from Chile has silvery rosettes of sword-shaped leaves, around 30cm (1ft) long and 2.5cm (1in) across, with short recurved thorns. Pinkish red stems are topped by short spikes of blue, twisted, tubular flowers, around 2.5cm (1in) long, in summer.
Cultivation As for *P. berteroniana*.
Height to 5m (16ft); spread to 3m (10ft). USZ 10–11, surviving -1°C (30°F) of overnight frost. Tolerant of summer drought. ◓

Left *Puya chilensis* in Tresco, Isles of Scilly

Above *Puya venusta*

Yucca (Agavaceae)

Most of the 30 *Yucca* species are perennials, evergreen shrubs, and trees, and are found in desert and semi-desert areas of the southern USA, Mexico, and the West Indies. Most species have stiff, leathery, and fleshy leaves and a tall, stiff, branched flowering stem with creamy white, bell-shaped flowers. Pollination is by the yucca moth, *Tegeticula spp.*, which lives in the flowers; it gathers up pollen from one flower, before flying to another and laying an egg in the stigma; it then puts one of the balls of pollen it has gathered on top of the egg. The pollen fertilizes the flower, and the larva feeds on some of the developing seeds, leaving others to ripen normally. For tree *Yuccas see p.18*.

Yucca gloriosa
This shrub, from North Carolina to Florida, has a woody trunk and stiff, spine-tipped leaves, to 50cm (20in) long and 5cm (2in) wide. The flower stem reaches 1.5m (5ft). Nodding, white or purplish flowers, 5–7cm (2–3in) long, open in autumn.
Cultivation Needs dry, sandy or clay soil in full sun. Give some water in summer.
Height to 6.5m (22ft); spread to 2m (6½ft). USZ 8–11, surviving -12°C (10°F) of overnight frost. Tolerant of summer drought. ◗

Yucca whipplei
OUR LORD'S CANDLE
This stemless shrub, from California and Mexico, has stiff, finely toothed leaves, to 1m (3ft) long and 1.5cm (½in) wide. Its flower stem, 2m (6½ft) or more long, is multi-branched. The scented, nodding, white flowers, 5–7cm (2–3in) long, open in spring (*see* p.19).
Cultivation Needs dry rocky soil in full sun. Water in winter.
Height to 3m (10ft); spread to 2m (6½ft). USZ 9–11, surviving -6.5°C (20°F) of overnight frost. Tolerant of summer drought. ◗

Above *Puya castellanosii*, Calchaqui Valley, Argentina

Above *Yucca gloriosa* at Kew, with the red trunks of ***Arbutus x andrachnoides*** behind
Left *Yucca whipplei* (Our Lord's candle) near Bakersfield, California

The Crassula Family

Above *Aeonium arboreum* 'Zwartkop'

Aeonium (Crassulaceae)

The genus *Aeonium* consists of 31 species, most of which are found wild in the Canary Islands and Madeira, but a few extend as far south and east as Tanzania and Arabia. The majority are short-stemmed succulent perennials, which build up a monocarpic rosette over several years. A few, such as *A. arboreum*, have branching stems, and this species has become a weed on the coast of New Zealand.

Aeonium arboreum
This succulent perennial is a native of Gran Canaria. The green rosettes are 12–20cm (5–8in) across. Flowering stems, around 30cm (1ft) long, with masses of yellow, star-shaped flowers, around 1cm (⅜in) across, are produced in late spring. 'Zwartkop' has dark purple leaves.
Cultivation Easily grown in rather dry soil.
Height to 1m (3ft); spread to 60cm (2ft).
USZ 10–11, surviving -1°C (30°F) of overnight frost. Tolerant of summer drought. ◑

Cotyledon (Crassulaceae)

Cotyledon contains nine species from South Africa to Arabia, of which six are to be found in the Cape. They are shrubby succulent perennials, often with waxy leaves and nodding tubular flowers.

Cotyledon orbiculata
KOUTERIE, VARKOOR
This succulent perennial has cylindical to inversely ovate, thick, white leaves, 8cm (3in) long. The red, hanging flowers, 1.2cm (½in) long, with recurved tips, appear from spring to autumn. *C. orbiculata* grows in dry rocky places from Namibia to the Cape, the Karroo, and eastwards in dry areas to high in the Drakensberg.
Cultivation Easily grown in sandy soil. Water infrequently in the growing season.
Height to 1m (3ft); spread to 60cm (2ft).
USZ 10–11, surviving -1°C (30°F) of overnight frost. Tolerant of summer drought. ◑

Crassula (Crassulaceae)

Crassula is an important genus of succulent annuals, herbaceous perennials, evergreen subshrubs, shrubs, and trees. There are around 200 species, mostly in the southern hemisphere, of which 105 occur in the winter-rainfall region of the Cape, South Africa. Some are moss-like aquatics, and one, *C. helmsii* from New Zealand, has

Above *Cotyledon orbiculata* (kouterie)

become a weed in pools and reservoirs in England. Others are minute desert succulents, and many, such as *C. coccinea*, have large flat heads of red or pink flowers.

Crassula ovata
This evergreen succulent shrub can eventually make a small, much-branched tree, and is also a popular houseplant in Europe. It is wild from the Swartberg in the Cape to Natal, in South Africa. The green ovate leaves, 2–4cm (¾–1½in) long, have a red edge. White, star-shaped flowers, 2cm (¾in) across, in a rounded head, are borne in winter. The rather similar *C. arborescens* has white leaves, and flowers in summer.
Cultivation Easily grown in any soil. Position where the plant will receive sun in late summer, to encourage flowering.
Height to 9m (30ft); spread to 6m (20ft).
USZ 9–11, surviving -3°C (27°F) of overnight frost. Tolerant of summer drought. ◑

Above *Crassula ovata*

Above *Kalanchoe pumila*

Dudleya (Crassulaceae)

This genus comprises approximately 40 species of succulent perennials, which are natives of dry parts of California and elsewhere in southwestern North America. Many have white, wax-covered leaves and masses of small fleshy rosettes.

Dudleya pulverulenta
This rosetted succulent perennial is found wild in dry coastal hills from San Luis Obispo county in California to Baja California, Mexico. The stem has broad clasping leaves, 8–25cm (3–10in) long, to 10cm (4in) wide, covered with white waxy blooms. The deep red flowers, 1.2–2cm (½–¾in) long, are tubular nearly to the middle, and are borne in early summer.
Cultivation Needs dry soil in partial shade. Water in late winter and spring.

Above *Dudleya pulverulenta* in California
Right *Kalanchoe thyrsiflora*

Height and spread to 80cm (32in). USZ 10–11, surviving -1°C (30°F) of overnight frost. Tolerant of summer drought. ◑

Kalanchoe (Crassulaceae)

Kalanchoe consists of 200 species of succulents from annuals and perennials to trees, from Africa, Asia, and Australasia, with many beautiful species in Madagascar.

Kalanchoe pumila
This Madagascan subshrub has greyish green leaves, 2.5cm (1in) long, and pink, four-petalled flowers, 2cm (¾in) long, in spring.

Cultivation Grow in sandy soil in sun. Height to 15cm (6in); spread to 30cm (1ft). USZ 9–11, surviving -3°C (27°F) of overnight frost. Tolerant of summer drought. ◑

Kalanchoe thyrsiflora
This succulent perennial has flat, red-edged, green leaves, 7.5cm (3in) across, and spikes of white tubular flowers, to 1cm (⅜in) long, in spring. It is wild in South Africa, from Eastern Cape to Natal and Transvaal.
Cultivation Easily grown in dry soil. Give some water in summer.
Height to 60cm (2ft); spread to 30cm (1ft). USZ 10–11, surviving -1°C (30°F) of overnight frost. Tolerant of summer drought. ◐

231

Mesembryanthemums

Carpobrotus (Aizoaceae)
HOTTENTOT FIG

Carpobrotus has 13 species of succulent perennials, six in the Cape, others in Natal and Australia, with one species (*C. chilensis*) in Chile and California. Some species have become pests on coastal cliffs in southwest England and the Mediterranean region. *C. edulis* (Hottentot fig), with its edible fruit, is also common.

Carpobrotus acinaciformis
This succulent perennial grows wild on the coast of the Cape peninsula and adjacent areas, in South Africa. Its curved leaves are 1.5–2.5cm (½–1in) across. Purple flowers,

7–10cm (3–4in) across, appear in summer. The fruit is egg-shaped.
Cultivation Easily grown in sandy soil. Is good to cover a dry sandy bank.
Height to 15cm (6in); spread 6m (20ft) or more. USZ 9–11, surviving -6.5°C (20°F) of overnight frost. Tolerant of summer drought. ☽

Conicosia (Aizoaceae)

This genus consists of two species of succulent perennials, natives of Western and Southern Cape, South Africa.

Conicosia elongata
This tufted succulent perennial has white to yellow flowers, 6–8cm (2½–3in) across. It is

Above *Disphyma crassifolium* on Tresco, Isles of Scilly

found in mainly in Western Cape. The leaves, around 10cm (4in) long, are bluish green and triangular in section. The very similar *C. pugioniformis* is more widespread, as far east as Port Elizabeth, growing on sandy plains. Both flower in spring.
Cultivation Grow in open, sandy or light clay soil. Water in winter.
Height to 15cm (6in); spread to 30cm (1ft). USZ 10–11, surviving -1°C (30°F) of overnight frost. Tolerant of summer drought. ☽

Disphyma (Aizoaceae)

The genus *Disphyma* has around four species of succulent perennials, natives of the Cape, Australia, and New Zealand.

Disphyma crassifolium
This succulent perennial is found in South Africa and South Australia, growing on

Above *Conicosia elongata*
Left *Carpobrotus acinaciformis* at the Cape of Good Hope

Above *Lampranthus haworthii*

rocks just above high tide, and it has become naturalized in similar places in Cornwall and California. The dark green leaves, 2.5–3.5cm (1–1½in) long, are triangular in section. White to pinkish red flowers, 4cm (1½in) across, are produced during spring.
Cultivation Easily grown in sandy soil. High tolerance of salt spray means that this species is useful for seaside plantings.
Height to 10cm (4in); spread to 50cm (20in). USZ 10–11, surviving -1°C (30°F) of overnight frost. Tolerant of summer drought. ◑

Lampranthus (Aizoaceae)

Lampranthus comprises around 155 species of succulent perennials and evergreen subshrubs; one species is in Australia and the rest in South Africa. The genus contains some of the mostly brightly coloured members of the family Aizoaceae. They are usually shrubby, with wiry stems and narrow, succulent leaves. The fruits have five valves, with distinct points.

Lampranthus aureus
This succulent perennial has greyish leaves, around 5cm (2in) long and joined at the base and orange flowers, to 6cm (2½in) across, in spring. It is from the southwestern Cape, South Africa, usually growing on granite.
Cultivation Grow in sandy soil. Give some water in winter; keep dry in summer.
Height to 40cm (16in); spread to 60cm (2ft). USZ 10–11, surviving -1°C (30°F) of overnight frost. Tolerant of summer drought. ◑

Lampranthus haworthii
This succulent perennial has pale greyish leaves, around 3cm (1¼in) long, spreading from a fused base. It is found wild around Clanwilliam, in South Africa, The pale purple flowers, to 7cm (3in) across, appear in spring.
Cultivation Easily grown in sandy soil. Water in winter; keep dry in summer.
Height to 60cm (2ft); spread to 1m (3ft). USZ 10–11, surviving -1°C (30°F) of overnight frost. Tolerant of summer drought. ◑

Lampranthus saturatus
This much-branched succulent shrub has green leaves, to 4cm (1½in) long, and magenta flowers, to 6cm (2½in) across, produced in winter and spring. It is found wild on sandstone rocks in the Olifants river valley in South Africa.
Cultivation Grow in sandy soil, with good drainage. Water infrequently.
Height to 50cm (20in); spread to 60cm (2ft). USZ 10–11, surviving -1°C (30°F) of overnight frost. Tolerant of summer drought. ◑

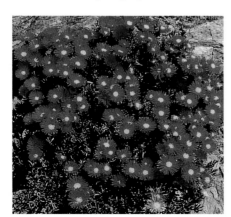

Above *Lampranthus saturatus*

Above *Lampranthus aureus*

Desert Shrubs

Adenium (Apocynaceae)

The genus *Adenium* contains around five species of deciduous succulent perennials to small trees, which grow in deserts and semi-deserts, from South Africa (Natal) and Zimbabwe through eastern Africa to Socotra. They are very poisonous, and are used to kill fish, to put on the tips of arrowheads, or as a means of torture. Their most beautiful flowers are particularly striking when they appear in an otherwise parched landscape.

Adenium obesum

This succulent perennial, from southern to eastern Africa and Socotra, eventually looks like a small tree. The leaves are inversely ovate, to 15cm (6in) long. Pink to red flowers, 2–5cm (1–2in) across, with a short tube and five lobes, are borne in summer.
Cultivation Grow in sandy soil in a dry site. Needs very little water, mainly in summer. Plant away from any irrigation.
Height to 5m (16ft); spread to 1.5m (5ft). USZ 10–11, surviving -1°C (30°F) of overnight frost. Tolerant of summer drought. ◑

Euphorbia (Euphorbiaceae)

Though this genus contains annual and perennial herbaceous species, and leafy shrubs, most of the 1,500 or so species are cactus-like succulents from subtropical areas, and in Africa many species have similar shapes to American Cactaceae. A good example is shown on p.15.

Above *Pachypodium succulentum* (Dikvoet)

Euphorbia caput-medusae

This succulent perennial has a stout central stem and a number of branches, 1–3cm (⅜–1¼in) in diameter, so that it reminded Linnaeus of the smelly head of the Medusa, with snakes coiled in her hair. It is wild in South Africa, particularly in sandy places near the south and west coasts, northwards to Namibia. The creamy white flowers, 1–2cm (⅜–¾in) across, with pale yellow, palmate glands, are produced in winter.
Cultivation Requires sandy soil. Water during winter.
Height to 75cm (30in); spread to 1m (3ft). USZ 10–11, surviving -1°C (30°F) of overnight frost. Tolerant of summer drought. ◑

Fouquieria (Fouquieriaceae)

The genus *Fouquieria* comprises seven species of deciduous succulent shrubs and trees, which are natives of deserts in Mexico and the southwestern USA eastwards to Texas. The stems are little branched, thin, and cane-like, with a spine from each node.

Above *Adenium obesum* near the Tsavo, central Kenya

The leaves appear in winter, falling in early summer as the flowers open.

Fouquieria splendens
OCOTILLO
This shrub from southwestern North America has arching branches densely set with spines and clusters of fleshy, elliptic to inversely lance-shaped leaves, to 2.5cm (1in) long. The red, tubular flowers, to 2.5cm (1in) long, have recurved lobes and are borne in spring and summer.
Cultivation Needs dry sandy soil. Give some rain in winter, very little in summer.
Height to 7m (23ft); spread to 6m (20ft). USZ 10–11, surviving -1°C (30°F) of overnight frost. Tolerant of summer drought. ◑

Pachypodium (Apocynaceae)

Pachypodium, with 13 species of succulent perennials in southern Africa and Madagascar, is very similar to *Adenium* but has an extremely thick underground stem and thin spiny branches.

Above *Pelargonium praemorsum*
Left *Euphorbia caput-medusae*

Above *Fouquieria splendens* (ocotillo) in the Anza-Borrego desert, southern California

Pachypodium succulentum

DIKVOET

This desert succulent perennial has a turnip-like underground stem, to 50cm (20in) long. From this emerge a variable number of spiny stems, with numerous narrow leaves, to 5cm (2in) long, hairy beneath, and pink, purple, or white, tubular flowers, in spring. The flowers have a narrow tube, around 7.5cm (3in) long, with slender lobes slightly shorter than the tube. *P. succulentum* is found in South Africa, mainly in Eastern Cape north to Orange Free State.
Cultivation Needs dry sandy soil. Give some rain in winter, very little in summer.
Height and spread to 60cm (2ft). USZ 10–11, surviving -1°C (30°F) of overnight frost. Tolerant of summer drought. ◑

Pelargonium (Geraniaceae)

The genus *Pelargonium* is described on pp.184–7. In addition to leafy subshrubby species, which live in damp environments, there are many with underground tubers and stems that appear in winter, and other succulent species with small fleshy leaves, which live in harsher, drier, desert-like places and require the same treatment as other succulent plants.

Pelargonium praemorsum

This twiggy succulent perennial, from western South Africa, has a large tuber and deeply divided leaves, 2.5cm (1in) across. Purple or cream, star-shaped flowers, 2cm (¾in) across, appear in spring and summer.
Cultivation Grow in dry sandy soil. Water mainly in winter.
Height to 60cm (2ft); spread to 1m (3ft). USZ 10–11, surviving -1°C (30°F) of overnight frost. Tolerant of summer drought. ◑

Plumeria (Apocynaceae)

Plumeria has around 17 species in tropical America and the West Indies. They are deciduous succulent shrubs or trees, with narrow leaves mainly on the branch tips.

Plumeria rubra

FRANGIPANI

This shrub or small tree is from Mexico to Panama. The scented, red, pink, white, or yellow flowers, to 7cm (3in) across, often with a yellow centre, are used to decorate Buddhist temples, in summer and autumn. The leaves are smooth, to 30cm (1ft) long.
Cultivation Easily grown in sandy soil.
Height and spread to 6m (20ft). USZ 10–11, surviving -1°C (30°F) of overnight frost. Needs some water in summer. ●

Above *Fouquieria splendens* (ocotillo)

Above A cultivated *Plumeria rubra* (frangipani)

Epiphytic Cactuses

Disocactus (Cactaceae)

A genus of 10 species from Mexico and Central America, like *Epiphyllum* but with coloured day-flowers lasting for several days. Many hybrids between the species exist.

Disocactus 'Ackermannii'
An ancient cactus hybrid, grown before the Spanish arrival in Mexico. Scarlet flowers, to 15cm (6in) across, are borne on flattened arching stems in early summer.
Cultivation Grow in a pot of well-drained soil with stones, charcoal, bark, and shredded dry leaves. In hot climates, hang in the shade. Water in hot weather. In cold areas overwinter dry on a light windowsill. *Height and spread to 1m (3ft). USZ 10–11, surviving -1°C (30°F) of overnight frost. Tolerant of summer drought.* ◑

Above *Disocactus* 'Astronaut'

Disocactus 'Astronaut'
This large-flowered hybrid cactus has slightly scented flowers, to 23cm (9in) across, on flattened arching stems during early summer. The outside segments are deep scarlet; the inner ones red.
Cultivation As for *D.* 'Ackermannii'. *Height and spread to 60cm (2ft). USZ 10–11, surviving -1°C (30°F) of overnight frost. Tolerant of summer drought.* ◑

Epiphyllum (Cactaceae)

This genus consists of around 15 species of cactuses in tropical America. They are all

Above *Disocactus* 'Ackermannii'
Right *Epiphyllum crenatum*

Above *Hatiora gaertneri* (Easter cactus)

epiphytic, growing on trees or rocks in areas that are hot and humid in summer and cooler and dry in winter. Most of those grown for their large flowers are hybrids. Protect the soft young stems, formed in summer, from snails.

Epiphyllum crenatum
This cactus has night-scented white flowers, to 30cm (1ft) long, on flattened stiff stems in early summer. This species grows wild on trees and rocks in Mexico and Honduras.
Cultivation As for *D.* 'Ackermannii'.
Height and spread to 50cm (20in). USZ 10–11, surviving -1°C (30°F) of frost. Tolerant of summer drought for short periods. ◗

Epiphyllum oxypetalum
A native of Mexico with flattened stems attached to a stiff, upright, cylindrical central stem. The white flowers, scented in the evening, can be 30cm (1ft) long and are produced from late spring to summer.

Cultivation As for *D.* 'Ackermannii'.
Height and spread to 3m (10ft). USZ 11, needing a minimum of 4.5°C (40°F). Tolerant of summer drought for short periods. ●

Hatiora (Cactaceae)

A genus of six epiphytic or lithophytic cactus species, natives of eastern Brazil.

Hatiora gaertneri
EASTER CACTUS
This Brazilian native has upright, arching or eventually pendulous stems, with each segment being around 7cm (3in) long. The red flowers, around 5cm (2in) across, open wide in sunny weather in spring.
Cultivation As for *D.* 'Ackermannii'.
Height to 17cm (6½in); spread to 15m (6in). USZ 10–11, surviving -1°C (30°F) of overnight frost. Tolerant of summer drought. ◗

Schlumbergera (Cactaceae)
CHRISTMAS CACTUS

This genus has six species of cactuses, all from Brazil. They grow on rocks or trees. Many hybrids have been raised.

Schlumbergera x buckleyi
This hybrid cactus features pendulous, branching, flattened stems and, in winter, pinkish red flowers, to 5cm (2in) long, with a protruding style and stamens.
Cultivation Grow in sandy leafy soil. Keep rather dry in winter. Tolerates shade.
Height and spread to 60cm (2ft). USZ 11, needing a minimum of 4.5°C (40°F) overnight. Tolerant of summer drought. ◗

Schlumbergera 'Gina'
This hybrid cactus produces white flowers with a magenta style, in winter, on flattened stems. Its colour develops best in warm conditions, around 15°C (59°F).
Cultivation As for *S. x buckleyi*.
Height to 15cm (6in); spread to 40cm (16in). USZ 11, needing a minimum of 4.5°C (40°F) overnight. Needs water in summer. ◗

Above *Schlumbergera* 'Gina'

Above *Epiphyllum oxypetalum*
Right *Schlumbergera x buckleyi*

237

Western American Cactuses

Echinocactus (Cactaceae)

Echinocactus has around six species of cactuses, from southwestern North America.

Echinocactus grusonii
This barrel-shaped cactus from central Mexico is often grown for its golden spines and large stem, 80cm (32in) in diameter. Yellow flowers, to 6cm (2½in) long and 5cm (2in) across, appear in summer.
Cultivation Needs sandy rocky soil. Water infrequently, mostly in spring.
Height to 1.3m (4ft); spread to 1m (3ft). USZ 10–11, surviving -1°C (30°F) of overnight frost. Tolerant of summer drought. ◑

Echinocereus (Cactaceae)

The genus Echinocereus consists of about 60 species of cactuses, natives of Mexico and the southwestern USA. Many survive freezing if they are kept dry in winter.

Echinocereus engelmannii
This usually clump-forming cactus has long spines and purplish red to magenta or lavender flowers, 9cm (3½in) long and wide, in spring. It is wild in northwest Mexico, California, Utah, and Arizona, growing on stony slopes in the desert. The stem has a diameter of around 9cm (3½in).
Cultivation Needs sandy rocky soil. Water infrequently, mostly in spring.
Height to 15cm (6in); spread to 30cm (1ft). USZ 9–11, surviving -6.5°C (20°F) of overnight frost. Tolerant of summer drought. ◑

Echinocereus triglochidiatus
This usually clump-forming cactus has long spines and bright red flowers, around 7cm (3in) long and wide, in spring. It is wild in the mountains of California, Nevada, and Arizona, growing on dry rocky slopes. The stem has a diameter of around 9cm (3½in).
Cultivation As for E. engelmannii.
Height to 20cm (8in); spread to 30cm (1ft). USZ 9–11, surviving -6.5°C (20°F) of overnight frost. Tolerant of summer drought. ◑

Ferocactus (Cactaceae)

Ferocactus has 25–30 species of cactuses, found in Mexico and the southwestern USA. Many are very spiny, with the central spine being curved or hooked.

Ferocactus cylindraceus
BARREL CACTUS
This globular, later cylindrical, cactus has red, white, pink, or yellowish spines, to

Above *Ferocactus cylindraceus* (barrel cactus)

17cm (6½in) long, and yellow flowers, 3–6cm (1¼–2½in) long, in spring. It is wild in the Mojave Desert in Mexico, southern California, and east to Utah and Arizona. The stem has a 40cm (16in) diameter.
Cultivation Needs sandy rocky soil. Water infrequently, mostly in spring.
Height to 2m (6½ft); spread to 1m (3ft). USZ 10–11, surviving -1°C (30°F) of overnight frost. Tolerant of summer drought. ◑

Ferocactus peninsulae
This cactus originates in the central and southern part of Baja California, where it flowers mainly from summer to autumn. The stem usually has a diameter of around 50cm (20in) in mature specimens. The spines are particularly long, and some are flattened and hooked. The flowers are red,

Above *Echinocereus triglochidiatus*

Above *Ferocactus peninsulae*

Above *Hylocereus undatus*

orange, or yellow, to 7.5cm (3in) long and 6cm (2½in) across.
Cultivation Grow in dry sandy soil. Needs some rain in spring, and otherwise at irregular intervals.
Height to 2.4m (8ft); spread to 50cm (20in). USZ 10–11, surviving -1°C (30°F) of overnight frost. Tolerant of summer drought. ☾

Hylocereus (Cactaceae)

The genus *Hylocereus* consists of around 15 species of cactuses, which are natives of Central America, the West Indies, Colombia, and Venezuela to eastern Brazil. Most species grow in forests and are epiphytic climbers, or scramble over rocks and through shrubs.

Above *Mammillaria compressa*

Above *Echinocereus engelmannii* in California
Left *Echinocactus grusonii*, with grey-leaved *Senecio serpens* and a *Dudleya* species

Hylocereus undatus
This beautiful and commonly cultivated cactus is now widespread in South America, usually as a relic of cultivation. Its native range is uncertain, but it probably originated in Mexico and Central America. It grows on trees in the forest, and also scrambles on coastal rocks and in scrub. The stems are three-angled or winged, with each section around 1m (3ft) long and around 5cm (2in) wide. The sweetly scented flowers open at night during summer, and are 30cm (1ft) across, with a tube around 12.5cm (5in) long, and segments to 14cm (5½in) long, the outer ones fleshy and reddish on the back, the inner ones white.
Cultivation Grow in sandy soil. Needs space to grow well, and will climb over buildings or rocks and into trees or shrubs. A dry cool season will encourage the production of flowers.
Height to 5.5m (18ft); spread to 6m (20ft). USZ 11, needing a minimum of 4.5°C (40°F) overnight. Tolerant of summer drought. ⬤

Mammillaria (Cactaceae)

Mammillaria comprises around 150 species of cactuses, found mostly in Mexico but with several species in the southern USA, including California, and a few as far south as the West Indies and northern South America. Most can be recognized by their fleshy tubercles (Latin *mamilla* = nipple) with spines on the tip. The flowers are generally small, around the rim of the stem, and form berry-like, often red fruit.

Mammillaria compressa
This clump-forming cactus is a native of central Mexico. Each stem is 8cm (3in) in diameter. The purplish pink flowers, 1–1.5cm (⅜–½in) across, appear in spring, followed by red fruits.
Cultivation Easily grown in sandy soil, dry in winter, with some water in summer.
Height to 15cm (6in); spread to 60cm (2ft). USZ 10–11, surviving -1°C (30°F) of overnight frost. Tolerant of summer drought. ☾

Opuntias

Above *Opuntia basilaris* (beavertail) in the Mojave Desert, California

Above *Opuntia basilaris* (beavertail)

Above *Opuntia* 'Cantabrigiensis'

Opuntia (Cactaceae)

The genus *Opuntia* consists of around 100 species of cactuses found throughout the warmer regions of North and South America, from British Columbia and Massachusetts to the Strait of Magellan. In addition, species have gone wild in most other semi-desert areas of the world, and in dry valleys in the Himalayas or in Switzerland; they have often become serious weeds. Opuntias can be trees, large shrubs, or creeping succulents, sometimes viciously spiny, at other times with tufts of loose, irritant hairs. Stems can vary from unjointed and tree-like, to flattened pads and jointed cylindrical stems; the last, called chollas, are sometimes put in a separate genus, *Cylindropuntia*. The stems are densely covered with spines, which embed themselves in passing animals, and later root where they fall to the ground.

Opuntia basilaris
BEAVERTAIL
This beautiful cactus is found wild in the Mojave and Colorado deserts in California, Utah, Arizona, and in northern Mexico, growing on flat sandy places. It forms sprawling clumps of greenish grey flattened

pads, 8–20cm (3–8in) long and 6–15cm (2½–6in) across. These often have purplish edges and few spines but short brown glochids (barbed, stiff hairs). Purplish pink, rarely paler or white, flowers, around 7.5cm (3in) across, appear in spring.
Cultivation Needs dry sandy soil. Water mainly in spring and early summer.
Height to 60cm (2ft); spread to 1m (3ft). USZ 9–11, surviving -6.5°C (20°F) of overnight frost. Tolerant of summer drought. ◐

Opuntia 'Cantabrigiensis'
This sprawling cactus has bluish green flattened pads, around 20cm (8in) long and 15cm (6in) wide, and whitish spines. The pale yellow flowers, 7.5cm (3in) wide, appear in summer. This cultivar is named after Cambridge, England, where it has survived outdoors in the University Botanic Garden for around 100 years. It is now considered to belong to the variable *O. engelmannii* from the southwestern USA and Mexico.
Cultivation Easily grown in dry sandy soil. In areas with wet winters, protect this species by covering it with a large sheet of glass to keep off the rain.
Height to 60cm (2ft); spread to 1m (3ft). USZ 9–11, surviving -6.5°C (20°F) of overnight frost. Tolerant of summer drought. ◐

Above *Opuntia echinocarpa* at the Hanbury Botanic Gardens, La Mortola, in northwestern Italy

Opuntia echinocarpa

This cactus has dark green, cylindrical stems, 2.5cm (1in) thick, with silvery or golden spines. It is a native of deserts in California, Utah, and Arizona. The greenish flowers, 5cm (2in) across, appear in spring.
Cultivation Easily grown in dry sandy soil. *Height to 1.5m (5ft); spread to 2m (6½ft). USZ 9–11, surviving -3°C (27°F) of overnight frost. Tolerant of summer drought.* ☽

Opuntia erinacea

This cactus is wild in dry mountains, from California to Utah and Arizona. Greenish flattened pads, to 15cm (6in) long, 7cm (3in) wide, are densely covered with long greyish spines. Yellow flowers, 5cm (2in) wide, in spring, fade to reddish.
Cultivation Easily grown in dry sandy soil. *Height to 30cm (1ft); spread to 1.2m (4ft). USZ 9–11, surviving -6.5°C (20°F) of overnight frost. Tolerant of summer drought.* ☽

Opuntia gosseliana (syn. *O. macrocentra*)

This cactus is found from Arizona to Texas and Mexico, in sandy deserts and dry woods. The greyish purple flattened pads to 20cm (8in) long, 18cm (7in) wide, bear pale brownish grey spines. Yellow flowers, 6cm (2½in) wide, in spring, fade to reddish.
Cultivation Easily grown in dry sandy soil. *Height to 1m (3ft); spread to 2m (6½ft). USZ 9–11, surviving -6.5°C (20°F) of overnight frost. Tolerant of summer drought.* ☽

Opuntia littoralis

This cactus grows near the sea in southern California. The bluish green flattened pads, 15cm (6in) long and 7cm (3in) wide, bear greyish spines. Orange-yellow to red flowers, 5cm (2in) wide, appear in spring.
Cultivation Easily grown in dry sandy soil. *Height to 60cm (2ft); spread to 6m (20ft). USZ 9–11, surviving -3°C (27°F) of overnight frost. Tolerant of summer drought.* ☽

Left *Opuntia gosseliana* in California

Above *Opuntia littoralis* on the coast near Los Angeles

Above *Opuntia erinacea*

241

South American Cactuses

Aporocactus (Cactaceae)

Aporocactus consists of two species of trailing cactuses, natives of Mexico, both epiphytic or growing over rocks. They are sometimes included in *Disocactus*.

Aporocactus flagelliformis
This cactus, which grows wild in Hidalgo, has short, bristly, cylindrical, trailing stems, 1cm (⅜in) in diameter, and purplish pink flowers, in spring. The flowers are 5–8cm (2–3in) long, 2.5–4cm (1–1½in) wide.
Cultivation Easily grown in well-drained, leafy soil. Is good hanging under a tree. *Length to 1m (3ft); spread to 60cm (2ft). USZ 10–11, surviving -1°C (30°F) of overnight frost. Needs some water in summer.* ◗

Above *Aporocactus flagelliformis* in a hanging basket

Above *Cleistocactus baumannii*

Cleistocactus (Cactaceae)

Cleistocactus is a genus of around 50 species of cactuses, which are found growing wild from Peru to Bolivia, northern Argentina, and Paraguay.

Cleistocactus baumannii
This upright or arching cactus is found growing wild in Argentina, Paraguay, and Bolivia. It has hairy stems, 3cm (1¼in) in diameter, branching from the base, and spines to 4cm (1½in) long. The tubular, orange to scarlet flowers, 5–7cm (2–3in) long, are borne in spring. They are curved from the base, and have a protruding style and stamens.
Cultivation Easily grown in dry rocky soil. Give some water in summer.

Above *Cleistocactus samaipatanus*

Height to 2m (6½ft); spread to 1m (3ft). USZ 10–11, surviving -1°C (30°F) of overnight frost. Tolerant of summer drought. ◑

Cleistocactus samaipatanus
This upright cactus, from Bolivia, has hairy stems, 4cm (1½in) in diameter, and spines to 3cm (1¼in) long. Bright red, S-shaped flowers, 3.5cm (1½in) long, with a protruding style and stamens, appear in spring.
Cultivation As for *C. baumannii*.
Height to 1.5m (5ft); spread to 1m (3ft). USZ 10–11, surviving -1°C (30°F) of overnight frost. Tolerant of summer drought. ◑

Echinopsis (Cactaceae)

This South American genus has around 60 species, although hundreds have been

Above *Echinopsis terscheckii* flowering in January in a valley in northern Argentina

named. Some may be found under the generic names *Trichocereus*, *Lobivia*, *Helianthocereus*, *Chamaecereus*, and other smaller genera. Some are large and woody enough to be used in building; others contain mescaline. In some species the flowers are open in the day, others open at night. Many species are cultivated, and hybrids are grown in collections.

Echinopsis pasacana

This is a high-altitude cactus from the dry altiplano of the Andes of northern Argentina, and is closely related to *E. terscheckii*. The little branched, columnar stems, 30cm (1ft) in diameter, have more than 20 ribs, numerous soft spines, and hairs. The bell- to funnel-shaped flowers, 10cm (4in) across, in summer, are greenish or red outside, with white petals inside.

Cultivation Needs well-drained, deep, sandy soil, with a little rain, mostly in summer. It should tolerate winter cold, provided that it is dry.
Height to 3m (10ft); spread to 60cm (2ft). USZ 10–11, surviving -1°C (30°F) of overnight frost. Tolerant of summer drought. ☾

Echinopsis tarijensis

This beautiful cactus is found on high passes in northern Argentina and Bolivia, growing on steep rocky slopes at around 3,600m (12,000ft). The little-branched stems, 40cm (16in) in diameter, are columnar with around 25 ribs, soft spines, and dense white hairs. The upright, bell-shaped, pinkish or red flowers, around 10cm (4in) across, appear in summer.
Cultivation Needs well-drained, deep, sandy soil, with a little rain, in summer.

Height to 5m (16ft); spread to 40cm (16in). USZ 9–11, surviving -6.5°C (20°F) of overnight frost. Tolerant of summer drought. ☾

Echinopsis terscheckii

This cactus is found in river valleys in the Andes of northern Argentina. The bluish green, columnar trunk, 45cm (18in) in diameter, is much branched well above the ground, and has 8–18 ribs and rather few dark spines. The trumpet-shaped flowers, 15–20 (6–8in) long, are reddish and greenish outside, with white petals; they are produced in summer.
Cultivation Needs deep sandy soil. Water intermittently in summer.
Height to 9m (30ft); spread to 4.5m (15ft). USZ 9–11, surviving -3°C (27°F) of overnight frost. Tolerant of summer drought. ☾

Above *Melocactus intortus*

Melocactus (Cactaceae)

The genus *Melocactus* comprises around 34 species of cactuses, which are natives mainly from eastern Brazil, Peru, Venezuela, Central America, and the Caribbean. On top of a cylindrical, spiny stem is a white, woolly topknot (known as the cephalium), in which are produced the red or pink flowers and then the juicy, white or pink fruit.

Melocactus intortus

This unusual cactus is found on desert islands in the Caribbean, from the Turks and Caicos islands, south to Martinique. The bluish green stems have 12–24 ribs. The cephalium, to 50cm (20in) long, bears white wool and red spines. Pink flowers, around 1cm (⅜in) across, in summer, are followed by small, pink or red fruit.
Cultivation Needs dry rocky soil. Water intermittently, mainly in summer.
Height to 60cm (2ft); spread to 30cm (1ft). USZ 11, needing a minimum of 4.5°C (40°F) overnight. Tolerant of summer drought. ☾

Above *Echinopsis tarijensis* at 3,700m (12,150ft)
Left *Echinopsis tarijensis* at Jujuy, in Argentina
Far Left *Echinopsis pasacana* in Argentina

Plants for special uses in the garden

PLANTS FOR VERY DRY OR DESERT GARDENS

Adenium obesum
Agave (all)
Aloe (all)
Argemone platyacantha
Argyranthemum gracile
Bismarkia nobilis
Bromelia balansae
Calliandra californica
Capparia aphylla
Chilopsis linearis

Choisya arizonica
Cotyledon orbiculata
Echinopsis (all)
Elaeagnus angustifolia
Encephalartos horridus
Euphorbia bravoana
Euphorbia millii
Loeselia mexicana
Nerium oleander (by a spring)
Oenothera speciosa

Opuntia (all)
Pelargonium acetosum
Pelargonium praemorsum
Phoenix sylvestris
Plumbago auriculata
Puya (all)
Sphaeralcea ambigua
Sphaeralcea emoryi
Washingtonia filifera

PLANTS FOR DRY COASTAL GARDENS

Acacia saligna
Agapanthus praecox
Capparis spinosa
Ceanothus 'Concha'
Ceanothus thrysiflorus
Cistus (all)
Hyophorbe verschaffeltii

Lavandula (all)
Lilium candidum
Lupinus albifrons
Lupinus pilosus
Matthiola incana
Myrtus communis
Nerine sarniensis

Pancratium canariense
Pelargonium cucullatum
Phoenix canariensis
Pinus halepensis
Pinus pinea
Rosmarinus (all)

PLANTS FOR WET COASTAL GARDENS

Agapanthus praecox
Astelia chathamica
Carpobrotus acinaciformis
Clematis indivisa
Cordyline australis
Disphyma crassifolium

Eucryphia cordifolia
Euphorbia x pasteurii
Hibiscus tiliaceus
Leucodendron argenteum
Lobelia tupa
Lonicera sempervirens

Metrosideros excelsa
Pandanus utilis
Phormium (all)
Zantedeschia aethiopica

TREES & SHRUBS FOR MEDITERRANEAN & SUMMER-DRY GARDENS, NEEDING LITTLE EXTRA WATER

Acacia (all)
Aloe plicatilis
Alogyne huegelii
Arbutus andrachne
Bauhinia variegata
Callistemon viminalis
Cistus (all)
Cupressus sempervirens
Dendromecon rigida

Dracaena draco
Eucalyptus ficifolia
Fremontodendron californicum
Halimium (all)
Lavandula (all)
Lupinus albifrons
Nerium oleander
Olea europaea
Phlomis (all)

Phoenix canariensis
Protea cynaroides
Salvia x jamensis
Stipa gigantea
Trichostema lanatum
Zauschneria californica

CLIMBING PLANTS FOR WALLS & ARBOURS IN SUMMER-DRY CLIMATES

Allamanda cathartica
Bougainvillea
Campsis grandiflora
Canarina canariensis
Clematis cirrhosa

Distictis buccinatoria
Hardenbergia violacea
Lonicera pilosa
Rosa banksiae
Rosa gigantea and cvs

Thunbergia grandiflora
Tropaeolum azureum
Tropaeolum pentaphyllum
Wisteria sinensis

CLIMBING PLANTS FOR WALLS & ARBOURS IN SUMMER-WET CLIMATES

Bomarea multiflora
Bougainvillea (all)
Campsis grandiflora
Clematis indivisa
Clematis urophylla

Distictis buccinatoria
Ipomoea alba
Passiflora (all)
Quisqualis indica
Rhodochiton atrosanguineus

Rosa banksiae
Solandra longiflora
Solandra maxima
Thunbergia grandiflora
Wisteria floribunda

PLANTS FOR WET OR HUMID GARDENS

Agapetes serpens
Bamboos (all)
Begonia luxurians
Clematis urophylla
Clianthus puniceus
Cordyline indivisa
Cupressus cashmiriana
Cyathea medullaris
Cymbidium (all)

Daphne bholua
Dicksonia antarctica
Embothrium coccineum
Epiphyllum (all)
Fuchsia (all)
Lapageria rosea
Luculia intermedia
Magnolia campbellii
Orchids (most)

Philadelphus mexicanus
Pinus montezumae
Pinus patula
Rhodochiton atrosanguineus
Rhododendron (all)
Schlumbergera (all)
Telopea truncata

PLANTS FOR SHADY GARDENS

Abutilon (all)
Acanthus mollis
Begonia (all)
Brugmansia insignis
Campanula incurva
Clivia miniata
Crinum moorei

Cyclamen repandum
Dudleya pulverulenta
Dypsis lutescens
Echium pininana
ferns (all)
Fuchsia boliviana
Fuchsia denticulata

Heliconia rostrata
Hoya carnosa
Isoplexis sceptrum
Mahonia siamensis
Musa (all)
Neoregelia carolinae

TREES FOR SMALL GARDENS

Acacia dealbata ssp. *subalpina*
Acacia fimbriata
Aesculus californica
Arbutus andrachne
Bauhinia tomentosa
Cercis siliquastrum
Chamaerops humilis

Cornus capitata
Crataegus pubescens
Cupressus cashmiriana
Cycas revoluta
Dypsis lutescens
Erythrina crista-gallii
Eucalyptus ficifolia

Eucryphia cordifolia
Ficus carica
Magnolia yunnanensis
Olea europaea
Pinus bungeana
Punica granatum

PLANTS WITH SCENTED FLOWERS

Amaryllis belladonna
Brugmansia candida
Brugmansia insignis
Brunfelsia americana
Cordyline australis
Coronilla valentina
Cosmos atrosanguineus
Daphne (all)
Dianthus caryophyllus
Elaeagnus (all)
Epiphyllum crenatum
Epiphyllum oxypetalum

Gardenia augusta
Gladiolus callianthus
Gladiolus tristis
Hedychium (all)
Heliotropium arborescens
Hoya carnosa
Hyacinthus orientalis
Impatiens tinctoria
Ipomoea alba
Jasminum (all)
Lilium formosanum
Luculia gratissima

Mahonia siamensis
Mandevilla laxa
Matthiola incana
Nicotiana alata
Philadelphus (all)
Plumiera rubra
Rhododendron 'Fragrantissimum'
Rhododendron jasminiflorum
Rhododendron veitchianum
Trachelospermum (all)
Verbena platensis

PLANTS WITH AROMATIC LEAVES

Choisya (all)
Cistus ladanifer
Citrus (all)
Eucalyptus (all)

Laurus nobilis
Lavandula (all)
Myrtus communis
Pelargonium tomentosum

Prostanthera (all)
Rosmarinus (all)
Salvia (most)
Trichostema lanatum

PLANTS SUITABLE FOR LARGE POTS OR CONTAINERS

Agapanthus praecox
Astelia chathamica
Astelia nervosa
Campanula incurva
Convolvulus cneorum
Cymbidium (all)

Gardenia augusta
Jasminum grandiflorum
Jasminum polyanthum
Lilium (all)
Matthiola incana
Nerium oleander

Pelargonium (all)
Tropaeolum azureum
Vriesea splendens

PLANTS FOR EVERGREEN HEDGES

Arbutus unedo
Camellia japonica
Cupressus macrocarpa
Fortunella margarita
Gardenia augusta

Jasminum grandiflorum
Jasminum nitidum
Laurus nobilis
Murraya paniculata
Myrtus communis

Nerium oleander
Photinia arbutifolia
Rhaphiolepis umbellata

PLANTS THAT ATTRACT BUTTERFLIES, SUNBIRDS, & HUMMINGBIRDS

Abelia floribunda
Aloe (all)
Buddleja (most)
Calliandra californica
Cestrum elegans
Chilopsis linearis

Escallonia bifida
Eupatorium ligustrinum
Grevillea (all)
Heliotropium arborescens
Lantana camara
Leonotis ocymifolia

Lobelia tupa
Lonicera sempervirens
Sutherlandia montana
Verbena platensis
Zauschneria californica

Glossary

anther: the organ that holds the pollen

awn: a long, stiff projection from the flower of a grass

bract: leaf close to or protecting a flower, sometimes coloured

calyx: usually green parts of a flower, often cup-shaped

corm: swollen base of a stem, as in crocuses

corolla: the petals of a flower, used when they are all joined into a tube or bell

epilithic [usually of orchids or cactuses]: grows on rocks.

epiphytic: grows on trees

falls [of irises]: the part of the iris flower which hangs down, usually the inner perianth segments

glochids: clusters of spines or hairs on a cactus

inflorescence: the flowering stem, bracts, and flowers of a plant

internode: space between the nodes, usually a bare stem

lance-shaped: usually called lanceolate; narrow (3–4 times as long as wide) and pointed, widest towards the base

lithophytic: grows on rocks

monocarpic: flowers once, then dies

oblanceolate: narrow & pointed, widest towards the apex

obovate: broad and pointed, widest towards the apex

ovate: broad and pointed, widest towards the base

panicle: a much-branched inflorescence, the lowest flowers opening first

papillose: with small, soft thick hairs

perianth segments: petal-like parts of a flower, used where sepals and petals are little different (as in lilies)

pinnate: a leaf with leaflets on either side of the axis

pseudobulb [in orchids]: a swollen, often bulb-like stem

raceme: a branched inflorescence, the lowest flowers opening first, as in a bluebell

rhachis: the axis of a compound leaf, particularly of a fern

rhizome: an underground stem, usually swollen

sporangium: an organ that holds spores

staminodes: sterile, sometimes petal-like stamens

standards [in irises]: the parts of the flower that stand up, usually the outer perianth segments

style: the part of a flower which receives the pollen, usually in the centre

tank plant [of a bromeliad]: a plant that holds water in the centre of its leaves; common in Bromeliaceae in the South American tropics

tuber: a swollen rhizome (underground stem)

tubercules: small tubers

tunic: the usually papery covering of a corm or bulb

umbel: a usually flat-topped inflorescence in which all the branches arise from one point

vase plant: another name for a tank plant

whorl: a group of three or more leaves or flowers arising from the same level on a stem

Recommended Further Reading

The Gardens of Roberto Burle Marx
Sima Eliovson. Saga Press Inc/Timber Press with
Thames & Hudson, 1991.
*An account of the work of the great Brazilian landscape
architect, with lists of plants used in tropical South America.*

**Cultivated Plants of the World: Trees,
Shrubs, Climbers**
Don Ellison. Flora Publications International, 1995.
*Illustrations of numerous subtropical garden plants, as well
as many hardy ones, with an Australian bias.*

Flowering Tropical Climbers
Geoffrey Herklots. Dawson Science History
Publications, 1976.
*An excellent illustrated first-hand account of many rare and
interesting climbers.*

The Mediterranean Gardener
Hugo Latymer. Frances Lincoln, in association with the
Royal Botanic Gardens, Kew, 1990.
A practical guide to gardening on the Mediterranean coast.

Mediterranean Gardening: A Practical Handbook
Yves Menzies. John Murray, 1991.
*An excellent first-hand account of how to establish and keep
a garden in the Mediterranean.*

Gardens of the Sun
Trevor Nottle. Kangaroo Press, 1994.
*A philosophical and practical book by the Australian
plantsman and gardener, filled with good ideas.*

Conservatory and Indoor Plants
Roger Phillips & Martyn Rix. Pan Books, 1998.
*Many plants suitable for Mediterranean or subtropical
gardens are covered here.*

The English Garden Abroad
Charles Quest-Ritson. Viking, 1992.
*An inspirational account of English-made gardens, mostly in
the Mediterranean region.*

Sunset Western Garden Book
Lane Publishing Company, Menlo Park,
California, 1988.
*An excellent source book for gardening in California, with
details of Californian climates.*

Index

Please note that page numbers in
italics refer to illustrations in the
introduction only

Acknowledgments

Martyn Rix would like to thank the following people: Jill Bryan, Michele Byam, Aljos Farjon, John Fielding, Gina Fullerlove, Peter & Barbara Knox-Shaw, John Marston, Mike Nelhams, Roger Phillips, Charles Quest-Ritson, Alison Rix, Anthony Rix, Richard Rix, Nigel Taylor, Peter Taylor, William Waterfield.

Photographic Credits

Jacket: front, clockwise from top left: John Fielding; Royal Botanic Gardens, Kew, above and below; John Fielding; Harpur Garden Library/Jerry Harpur; back: all Royal Botanic Gardens, Kew; spine: Martyn Rix.

All the photographs are the copyright of Martyn Rix or Roger Phillips, with the exception of the following:

Pages 4–5: The Garden Collection/Gary Rogers; 11 left, 13 above John Fielding; 26 right Board of Trustees of the Royal Botanic Gardens, Kew; 27 below, 30 above right John Fielding; 45 left Photos Horticultural.

DATE	ISSUED TO
6/29/16	Quirico